COMING OF AGE(NCY) ON THE MIGRANT TRAIL

GLOBAL LATIN/O AMERICAS

Frederick Luis Aldama and Lourdes Torres, Series Editors

COMING OF AGE(NCY) ON THE MIGRANT TRAIL

ADOLESCENT JOURNEYS IN CONTEMPORARY LATINX YOUNG ADULT LITERATURE

Susana S. Martínez

THE OHIO STATE UNIVERSITY PRESS
COLUMBUS

Library of Congress Cataloging-in-Publication Data

Names: Martínez, Susana S., author

Title: Coming of age(ncy) on the migrant trail : adolescent journeys in contemporary Latinx young adult literature / Susana S. Martínez.

Other titles: Global Latin/o Americas

Description: Columbus : The Ohio State University Press, [2025] | Series: Global Latin/o Americas | Includes bibliographical references and index. | Summary: "Maps agency in young adult literature involving Latinx migrant youth, showing how these narratives combat stereotypes and contribute to antiracist pedagogical discussions where young people emerge as catalysts for social change. Analyzes novels published between 1981 and 2024 and by authors such as Jennifer De Leon, Alexandra Diaz, and Jonny Garza Villa"—Provided by publisher.

Identifiers: LCCN 2025031787 | ISBN 9780814216026 hardback | ISBN 0814216021 hardback | ISBN 9780814284636 ebook | ISBN 0814284639 ebook

Subjects: LCSH: Immigrant youth—United States—Social conditions | Emigration and immigration in literature | Young adult fiction, American—History and criticism | American fiction—Mexican American authors—History and criticism | American fiction—Hispanic American authors—History and criticism | American fiction—History and criticism | Agent (Philosophy) in literature | Mexico—Emigration and immigration | Central America—Emigration and immigration

Classification: LCC PS374.Y57 M37 2025

LC record available at https://lccn.loc.gov/2025031787

Other identifiers: ISBN 9780814259658 (paperback) | ISBN 0814259650 (paperback)

Cover design by adam bohannon

Text composition by Stuart Rodriguez

Type set in Minion Pro

∞ The paper used in this publication meets the minimum requirements of the American National Standard for Information Sciences—Permanence of Paper for Printed Library Materials. ANSI Z39.48-1992.

Para Lupita

And for my parents, José Luis and Clara,
who migrated as young adults

CONTENTS

INTRODUCTION

A Road Map and Chronology of Latinx YA Literature on the Migrant Trail

With wars and political crises brewing worldwide, forced migration is a global phenomenon that deeply affects youth. In mainstream media, Central America is notorious for its Darien Gap serving as a corridor for migrants from around the world and for expelling mostly Guatemalans, Salvadorans, Hondurans, and Nicaraguans due to poverty and violence. For decades, the so-called Northern Triangle has drawn attention for outmigration, either in the form of caravans of people seeking safety in numbers or for unaccompanied migrant children crossing Mexico to reach the United States to reunite with a parent or close relative. The Administration for Children and Families, a division of the US Department of Health and Human Services, defines an unaccompanied migrant child as a "child who has no lawful immigration status in the United States; has not attained 18 years of age; and, with respect to whom, there is no parent or legal guardians in the United States, or no parent or legal guardian in the United States available to provide care and physical custody" (Administration for Children and Families).

Situated within this transnational context, *Coming of Age(ncy) on the Migrant Trail* offers a critical analysis of Latinx young adult (YA) novels about Central American and Mexican migrant journeys. I focus on this particular journey because unaccompanied migrants from Central America and Mexico are either demonized in US political discourse as potential gangbangers and drug dealers or viewed as traumatized victims of violence and poverty. The book's central argument is that the popular genre of Latinx YA literature is an ideal medium from which to examine the often invisibilized root causes of migration and through which youth emerge as powerful agents of change to counter hate.

The middle-grade and YA novels I study are written in English for a predominantly US youth audience, primarily intended for readers whose ages mirror those of the protagonists, ranging from early adolescence to teens and young adulthood. Yet increasingly, readers like me form part of a growing crossover market because as youth of color growing up in the US, we never saw our Central American and Mexican immigrant stories represented in literature.[1] Given the political hostilities Black and Brown people face in the US amid anti-immigrant white nationalism, LGBTQ+ book bans, and debates around teaching about race in K–12 curricula, this book amplifies marginalized voices by drawing from several interdisciplinary fields—the predominantly white field of children's and YA literature along with Latinx studies and Central American studies.

As the center of the Americas (Cornejo 15), the region has experienced US colonialism, imperialism, and political intervention for centuries, so Central Americans and the diaspora have much to say about the root causes of migration. In *Teaching Central American Literature in a Global Context,* Gloria Chacón and Mónica Gil affirm the isthmus's infrequently acknowledged geopolitical importance and its interconnectedness to the United States:

> The region enabled the accumulation of wealth in the United States by facilitating and speeding up the transport of commodities and peoples from the East Coast to California during the gold rush via its territories. The route also expedited South American travel to the United States, adding to the Latinization of California in the nineteenth century, and facilitating the transportation of goods and ideas, uniting the Pacific and Atlantic Oceans till this day via the Panama Canal. Central American cultural texts and people have enriched the cultural fabric of the United States. (18)

To trace the understudied representation and agency of migration stories from Guatemala, El Salvador, and Honduras in the booming industry of YA publishing, I gather an array of YA novels that play a key role in building historical memory by introducing younger generations of the diaspora to the United

1. Referring to general adult interest, Dimitrije Curcic reports that 51 percent of people who purchase YA books are between 30 and 44 years old, accounting for 28 percent of all buyers. Also, 78 percent of the over-18 buyers are purchasing YA books with the intention of reading them themselves.

States' past and present role in destabilizing the communities the protagonists are forced to flee. The harrowing stories of characters who come of age and come into their own sense of agency on the dangerous trek from Central America, across Mexico, and into the United States embody renowned scholar Rudine Sims Bishop's theory of literature's power to serve as "mirrors, windows, or sliding glass doors" ("Mirrors"). They can serve as valuable mirrors that reflect real life migration experiences to youth who have themselves fled home and survived the crossing, or whose parents or grandparents undertook the journey to provide them with more opportunities in the US. Increasing awareness and access to these stories is crucial because educators often forewarn that when children don't see themselves regularly in books, they may lose interest in reading and feel that their lives don't matter (G. Enriquez 103). Likewise, they can also act as much-needed windows that introduce a more privileged readership to life-and-death experiences they are unfamiliar with. As readers accompany the characters along their frightening journeys, feelings of empathy, solidarity, or curiosity might propel them to open the sliding glass door: "Readers have only to walk through in imagination to become part of whatever world has been created and recreated by the author" (Bishop, "Mirrors" ix).

Coming of Age(ncy): Reading Latinx YA Literature as Accompaniment

As the daughter of a Guatemalan mother who migrated to Los Angeles as a young adult and married my Mexican father, who also emigrated at a young age as the oldest of six children raised by a single mother, I have felt strongly drawn to YA novels about the Central American and Mexican migration experience that I never had access to during adolescence. As a bilingual and bicultural child born and raised in Los Angeles, I often heard my parents reflecting on their coming-of-age experiences with their Mexican, Guatemalan, and Salvadoran friends and extended family. During summer trips to northern Mexico or Guatemala City, the colonial city of Antigua, Lake Atitlán, and my mother's hometown of Gualán, Zacapa, throughout my childhood and teenage years, I would hear family members whisper about "La Situación" or "La Violencia" and assumed they were discussing crime or stressful financial times. Unaware that they were actually referring to the US-supported civil conflict that lasted thirty-six years and included genocide against Indigenous Maya communities in the highlands, I was oblivious to the violence and human rights abuses that the US was enabling through military dictatorships.

My predominantly white Catholic middle schools and progressively liberal high school in Los Angeles didn't offer history classes on Latin America, but I distinctly remember a screening of the documentary *Roses in December* (1982) during a school assembly. It featured the solidarity and accompaniment work of four American church women in the context of liberation theology. Learning about the rape and murder of sisters Dorothy Kazel, Ita Ford, and Maura Clark and Jean Donovan, a young laywoman, ordered by the right-wing dictatorship of El Salvador, made such an impact on me because it was the first time that Central America was addressed at school, as opposed to activities that had to do with Mexico or Chicana/o history.

When I attended the University of California at Los Angeles, my Latin American literature courses never covered Central America. I started graduate school at Yale in 1992, the year Mayan activist Rigoberta Menchú was awarded the Nobel Peace Prize. Her moving testimonio named the long history of injustice and impunity in Guatemala, including genocide against the Maya. Based on her first-person account and the academic controversy that ensued, I wrote my dissertation on Latin American testimonio and regularly teach college courses on human rights, historical memory, and peace activism to students much like my younger self, who are initially shocked to learn about the US role in Central American violence. When my students share that their grandparents, parents, or they themselves crossed several borders to seek safety in the US, they raise important questions about US complicity in the root causes driving migration and often express feeling seen for the first time. This ties back to Bishop's concept of books as indispensable windows and sliding glass doors that invite others into an unknown world, sparking many questions about identity, agency, and solidarity as they work for social change.

As a professor at a private university with a social justice mission, I have had the privilege of leading study abroad and service immersion trips to Mexico, El Salvador, and Peru. I traveled to Honduras in August 2014 as part of a human rights delegation with Witness for Peace Southwest, US–El Salvador Sister Cities, and School of the Americas Watch, member groups of the Honduras Solidarity Network. The delegation was framed as accompaniment because we would visit communities in resistance, listening and learning from their testimonies. The trip took place during the media frenzy over a surge in unauthorized crossings at the Mexico-US border by unaccompanied minors from Guatemala, El Salvador, and Honduras. By the end of July 2014, some sixty thousand young people had made their way through Mexico and arrived at its northern border (Chávez and Masri). It was an eye-opening trip during the corrupt narco dictatorship of Juan Orlando Hernández (2014–22), whom the US supported after the 2009 coup. We met with human rights advocates in Tegucigalpa, San Pedro Sula, the Bajo Aguán, and Garifuna communities, which are under attack by militarized police.[2] Several grassroots organizations in resistance helped us see migration in a wider context, such as how the government prioritized local and transnational business ties while repressing Afro-Indigenous communities defending their rivers and ancestral lands. On our last night, we had a special dinner guest, the environmental activist and Indigenous leader Berta Cáceres (1971–2016), who was herself under continuous attack for denouncing transnational megaprojects and corruption. She talked with us about her work as cofounder of the Council of Popular and Indigenous Organizations of Honduras and their struggles in the Lenca region of Río Blanco denouncing a transnational dam project while drawing important connections to US and Canadian interventions that were forcing people to flee Honduras. Since I hadn't been up to date on the news, I was surprised when Berta turned to me, pointed to the television, and asked, "Are you ready to go back to that?" At the time, I didn't understand what she was asking me or what I was seeing on the screen, but the heavily armed US police units in riot gear looked exactly like the military trained officers I'd been seeing all over Honduras. When I returned home the following day, I realized that Berta was referring to the uprisings in Ferguson over the police killing of an unarmed Black teenager named Michael Brown, and I've reflected on her question ever since. What transnational economic and racialized political connections was she challenging me to see between authoritarian forces acting with impunity in Honduras and the US? Was I prepared to exert agency as a citizen and taxpayer when state forces repress and kill people at home and abroad with impunity? I followed her work and celebrated when she was awarded the Goldman Environmental Prize a year later. In her acceptance speech, Cáceres urged and warned,

> Let us wake up! We're out of time. We must shake our conscience free of the rapacious capitalism, racism, and patriarchy that will only assure our own self-destruction. The Gualcarque River has called upon us, as have other gravely threatened rivers. We must answer their call. Our Mother Earth—militarized, fenced-in, poisoned, a place where basic rights are systematically violated—demands that we take action. Let us build societies that are able to coexist in a dignified way, in a way that protects life. Let us come together

2. Honduran ex-President Juan Orlando Hernández is currently serving a forty-five-year sentence in a US prison for narcotrafficking.

> and remain hopeful as we defend and care for the blood of this Earth and of its spirits.

I naively thought this prestigious award would offer her much-needed protection, so I was devastated when she was gunned down in her home on March 3, 2016. Her brutal assassination went beyond the media's portrayal of Honduras as a danger zone; it implicated underreported national and state-backed extractivist developments in energy, agribusiness, and tourism (Loperena 168).

Centering Berta Cáceres's question, my literary analysis is shaped by being in community with immigrant justice activism in Chicago. Before the COVID-19 pandemic, I volunteered in an interfaith arts program in two migrant "shelters" with tender-age children and adolescents. Although they were called "shelters," they were in reality youth detention centers contracted by a local nonprofit under the government's Office of Refugee Resettlement. If the children had not yet reunited with a family member or sponsor by the time they turned eighteen years old, they were transferred to an adult detention facility, where the deportation process would begin.

The array of nationalities and languages represented made singing into a portable microphone particularly joyous. There were always Spanish-speaking youth from Central and South America and the Caribbean. Many were visibly traumatized due to violence during the migrant journey or separation from a loved one at the border. Sometimes, after they were allowed to talk on the phone with a relative, they returned visibly upset. It was always moving to see how the kids comforted each other, but it was heartbreaking to see them languish there for months. As we packed up, they would often ask when we were coming back. With wry humor, teens would say, "I hope I'm not here next time you come." I'd smile sadly, saying, "Yes, I hope I don't see you next time."

Given the range of emotions and trauma the children were experiencing in detention, we were instructed to stay in the present moment as we sang, played games, worked on art projects, and ended our visits with a final reflection or blessing. During our accompaniment, I'd peek at the bookshelves to see if the kids had access to any of the YA books I was reading on Central American and Mexican migrant journeys. Although I never saw them on the bookshelves, I wonder if kids in detention today have access to a growing number of titles, like the ones included in this study, that have been translated into Spanish. If they have access to them, would it feel too soon to read about leaving home, and would they consider them "mirror books"? Would it feel comforting or triggering to see themselves in those books while confined in a detention shelter? For those who eventually reunite with their parents or sponsors in the US and enroll in school, how would it feel if they came across these YA novels in the curriculum or library shelves? Would they eventually feel comfortable sharing their personal migration experiences with teachers, counselors, classmates, or friends?

With the same interfaith organization, I served as an immigration Court Watch volunteer in downtown Chicago, following cases of people in detention and deportation proceedings. I witnessed many people opting for "early departure" because they had spent too much time away from the families they journeyed to provide for. During the pandemic, I was paired up with a Spanish speaker in detention for weekly video calls. This accompaniment consisted of conversations focused on the present moment that often included reflections on the terrible conditions inside and longing to reunite with family, especially their children. Thankfully he was released and reunited with family.

After the pandemic, I participated in a week-long service trip to the lands of the Tohono O'odham Nation and crossed into Mexico with university students. The time I spent witnessing the testimonio of a Salvadoran survivor who was abandoned by a coyote in the Sonoran Desert as a nineteen-year-old and watched several people in her group perish from dehydration as well as the time I spent hiking to participate in water drops along the migrant path with Tucson Samaritans and No More Deaths volunteers reinforced the belief that no one is illegal on stolen land.

My interdisciplinary reading of youth literature is also shaped by three experiences accompanying migrant families in Chicago. The first was a Guatemalan family that eventually received asylum, the second was a refugee family from the Democratic Republic of the Congo, and the third was a Colombian family that spent more than six months in shelters before finding housing. Their agency and resistance have taught me the power of storytelling and witnessing.

Over the years, our community of volunteers has witnessed increased militarization of the border, exponential detention and deportations in addition to a global pandemic, and mass social protests in solidarity with the Black Lives Matter movement, demanding #AbolishthePolice, #AbolishICE, and #FreePalestine. This intergenerational community has taught me that youth care deeply about how issues of migration intersect with race, class, gender, sexuality, ableism, and state-sponsored genocide. My hope is that this book will serve as a springboard for antiracist conversations and curriculum building among academics, parents, teachers, librarians, and volunteers along with graduate and undergraduate students interested in raising critical awareness about immigrant justice.

Latinx YA Literature Matters! But What Counts as Latinx YA? And Who Gets to Tell These Stories?

Adolescence has always been considered a transitional period of questioning self-identity and searching for connections to the larger world outside the home. Pam B. Cole defines adolescence as "a time of firsts: a period of rapid psychological, physical, and social change, a time of uncertainty, roller-coaster emotions, and conflict. It's a stage in which young people are separating from their parents, and trying out the identities they will carry into their adulthoods" (1). The titles I study, specifically written for youth and marketed as YA fiction, pose big questions about life and love as they portray the physical and emotional journeys of unaccompanied Central Americans and Mexicans on their trek to the United States, as well as the inward search for meaning while facing danger, always longing for a sense of home and belonging.

So who exactly are Latinx youth literature's target readers? Generally the intended audience is divided into middle schoolers between the ages of 11 and 14, high schoolers ranging from 14 to 18, and the category of "youth" assigned to those under the age of 25. The Latinx market is important and diverse. According to the Pew Research Center, they are the youngest major racial or ethnic group in the United States: "About one-third, or 17.9 million, of the nation's Hispanic population is younger than 18, and about a quarter, or 14.6 million, of all Hispanics are Millennials." The US Hispanic population reached 62.1 million in 2020, an increase of 23 percent over the previous decade, and they accounted for 51 percent of the nation's total population increase, a higher share than any other racial or ethnic group (Passel et al.). Moreover, "Among Hispanics ages 5 to 17, nearly all of whom are U.S. born, 88% are proficient English speakers, including 37% who speak only English at home and 50% who speak another language at home but speak English very well." Clearly Latinx teens are an important and diverse market, but how often do they see their stories reflected in books assigned at school?

I use *Latinx* as gender neutral, nonbinary alternative to *Latino/a* and *Hispanic.* As Zimmerman et al. stress, "Latinxs include a racially, culturally, and linguistically diverse group of people living in the United States who trace their ancestry to predominantly Spanish-speaking regions of Latin America and the Caribbean" (837). Like *Latine,* the term *Latinx* has generated debate, but I use it as a LGBTQ+-inclusive term that some young people have embraced; therefore, I respectfully follow their lead. According to Lopez et al., the pan-ethnic label Latine is also being used in Spanish. Importantly, Barillas Chón specifies that the terms Latino/a and Hispanic are colonial inventions in which the US is highly implicated and that flatten differences within different groups of the continent (295). Born and raised in Los Angeles, scholar Giovanni Batz writes about recovering his K'iche' Maya roots in a US educational system that pressures Indigenous youth to adapt to a predominantly Latino/Hispanic environment, while others adopt strategies to preserve their Maya identity, including a rejection of the Latino/Hispanic label. Bearing the range of terms in circulation, I use Latinx with an awareness that identities are continuously transforming and recovering as expressions of cultural resistance (Batz 202).

So why do I use the term *Latinx YA literature* if not all protagonists and authors are Latinx? I use this term to encompass the totality of the literary corpus since all texts are published in the US, and when the protagonists flee their homes in the Northern Triangle and Mexico, the US is their intended destination. While I identify characters as Indigenous Maya or Ladinos as Guatemalan, Honduran, Salvadoran, or Mexican during their journeys, I use "Latinx" to refer to protagonists who come of age in the US.[3] As undocumented youth, they experience the layered process of "becoming Latinx" among others who were born in the US and grapple with the privilege and responsibilities of citizenship in mixed-status homes. While I use *Latinx* to distinguish between the protagonists' and authors' US-based experiences, I refer to people and characters as Mexican or Central American when referring to their lived reality in Latin America. I make this place-based distinction to acknowledge differences in terms of poverty, gender, ethnicity, and access to health and education. As the novels illustrate, impoverished children, especially Indigenous youth in Mexico and Central America, are often expected to leave school to work in order to contribute to the household or to assume caregiving responsibilities for younger siblings.

Relatedly, I associate the decision to migrate for safety or to seek work to help family members with agency, which is defined as "the strategic making and remaking of ourselves, identities, activities, relationships, cultural tools and resources, and histories, as embedded within relations of power" (Lewis et al. 2007, 18, cited in Vaughn et al. 35). For Margaret Vaughn et al., agency "is the ability of individuals to exert influence and to create opportunities through intentions, decisions, and actions" (Vaughn 2018, 5, cited in Vaughn et al. 35). Vaughn et al. underscore that "as literature plays an important role in how agency is cultivated, a more varied representation of young children as agentic individuals is essential" (44). My analysis spotlights the specific

3. Referring to the terms *Ladino* and *mestizaje*, Barillas Chón stipulates, "Although born out of different historical junctures, I use *ladino* in a similar way that *mestizaje* is conceptualized in other parts of Abya Yala to refer to an ideology and political project of creating non Maya subjects for the purposes of maintaining unequal relationships of power in Guatemala" ("When Children" 288).

ways Central American migration narratives show young people finding what agency they can, and the specific need they have for agency while fleeing war, crossing through Mexico to reach the border, navigating life in the shadows, or finding their voices while exploring their cultural identities. In my view, agency matters particularly because the dominant narrative on child and youth migration is demonizing, victimizing, and invisibilizing, and the structural forces creating the root causes they flee are often normalized.

In terms of YA's literary history, Jackie White traces the genre's beginnings as an independent category to S. E. Hinton's novel *The Outsiders* (1967), noting that the title speaks "to the liminal or borderland sensibility most adolescents feel in being neither children nor adults" (193). Jennifer Buehler designates the 1970s as the golden age of YA, followed by a dormant period in the 1980s, and notes that in the mid-1990s YA publishing was starting to take off again (20). The foundation of the American Library Association's Young Adult Library Services Association and NCTE's Assembly on Literature for Adolescents along with the creation of literary prizes such as the Américas Award for Children's and Young Adult Literature in 1993, the Tomás Rivera Mexican American Children's Book Award in 1995, and the Pura Belpré Award in 1996 helped launch the field. Undoubtedly, in the last two decades, YA literature has become increasingly popular in the United States. In fact, YA has become the fastest-growing category, with 30.91 million YA fiction books sold in 2022, compared to 4.11 million nonfiction (Curcic). Literary critics Ebony Thomas and Marquise Griffin state that "the 1990s marked the start of the rise of books for children's and young adults as the most profitable arm of contemporary US publishing" (90).

Educator Nancy Larrick (1910–2004) pointed out the historical lack of diversity in the field in her 1965 article in the *Saturday Review* titled "The All-White World of Children's Literature." And in 2014 Walter Dean Myers reiterated in the *New York Times* the question that continues to haunt YA: "Where Are the People of Color in Children's Books?" (Chaudhri 35). Slowly, more authors of color are writing YA fiction, getting published, and finding their way to library shelves and classrooms across the country.

While the immediate audience for the novels I study might be adolescents and young adults, I believe these seemingly straightforward books challenge us as educators and social justice advocates to reflect on the interconnections between geopolitics and neoliberal capitalism. Given that YA literature remains primarily Eurocentric (Landt 690), I see these YA novels as specifically enriching discussions of diversity in the secondary and higher education curriculum because they urge students to think critically about and for themselves. Rooted in Paulo Freire's critical pedagogy, A. A. Akom's "Critical Hip

Hop Pedagogy as a Form of Liberatory Praxis" suggests that "resiliency and resistance can be developed that challenges the dominant mindset, increases academic engagement and achievement, and builds new understandings of the strength and assets of youth of color and the communities from which they come" (57). Likewise, Susan Landt characterizes young adolescents' encounter between self and other as "a kaleidoscope of opportunity" (697), while Steven Wolk affirms that teaching for social responsibility with YA literature empowers us all (664).

Out of the Shadows: Visibilizing US Central American Voices and Historical Memory in Latinx YA Literature and Scholarship

In her outstanding book *Side by Side,* children's and YA scholar Marilisa Jiménez García underscores that "the formation of Children's Literature Studies in the humanities during the 1980s contained a desire to steer away from arguments in Ethnic Studies movements" (11), so works by and for people of color were mostly left out of youth literary scholarship, dually marginalized in literary and Latinx studies (10). Jiménez García uses the designation "youth literature and culture" to move away from exclusionary scholarly practices. In "The Lens of Latinx Literature," she addresses the issue of commodification and "what gets seen and marketed as Latinx." Without mincing words, she asserts, "This is a system that makes diversity a viable market while still excluding creators and scholars of color" (4), and clarifies, "Latinx literature is a liminal space daring us to transcend disciplines and borders, asking us to go beyond our neat definitions. Latinx literature, thankfully, just never will behave. And that is why we need it more than ever" (7). I agree that we need Latinx YA literature more than ever before because of its capacity to affirm and reflect youths' diverse identities and migration stories during hostile times with threats of mass deportation. The books in this corpus can help youth navigate challenging conversations about race, inequality, violence, and racialized fears.

This study builds on the seminal work by Latinx and Chicanx scholars such as Cristina Rhodes's history of multiethnic representation in children's and YA literature published in the United States, "from racist representations in the nineteenth and twentieth centuries to activist futures today" ("Multicultural" 270). Other path breaking texts include Sonia Alejandra Rodríguez's "Conocimiento Narratives: Creative Acts and Healing in Latinx Children's and Young Adult Literature" (2019), Cristina Herrera's *ChicaNerds in Chicana Young Adult Literature: Brown and Nerdy* (2021), Trevor Boffone and Cristina

Herrera's *Nerds, Goths, Geeks, and Freaks: Outsiders in Chicanx and Latinx Young Adult Literature and Latinx Teens* (2020), and their *U.S. Popular Culture on the Page, Stage and Screen* (2022). *Coming of Age(ncy)* is also informed by the excellent *Tactics of Hope in Latinx Children's and Young Adult Literature* by Jesus Montaño and Regan Postma-Montaño (2022).

Building on this impressive and inspiring body of work, I aim to challenge the erasure of Central American lived experiences and make space for stories of the diaspora, thus further diversifying Latinx studies and young adult literary studies. By widening the chronology and road map to include non-Latinx authors who wrote about the Central American civil conflicts often as they were taking place, they also challenge us to reflect on white saviorism in a context of white supremacy. I seek to widen the Latinx YA lens so that younger generations, including Maya peoples in the diaspora, may learn about the Central American conflicts of the 1980s and 1990s and gain a critical awareness of their own agency alongside protagonists who vow to tell what they survived. Barillas Chón reminds us that Maya migrant populations are often invisibilized under the larger Latina/o racial category, "effectively rendering their experiences 'presently absent' in schools and in education studies" ("When Children" 287). In fact, Barillas Chón stipulates that in most cases, "unaccompanied Guatemalan minors are predominantly Indigenous or migrate from primarily Maya and rural regions within the country." Further, "Maya peoples' migration can be traced to the 1970s and that of Indigenous Zapotec and Mixtec Mexicans date back to the Bracero Program of the 1940s" (Barillas Chón, "K'iche'" 1225).

Methodological Framework and Data on Latinx YA Representation in US Publishing

Given the growing wealth of texts in YA literature in general and Latinx YA more specifically, for this study I selected novels that represent the Central American and Mexican migrant journey from the 1980s to 2024. While I searched for YA novels that feature unaccompanied migration from any of the seven Central American countries, I found novels that represent that journey only from Guatemala, El Salvador, and Honduras. Of these, the majority depict migration from Guatemala. Three novels portray migration from El Salvador, and three feature social conditions in Honduras, including the decision to migrate and deportation from the US. Of the forty-five novels I studied, published from 1981 to 2024, twenty-two books portray migration originating from Mexico.

For inclusion in my critical content analysis, the following criteria informed my text selection: (1) the book is a work of YA fiction written in English and marketed to a youth audience in the US; (2) the book spotlights the migrant journey by a protagonist from Central America or Mexico who crosses one or multiple borders to migrate clandestinely to the US; (3) the book features a Central American or Mexican protagonist or US-born youth raised by Central American or Mexican undocumented parents or siblings as part of a mixed-status home. I focus on the YA undocumented experience because undocumented minors are among society's most vulnerable population, and while they are deeply affected by larger power structures in their home countries and in the US as their intended destination, their stories challenge us to connect the direct violence they face with transnational neoliberal policies shaping forced displacement. Ultimately, their migration embodies agency and resistance as they strive to survive and imagine a better future.

As a road map and chronology of Latinx YA fiction centering Central American and Mexican migration, I want to address the fact that the authors discussed in the first three chapters are predominantly white or non-Latinx. Coinciding with the #WeNeedDiverseBooks and #OwnVoices social justice movements, the novels examined in chapter 4 point to a growing number of Latinx authors, and the writers discussed in chapter 5 are all Latinx. While the growth of Latinx representation is very positive and encouraging, I study their increasing presence within the larger context of the YA literary field and publishing industry that continue to be predominantly white.

To what extent do the authors' race and ethnicity as cultural insiders or outsiders really matter? As I see it, the authors' self-identification affects the cultural awareness and direct lived experience they bring to their writing. Although controversial, debates about "authenticity" are important in terms of the nuance some authors bring to the portrayal of youth migration and raising critical consciousness about their humanity. For this reason, I agree with Grace Enriquez's savvy revising of Bishop's mirrors metaphor: "Close approximations are not good enough. They are foggy mirrors that reflect only vague contours of the identities and lived experiences that comprise a child's reality. . . . If we present students with foggy mirrors, we might also be stereotyping them and their families" (104). With respect to the representation of Central American and Mexican migrant journeys to the United States, the white and Latinx authors featured in this book bring a wealth of lived experiences and perspectives to YA literature.

I collected data on the publishing industry from the University of Wisconsin's Cooperative Children's Book Center, which has tracked books by and about marginalized communities since 1985. The data shows that Latinx authors have historically had much smaller numbers regarding representation than have whites. According to the center's 2022 study, 39 percent of the total books they received (3,451) have at least one BIPOC primary character. But of these, only 6 percent of the primary characters are Latinx, as opposed to 12 percent Black/African, 22 percent animal, and 29 percent white. Of the books in the 2022 study, 7 percent were about Latinx characters. In terms of authorship, 11 percent had at least one Latinx creator, illustrator, or compiler, while 71 percent of books had at least one white creator. Thus, my study highlights that Central American and Mexican migration stories are making their way into a very marginalized space of Latinx representation, simultaneously diversifying Chicanx/Latinx studies and the white-dominated field of YA literature.

To gather texts for my study, I read book reviews and scholarly articles in children's and YA journals such as *Research on Diversity in Youth Literature,* magazines such as *School Library Journal* and *Horn Book Magazine,* and Goodreads lists. I regularly visited the We Need Diverse Books and Latinx in KidLit websites and followed YA authors on social media. I visited the Chicago Public Library's home page and catalog and reviewed the library's curated compilations of titles and blog posts, such as "New in Kids Books," "Teen Staff Picks," "Latinx History Month Reads for Teens," "Great Reads for Teens for Latinx History Month," and "La Frontera: Immigration Books for Teens." I visited library branches in Chicago and Los Angeles in person whenever possible to browse their children's and YA displays, and I visited Evanston Public Library's YA collection regularly. I combed through award lists such as the Américas Book Awards, Pura Belpré Award, and Tomás Rivera Book Award.

Working chronologically by date of publication, I found that the majority of YA novels were written by non-Latinx authors, several of whom have a range of travel or research experience in Latin America or the borderlands. According to authors' biographies and interviews I consulted, several authors have been or are themselves teachers in Latinx communities. Others have devoted time and energy volunteering with migrants at the border or working for nonprofits doing humanitarian work with refugees.

As for my findings, I examine a total of 45 YA novels written by 38 authors (Daniel Aleman, Omar Castañeda, Jennifer De Leon, Marie Marquardt, Marcia Mickelson, Ben Mikaelson, and Francisco Stork each wrote 2 novels, Alexandra Diaz wrote 3 novels, and 2 novels were cowritten by 2 authors). Of the authors, 26 are women (16 of whom are Latinx) and 12 are men (8 of whom are Latinx). Twenty-two authors identify as Latinx, and 16 are non-Latinx. These data point to the fact that significant systemic change must take place in order to achieve equity in the publishing industry. Educators and researchers have long stated the importance of having children and young adult readers see themselves in the books they read, in school or at home for pleasure. As prolific and prized Black YA author Jason Reynolds states in *The Guardian,* "For some of us, in order for us to see the world, we have to see ourselves first."

I maintain that although publishers are increasingly promoting more diverse titles, a diversity gap continues to exist as YA novels are still mostly written by white authors. Clearly, as educator Marie Ann Donovan states, referencing Rudine Sims Bishop's well-known metaphor of books as mirrors and windows, "it's impossible for any one book to be a full-length mirror. . . . No book can totally capture any one child's life, any one culture's breadth and depth" (178). M. J. Botelho agrees, underscoring that one mirror or one window is insufficient. The publishing industry must take significant steps to do better.

#WeNeedDiverseBooks, #OwnVoices, #Dignidad Literaria: Calling for Authenticity in the Neoliberal Marketplace

In an effort to push the publishing industry to do better in terms of diversity, equity, and inclusion, #WeNeedDiverseBooks (2014), #OwnVoices (2015), and #DignidadLiteraria (2020) galvanized social media to bring about more awareness. In 2021 We Need Diverse Books stopped using the term #OwnVoices, which was coined by author Corinne Duyvis, because they "believed it became a vague marketing term and created potentially unsafe situations for authors and illustrators who chose not to share parts of their identities." Instead, they use specific descriptions that authors use for themselves and their characters. Little Feminist uses the term internally, "as a shortcut to understand that the author or illustrator matches the identity of the main character." #OwnVoices took up the thorny issue of authenticity with full awareness that identities are intersectional, stipulating that if authors or illustrators "don't hold those identities they are representing, we expect them to listen to those who do." They make this pronouncement because "at worst, books not created by Own Voices may perpetuate white supremacy characteristics and harmful stereotypes. . . . Writing characters of color with a white gaze can be demeaning and sorely inaccurate if you are not immersed in that culture." Based on the research conducted by education scholar Rudine Sims Bishop, they maintain that "no representation is better than inaccurate representation." As children's literature scholar Karen Coats writes, "#ownvoices explicitly calls for writers to draw from their own experience," while noting, "apparently, the need for more diverse books is not as strong as the need by some to control the narratives of cultural identity" (26).

Although dated, a pertinent example regarding the need for greater Latinx representation was the uproar over the novel *American Dirt* (2020). This best seller put a spotlight on inequities in the publishing world with its depiction of the migrant journey through Mexico, which I cover in chapters 2 and 3. The controversy is reflective of my larger argument about the need for more Latinx representation on three interconnected levels.

Jeanine Cummins's *American Dirt* is an action-packed novel that immerses the reader in Mexico's drug war as a "window" book. It quickly rose to best-seller lists because readers such as Oprah Winfrey who were largely unfamiliar with forced migration were captivated by a plotline centered on a mother's need to flee to the US for safety with her young son. Despite the criticism the book received in the Latinx community, Oprah endorsed *American Dirt* because it helped her form a "newfound perspective about the migration process." She explained, "I really appreciated that book, and it helped me to see immigrants and the whole migration process differently than I had before. . . . So it opened up a space in me, allowed me to see things differently, and I appreciate that from the author and I thought the story was well told" (Aquilina and Wang). In Oprah's video for her Book Club, *American Dirt* functions as Bishop's "sliding glass door": "I was opened, I was shook up, it woke me up, and I feel that everybody who reads this book is actually going to be immersed in the experience of what it means to be a migrant on the run for freedom" (quoted in Alter). The book was lauded by acclaimed authors such as John Grisham, Stephen King, Ann Patchett, and YA author Julia Alvarez (studied in chapter 4) and cheered as "the great novel of Las Américas" by Chicana poet Sandra Cisneros. In fact, Cisneros defended her blurb in an interview with Chicanx novelist Yxta Maya Murray: "And I did it, and what do I get? Even if I was hyperbolic, I knew that book would be read by people who weren't in the choir. I didn't know what the advance was. I knew she did her homework, and she wrote a thriller. People got mad. A memoir will not get you a million-dollar advance, or if you write poetry—come on. You want your book to get sold? Write a thriller. Write a Y.A. book." Returning to Bishop's analogy, here the difference between a mirror and window book is that the latter appeals to those beyond the limited Latinx "choir."

The question of authenticity and representation became the focus of debate when Latinx authors spoke back to the publishing industry's privileging of whiteness. In her scathing review on Tropics of Meta titled "Pendeja, You Ain't Steinbeck: My Bronca with Fake-Ass Social Justice Literature," Chicanx author Myrian Gurba critiques *American Dirt* as a repackaging of Latinx writers' works "for mass racially 'colorblind consumption.'" Similarly, novelist Reyna Grande, who was born and raised in the Mexican state of Guerrero, where *American Dirt* begins, called out the immense border walls that the publishing industry erects for Latinx authors with lived experience. Pointing to the publish industry's racism, David Bowles, Gurba, and Roberto Lovato launched #DignidadLiteraria with the following objective:

> DignidadLiteraria is a network of committed Latinx authors formed to combat the invisibility of Latinx authors, editors and executives in the U.S. publishing industry and the dearth of Latinx literature on the shelves of America's bookstores and libraries. #DignidadLiteraria believes in the social and political power of wholly authentic Latinx voices and that it is the duty of the publishing industry and literati to use their full power and privilege to elevate these voices. ("#DignidadLiteraria and PRESENTE")

While I wholeheartedly agree with the need for more Latinx representation, the statement raises the question of determining who are "wholly authentic Latinx voices." Is prized Dominican American author Julia Alvarez a "wholly authentic Latinx voice" when she writes about the migration experience of an undocumented Indigenous protagonist from Chiapas, Mexico, as discussed in chapter 4? As the daughter of Cuban refugees and author of three YA novels examined in this book, is Alexandra Diaz a "wholly authentic Latinx voice" when she writes about Mexican and Guatemalan migrant journeys? I maintain that Alvarez's and Diaz's YA novels make valuable contributions to Latinx YA and the representation of the migrant journey in US fiction, as do non-Latinx authors who have done their "homework," to borrow from Cisneros. I view the critical backlash against *American Dirt* as instructive because Latinx authors spoke back to the white publishing industry for gatekeeping and profiting from immigrant pain.[4] Likewise, I hope to see many more novels and scholarship by US Central American voices.

The issue of authenticity and Latinx representation matters because of very active censorship campaigns against people of color and immigrants in general and, more specifically, an erasure of marginalized voices and their history with book bans. It's imperative that diverse YA books continue to be readily accessible in schools, integrated into the curriculum to help teachers reach their curricular goals, and prominently featured on public library

---

4. Adding insult to injury, the author and publisher used the barbed-wire motif on the book's cover as a decorative theme during the book's launch and promotion—Cummins in a manicure and the publisher in floral centerpieces at a celebration dinner. Immigration reporter Aura Bogado denounced it as a vulgar and oppressive fashion statement capitalizing on immigrant trauma. Flatiron Books later apologized for the barbed-wire centerpieces. See Alter and Lim.

shelves across the country. Given the book bans and white supremacist hostility toward "wokeness" and critical race theory, *Coming of Age(ncy)* aims to be a resource for teachers, librarians, graduate and undergraduate students, and fellow volunteers committed to advancing antiracist agency in our classrooms and communities. My deepest hope is that this book on Central American and Mexican youth migration will be useful to immigration justice advocates who carry out such important work supporting immigrants and refugees.

The Chapter Roadmap and Chronology: The Transnational Adolescent Migrant Journey in Latinx YA

Moving chronologically and geographically, *Coming of Age(ncy) on the Migrant Trail* provides a sociopolitical literary context for the representation of the Central American and Mexican youth migration journeys to the United States. I study how works of YA literature, published in English for a youth audience, represent political violence and state-sponsored repression taking place in the Northern Triangle, Mexico, and the US.

In chapter 1, I examine novels featuring Mayan protagonists who witness rape and genocide during the scorched-earth warfare of the early 1980s. This understudied corpus makes a significant contribution to US Central American studies, as well as Latin American and Latinx studies and YA literature, where content on Central American migration and youth more specifically have historically been absent. This literature is a noteworthy addition to what US Salvadoran scholar Yajaira M. Padilla calls the "Central American transnational imaginary," as works "marked by memories of war, settlement in the United States, and crossings through Mexico, and in which individual and communal identities are being continuously defined and renegotiated" ("Central American" 151). Here, I lay out my central argument that these stories of transmigration from Central America into Mexico en route to the United States are coming-of-age(ncy) survival narratives that contest the dominant narrative that vilifies migrants or views them solely as traumatized victims. Using a Latin American testimonio framework that combines personal and collective narratives to bring about social awareness, I study how the protagonists speak out against the terror and gendered violence they witness, thus contributing to historical remembrance. Sadly, the horrors of US-funded wars and impunity for crimes against humanity, including genocide, continue to spur mass migration and authoritarianism, threatening democracy for all.

In chapter 2, I analyze the literary representation of the adolescent migrant journey across Mexico to cross clandestinely into the United States.

The context of the North American Free Trade Agreement (NAFTA), which espouses a neoliberal politics of disposability where profits are prioritized over human dignity, is important for understanding the economic inequality and injustice portrayed in the novels, since immigration after September 11, 2001, is viewed as a national security issue, with increased hostility toward people who are pushed out of Central America and Mexico by racialized capitalism. As another example of neoliberal disposability, the Prevention through Deterrence policy funnels migrants away from border towns and into the Sonoran Desert, shifting the responsibility for thousands of deaths to an inhospitable environment. Given increasingly repressive policies that position Mexico as a vertical border enforcer, this chapter examines novels that illustrate youth agency amid the dire circumstances migrants endure as they flee home and cross Mexico on their way to the US border.

Chapter 3 explores the articulation of violence by studying the portrayal of criminal groups, the absent state, and youth agency. I study YA novels that take place in Mexico during the War on Drugs era and represent narcoviolence as a root cause for unauthorized migration to the US. Using the concepts of necropolitics and US anti-immigrant sentiment, I analyze how agency is depicted in the context of Mexican poverty and the violence of organized crime. I believe that this critical context can help teachers, parents, immigration advocates and undergraduate or graduate students gain deeper awareness about how neoliberal capitalism and impunity uphold what Canadian journalist Dawn Paley designates as "drug war capitalism." Read through this critical lens, the kidnappings, disappearances, femicides, and gendered violence portrayed in the novels reveal that impunity, corruption, and structural violence are the true culprits of forced migration given that the US and Mexico collude with organized crime to profit from drug war capitalism.

Continuing along the final leg of the migrant journey, in chapter 4, I examine stories that take place in the US, after surviving the crossing. These novels explore the protagonists' emotional and social experiences as undocumented residents in their new home. They illustrate the difficulties of coming of age in the shadow of illegality, constantly fearing family separation and deportation while also experiencing romantic love for the first time. The protagonists' first cross-racial friendships and romantic relationships invite reflection on white supremacy, the white savior complex, nativist anti-immigrant rhetoric, and problematic notions of deservingness.

Delving deeper into the social construction of "illegality," chapter 5 highlights a growing body of texts by Latinx authors that denounce the detention and deportation regimes, giving readers an inside look into the cruelty of US immigration policy. Despite the challenges the protagonists face at a young age, they find the inner strength to become agents of change who model empathy and dignity in a world that displays "zero tolerance" toward racialized others. Coming full circle, I end the chapter with an analysis of novels that portray US Central Americans exploring their identities and contributing to historical memory.

I conclude with a reflection on the larger implications of the increasing political and economic power that the United States exerts in Central America and Mexico to decrease the flow of undocumented migration, without addressing the root causes that are causing impoverished youth to flee in search of a more dignified life. Despite our politically divided times, these YA novels inspire my faith in youth agency and the power of storytelling to spark empathy, solidarity, and activism. I am hopeful that readers of all ages will see themselves in these passionately written stories and rise to the challenge of working for social change.

CHAPTER 1

Defying Death

Fleeing Salvadoran and Guatemalan Political Violence in Latinx YA Coming-of-Age(ncy) Narratives

In this chapter I explore the relationship between war and forced migration in young adult novels that take place during the violent civil wars in El Salvador and Guatemala. As realistic works of fiction set in the past, these "mirror" and "window" books invite today's youth to immerse themselves in the protagonists' perilous journeys as they flee injustice. These YA novels depict the harrowing experiences of Salvadoran and Guatemalan children and youth who witnessed and managed to escape state-sponsored genocide, fleeing political violence and defying death. The Salvadoran Civil War (1980–92) left more than 75,000 dead and 500,000 displaced. Salvadoran American scholar Leisy J. Abrego explains US ties to Central American violence: "In the 1970s and 1980s, US support for the military and elites of El Salvador set the conditions for the immensely devastating consequences of the civil war. Determined to prevent a communist victory in the region that would stand in the way of US corporations' profits there, as part of its Cold War operations, the Reagan administration armed and trained the military and paramilitary leaders of death squads with the goal of eliminating all opposition" ("On Silences" 74). By 1985 economic aid to El Salvador alone totaled $744 million, adding to the $744 million the country had already received between 1981 and 1983 for "security" measures (Smith 35, cited in Padilla, *From Threatening* 3).

On an even larger humanitarian scale, the Commission for Historical Clarification (CEH) established that 200,000 Guatemalans were killed or disappeared during the war (1960–96), including about 150,000 who sought refuge in Mexico (Manz, "Reflections" 313). The CEH's 1999 report of the truth commission documented the deaths of tens of thousands of children during Guatemala's thirty-six-year civil war, noting with "particular concern that a large number of children were among the direct victims of arbitrary execution, forced disappearance, torture, rape and other violations of their fundamental rights . . . [and the war] left a large number of children orphaned and abandoned . . . and the possibility of living a normal childhood within the norms of their culture, lost" (CEH 1999, 23, cited in Gibbons 149). Although the internal wars ended with the signing of peace treaties in Nicaragua in 1990, El Salvador in 1992, and Guatemala in 1996, extreme poverty and structural violence continue to be deadly forces in the region today. As we will see in the following chapters, the Central American postwar period, in fact, has proven even more violent than the armed conflicts. And sadly, impunity for past crimes against humanity and government corruption persists, driving many to migrate and seek asylum on an ongoing basis.

This chapter aims to provide educators, librarians, migration and human rights activists, and undergraduate and graduate students with the historical, political, and cultural contexts underlying YA works of fiction about the Central American civil wars and subsequent diaspora that often go unacknowledged in mainstream media and invisibilized in children's and YA scholarship. This critical overview will help educators guide young readers through a more nuanced understanding of the legacies of war and migration while making a wider audience aware of novels that address timely topics such as surviving genocide and recovering historical memory.

Importantly, eight of the nine YA novels I study in this chapter center Indigenous youth growing up in loving communities that instill pride in their Mayan languages and traditions amid violence. I believe they serve as much-needed "windows, mirrors, and sliding glass doors" (Bishop, "Mirrors" 9) for today's Central American migrant youth and US diaspora, particularly those of Maya descent. As renowned educator Rudine Sims Bishop wrote, "Literature transforms human experience and reflects it back to us, and in that reflection we can see our own lives and experiences as part of the larger human experience. Reading, then, becomes a means of self-affirmation, and readers often seek their mirrors in books. For many years, nonwhite readers have too frequently found the search futile" ("Mirrors" 9). Like Bishop, Poqomam migrant and educator David W. Barillas Chón emphasizes the importance of Central American representation: "Maya migrant populations are often invisibilized and subsumed under the larger Latina/o racial category[, e]ffectively rendering their experiences 'presently absent' in schools and education studies" ("When Children" 287). Given that only one of the authors discussed in this chapter was of Guatemalan descent, I acknowledge that this fiction "gives voice" to Indigenous characters from a non-Maya gaze. I include these works, however, because in my view their fiction gives visibility to Central American indigeneity in culturally responsible ways that aim to "honor Maya migrant students' lived realities" (Barillas Chón, "When Children" 288) while expanding diversity and antiracism within Latinx YA.

The non-Maya, non-Latinx authors discussed in this chapter have a range of experience visiting or temporarily living in Central America. Frances Temple (1945–95) and Canadian author, illustrator, and editor of children's books Alma Fullerton, for example, do not seem to have had lived experience in El Salvador or Guatemala, where their books take place. Temple was a primary school teacher whose books dealt with poverty and oppression in El Salvador, Haiti, and Jamaica. Author Ben Mikaelson identifies as Bolivian American since he was born in Bolivia and raised bilingual by missionary parents. The family moved to Minnesota when he was in the sixth grade. Skila Brown, who grew up in Kentucky and Tennessee, visited Guatemala several times and lived there for five months while she revised *Caminar.* Ann Cameron earned an MFA in English in 1972 and moved to Panajachel in Guatemala in 1983; she returned to the US during the armed conflict. As a teacher artist in the Southwest, for twenty years Marge Pellegrino coordinated programs for Owl and Panther, an organization in Tucson that works with refugees. Omar Castañeda (1954–97) was born in Guatemala and earned a BA and MFA from Indiana University and taught at Western Washington University. I concur with Karina Alma's assertion that although little has been written about Castañeda, "he might be the first published U.S. Central American writer from the diaspora."[1] Taken together, these authors give visibility to the survival experiences of Salvadoran and Guatemalan youth during a period of armed conflict when US capitalist interests and national elites supported the repression. For decades, Central Americans and the Maya in particular have exerted agency to migrate to the US, and these novels provide readers of the diaspora with valuable insight.

I highlight these works because YA literature as a genre is largely ignored or altogether absent from Latin American studies, Latinx studies, and US Central American studies. *Coming of Age(ncy) on the Migrant Trail,* therefore, seeks to address this gap in the scholarship, beginning chronologically with the representation of agency during the Salvadoran and Guatemalan conflicts and the legacy of state-sponsored violence that continues to drive youth

1. See Castañeda's children's book *Abuela's Weave* that takes place in Guatemala and his essay "Guatemalan Macho Oratory" in the collection *Muy Macho* (1996). See also Karina Alma's analysis of his short story "On the Way Out" in *Central American Counterpoetics: Diaspora and Rememory* (2024).

migration today. Drawing on the testimonio, a politicized literary genre with a history of resistance in Central America, as a decolonial feminist framework, I first examine four escape narratives featuring male protagonists using Henry A. Giroux's conceptualization of globalized neoliberalism's "politics of disposability" as part of a larger war on youth agency and democracy. Then I examine five YA novels featuring Guatemalan Mayan girls who witness rape and genocide during the scorched-earth warfare of the early 1980s. Although these characters bear similarities in their embodied knowledge of racialized violence as Indigenous youth, for the purpose of clarity, I discuss their gendered experiences separately, although I do not want to run the risk of essentializing or objectifying them. Instead, I pay particular attention to how they are rendered visible as vulnerable youth who exert agency to defy state-sponsored violence.

Like the twenty-three-year-old Maya Quiché Rigoberta Menchú, who fled and denounced Guatemalan state-sponsored violence in her foundational testimony *Me llamo Rigoberta Menchú y así me nació la conciencia* (1983), translated as *I, Rigoberta Menchú: An Indian Woman in Guatemala* (1984), these fictionalized Maya protagonists bravely speak out against the terror they witness, thus contributing to historical remembrance. *Keywords for Latina/o Studies* (2017) defines *testimonio* as a "product of an individual act of witnessing and/or experiencing an abject social state that is more than individual, that is indeed collective" (Cruz-Malavé 228). Menchú's hotly debated text, told from the perspective of a young Maya Quiché activist, connects her personal story in the highlands to a larger group struggle to denounce state-sponsored violence and build collective memory. Consequently, literary critic George Yúdice calls testimonio writing "first and foremost an act, a tactic by means of which people engage in the process of self-constitution and survival" (46).

Collectively, these YA novels take readers—of whatever age, nationality, or political stripe—on an unsettling journey from the personal to the communal, across a series of borders where death is always close at hand. They depict horrific state violence against marginalized civilians with chilling realism, including infanticide and the targeted death of children as "'the seed that has to be eliminated'" (Burt 2).

"What You've Seen Tonight Makes You a Man": Male Escape Narratives during the Salvadoran and Guatemalan Civil Conflicts

Set in the larger context of colonized white supremacist heteropatriarchal capitalism (Allweiss 223), this first set of novels portray coming-of-age(ncy) stories amid civil wars, characterized by racialized social exclusion along with a structural lack of social investment, such as equitable access to education, healthcare and dignified employment. *Grab Hands and Run* (1993) by Frances Temple, *Red Midnight* (2002) by Ben Mikaelsen, *Libertad* (2008) by Alma Fullerton, and *Caminar* (2014) by Skila Brown introduce readers to El Salvador and Guatemala through chilling first-person accounts. Set during armed conflicts, *Grab Hands and Run* and *Red Midnight* feature twelve-year-old boys using their agency to flee Salvadoran and Guatemalan state-sponsored death squads to ensure the survival of a younger sibling.

Grab Hands and Run by Frances Temple stands out as the only YA novel in this corpus to represent the civil war in El Salvador. It is also unique in its portrayal of a mestizo family; the other novels discussed in this chapter represent Indigenous Maya youth fleeing war in Guatemala. It is important to trace the family's mestizo identity to the 1932 massacre in El Salvador known as La Matanza under President General Maximiliano Hernández Martínez, who committed ethnic cleansing of the Indigenous population, killing ten thousand to end a largely peasant Indian uprising (Velásquez Estrada 46). Art historian Kency Cornejo explains, "As a result of La Matanza, many Pipiles in El Salvador hid their indigenous clothes and languages out of fear of execution, concealing not only their existence as a people but also their cultural legacy in a country that now considers itself the most mestizo of Central America" (192). Immersed in similar violence decades later, the title *Grab Hands and Run* refers to the command that Felipe's father issues to the family before he is forcibly disappeared by state agents and is later killed for speaking out against the authoritarian Salvadoran government. In Felipe's case, the order to flee the country underscores male-gendered violence, since boys were forcefully recruited into the army against their will. Anna Peterson and Kay A. Read attest, "In El Salvador until 1991 and . . . in Guatemala, the armed forces used roundups to fill ranks, taking teenage boys and young men from buses, churches, and marketplaces. The recruits were usually poor, often from the rural areas, and many were moved to posts far from home, making it harder for them to notify their families or to flee" (222). Forced recruitment into the army or civil patrols was often a death sentence for minors, who were already considered disposable by state forces. This detail is emblematic of the connection between historical reality and fictional representation that underlies these YA literary works.

As a twelve-year-old from Usulután, El Salvador, Felipe knows that boys his age are forcibly recruited by the army and guerrillas since his uncles were required to serve in the army and never returned. His hands are tough and his arms are muscular from stripping the fibers from maguey plants to be soaked, twisted to make twine, then traded for candles, rice, or medicine. He also knows that in the countryside, "work is life" (4), yet he is one of the few characters in this body of YA literature who attends school. His family believes that by attending school, he will be saved from forced recruitment, since "they seem to only want illiterates for the army" (6). When he is approached by a man five or six years older than him who asks for water and wants to buy dried corn, Felipe knows that the man is part of the guerrillas that authorities call "subversives" but that townspeople refer to as *muchachos,* or "guys," because they defend peasants from exploitative landowners and the military. Fearing danger, his grandmother insists that Felipe didn't see him, that it was a dream; she tells Felipe, "Forget he was here" (11). Her protective instinct proves correct when armored trucks take over the town and his parents order him to run to the lagoon and hide. There, he finds a man's severed arm and hand. Ignoring his grandmother's instructions to focus on personal safety, he shows agency in resistance by wrapping the body parts in his T-shirt, hoping that his father will take them to the Human Rights Office for a fingerprint, since this was most likely a political murder of someone who dared to speak out against the government. Traumatized, Felipe vomits, with a new awareness that his life has suddenly changed. He cries when he returns home and overhears that his father has received a death threat and wants the family to flee to Canada. When his father's motorcycle is found abandoned outside the city, Felipe and his mother know it is time to run.

While escaping on the roof of a bus, Felipe witnesses appalling violence. From this vantage point, he sees in the street a dead woman's body—a victim of the death squads that exhibited tortured bodies to warn others against engaging in "subversive" activities. Aldo A. Lauria-Santiago affirms that "the repeated public display of tortured and disfigured bodies was a method of terrorizing the living" (100). Felipe's "reading" of this dead body aligns with Cathy Caruth's theorization of trauma: "The event is not assimilated or experienced fully at the time, but only belatedly, in its repeated *possession* of the one who experiences it. To be traumatized is precisely to be possessed by an image or event" (*Trauma* 4–5). Moreover, the role of testimonio in the collective process of historical clarification resonates with Caruth's contention in *Unclaimed Experience* that "history, like trauma, is never simply one's own, that history is precisely the way we are implicated in each other's traumas" (24).

As they flee, Felipe sees teenage boys patrolling, dressed in army uniforms with dark sunglasses and automatic rifles. His mother takes a countercultural or subversive stance when she explains, "A border is nothing, just a line on a map between countries. But in the minds of the authorities, a border is as real as a rock. And if you don't have papers stamped in all the right places, the authorities don't let you cross" (48). Lacking official documentation, the family must hide from Salvadoran, Guatemalan, and Mexican authorities who use their power to prevent them from seeking refuge abroad. Felipe learns that "refugees" are "what they call all people who have to leave their home on account of war. Refugees or fugitives. People on the run" (60). Realizing that his mother risks sexual violence along the journey and that, as impoverished war victims, they are disposable nobodies, Felipe resolves to remember the painful images he witnesses to develop this memory into a social consciousness; his courage and agency to make life-saving choices will be his own form of resistance.

As El Salvador and Guatemala share a geopolitical border, the civil wars in those countries have inspired YA novels whose adolescent protagonists experience similar traumatic events. Mikaelsen's *Red Midnight* depicts the refugee journey of Santiago Cruz and Angelina, his little sister. As young Indigenous *campesinos* who speak Kekchi and know very little Spanish, they flee their ravaged Guatemalan village to perceived safety in the US. The title refers to the horrific night of May 18, 1981, when Guatemalan soldiers raped, tortured, and massacred everyone in the village of Dos Vías, setting everything on fire. Santiago witnesses soldiers kill his family and neighbors and declares, "I will always think of that night as the night that God turned his back on the indigenos [*sic*]" (20).

Fleeing this horrific scorched-earth tactic, Felipe runs into the night carrying Angelina and sees that the homes in the neighboring town have been burned down and a putrid smell fills the air. He sees coconuts on the ground, then suddenly realizes they are actually the skulls of people burned alive. Robert Jay Lifton's comment to Caruth in an interview positions Santiago as a survivor and highlights testimonio's role in that survival: "When one witnesses the death of people, that really is the process of becoming a survivor, and the witness is crucial to the entire survivor experience" (Caruth, *Trauma* 138). His uncle in another town reinforces the power of witnessing, insisting that Santiago escape immediately to denounce the horror: "Leave Guatemala. Go as far away as you can and tell what has happened this night. . . . What you've seen tonight makes you a man. You are the only person who can tell of this evil" (3). As a survivor who comes of age by using his agency to denounce the violence and bear witness for the dead, he embodies the mission of testimonio. Because the Guatemalan state considers Santiago a "disposable youth" marked for death, his testimony in turn transforms the reader into a survivor by proxy so that others may grow in awareness and work for social change. Dori Laub and Shoshana Feldman stress the importance of this role: "the listener to trauma comes to be a participant and co-owner of the traumatic event" (57). Knowing that this violence is an injustice, Santiago feels abandoned, as the heinous acts he witnesses shatter his faith in a loving God: "If there is a God, then tonight I think he is like the soldiers and does not care about us. He does not care about the poor campesinos from the mountains who do not have money to wear fancy clothes or to shine their shoes. Here in Guatemala, there is not a God to protect us" (26). By equating God's indifference to soldiers' cruelty, he critiques not only structural violence and how power aligns itself with the privileged but also how the poor and vulnerable are abandoned and unprotected.

Having denounced what he has witnessed, Santiago receives food, a compass, and a *cayuco,* or canoe, from a fellow *campesino* to get across Lake Izabal in hopes of reaching US shores as child refugees. He knows he must protect his sister from additional gendered harm because structural and racialized violence inflicts additional harm on Indigenous girls. Like Felipe in *Grab Hands and Run,* Santiago is warned that their lack of passports or immigration papers will make the siblings "illegal," but facing death on the ocean engenders a coming-of-age consciousness with a new sense of agency to battle the winds, currents, hunger, and thirst. After twenty-three agonizing days at sea, the siblings drift onto the shore of a private American beach club. As Indigenous child migrants, like in Guatemala, they are viewed as superfluous trash, yet their harrowing escape from terror and death is documented in the media, and their eyewitness testimony of a Guatemalan massacre is used both to denounce state-sponsored violence and to plead for asylum.

As in *Red Midnight,* witnessing in *Grab Hands and Run* provides a lifeline for the Salvadoran mother and children who eventually make it across the Guatemalan-Mexican border but end up in a US family detention center along with thousands of other Central American refugees. Here, they cross a semantic border; instead of refugees, they are now considered "illegal aliens." As Arturo Arias and Claudia Milian remark of others in the shadows, "they are objectified as abject 'illegals,' condemned to erasure from US visual memory and into nonexistence" (142). Linda Green contextualizes the change in designation, concluding that this "legalization discourse, promoted by the far right and emphasized in the mainstream media, overrides any moral or political language as the basis for human rights and shifts the burden of complicity from the state to the people least able to defend themselves" ("Wink," 167). Fortunately, when Felipe and his mother give their haunting testimony to representatives of Project Canada, they are recommended for asylum and Canadian citizenship. While waiting for their documents to arrive, they experience solidarity and sanctuary in the American Midwest, prompting Felipe to reflect on the contradiction between the complicit role of the US in Central American violence and citizens' willingness to defy official policy: "It seems that although the U.S. government does bad things in El Salvador and supplies the weapons with which we are killed, many North Americans have good hearts" (159). This ability to hold opposing perspectives while offering their testimonios as a counterhegemonic tool of resistance, denouncing state violence, marks Felipe and Santiago's transition into manhood as they exert agency to protect their younger siblings while struggling to understand the global forces shaping their lives.

Similar to *Red Midnight,* Skila Brown's *Caminar* (2014) takes place in Guatemala in 1981. Brown writes this free verse YA novel "in memory of the more than 200,000 people who were killed or disappeared in Guatemala between 1960 and 1996. May they always be remembered." In "A Note to the Reader," Brown stands out as one of the few authors to explicitly situate the novel's violence in the aftermath of the 1954 coup that overthrew the democratically elected government with US support. According to Aviva Chomsky, "After the 1954 coup, the first order of the day for the United States was to crush the political and social movements that had threatened its goals in Guatemala" (74). Setting the novel in 1981 is equally important because it points to the genocidal period known as La Violencia under the regimes of General Fernando Romeo Lucas García (1978–82) and General Efraín Ríos Montt (March 1982–August 1983), which received significant US support (Sanford, *Buried Secrets* 14).

As an only child, Carlos helps his mother by chopping wood, keeping the stove warm, feeding the chickens, and gathering eggs, but she won't allow him to cut down a tree or wring the chicken's neck, saying "Not yet" when she wipes her brow, "feathers stuck to her arm with blood" (5). By taking on these chores herself, she protects Carlos's childhood innocence as long as she can, shielding him from more violent actions that would signify his readiness for military or guerrilla recruitment in Guatemala's heteropatriarchal society.

A keen observer, Carlos notices that soldiers have set up camp in his village and that they pay four hundred quetzales for the names of communists. Although he's never heard that word expressed in his fictional village of Chopán, he sees Juan Choc Túc dangling from a tree with a sign that says "Communist" around his neck. The army hangs him so villagers will learn a lesson, but Carlos is critical of the division the army sows in the community by having people sell each other out: "They were not calling him a Communist, instead they spoke of land he owned, land others wanted, land no one could afford, unless they earned a few quetzales selling names to the army" (12). Here Brown acknowledges that the root cause for violence is unequal land distribution and income inequality. The soldiers further disrupt Indigenous life in the village with their divisive rhetoric and indoctrination that impacts Carlos's emerging sense of masculinity; after the army leaves, he skips school to work in the fields picking coffee. He shows off the coins he earned "for a day of being a man" and gives them to his mother, saying "school is for children, Mama. Today, I am a man" (21). An elder acknowledges his transition into manhood, stating, "I was your age when I stepped away from Child, stepped into Man" (22). Despite his mother's fears, Carlos embraces his newfound masculinity by proudly becoming the family breadwinner.

Carlos's coming of age(ncy) is influenced by the portrayal of heteronormative masculinity as embodied by soldiers and guerrilla fighters. The community of Chopán is fearful when the guerrillas enter the village because they have been warned by the army not to associate with them. Despite the army's instructions, Carlos's mother gives them tortillas for their journey into the jungle because "everyone has to eat" (35). When he goes up the mountain to gather mushrooms for soup, he hears bullets raining down from a helicopter. He climbs a tree to hide: "I stayed in my tree even when the pops of their rifles, laughter of the soldiers, screams of my neighbors all died down" (50). Traumatized, he finally gathers the strength to walk, repeating "it did not happen" multiple times (63). As he searches for food and water, he debates whether he should return to the village or keep climbing the mountain to reach his grandmother in Patrichál. He screams when he hears voices, fearing it's the army, but instead he encounters young guerrilla rebels from a different Maya ethnolinguistic group, so they communicate in Spanish. Miguel, the friendly leader, flirts with his comrade Ana and introduces Carlos to her brother Hector and cousin Paco, who seems to be Carlos's age but carries a gun. They tell Carlos about the massacre and mass grave, and that soldiers burned the village down. They remember seeing the woman who gave them tortillas "among the heads in the pile" (103). Carlos feels terrible guilt for not having done anything to stop the army from killing everyone, including his mother. Miguel explains, "That is why we fight, Carlos, against the rich man whose fathers' fathers took our land, who give us just a handful of beans, centavos, for cutting sugarcane or picking cotton from the earth, the cotton that is the grandchild of our grandfathers' seeds. One day, amigo, we campesinos will defeat the men who hold us down, take back our Guatemala" (126). When the helicopters return, Carlos wakes the rebels and runs to warn his grandmother, yelling for everyone to hide among the trees. This time when the village is set on fire, he does not hesitate to ensure the community's safety. Miguel honors Carlos's bravery, expressing that they are lucky to have found him and to have been helped by such a man. Abuela feeds the guerrillas but wants them to leave for the village's safety. All eyes are on Carlos—will he continue on with the rebels or stay in his grandmother's village? He decides to stay to help rebuild and to serve as a linguistic bridge since nobody in Patrichál speaks Spanish.

Caminar ends with the exhumation of the Chopán massacre victims in 2014, when Carlos searches through a list of more than one hundred names to show his young daughter who she is named after—Maria Catalina Ramón Có, her grandmother. His return highlights the importance of testimonio and historical memory for the next generation. YA novels such as *Grab Hands and Run, Red Midnight,* and *Caminar* serve as valuable mirrors and windows for the Central American diaspora by keeping history alive, as Carlos passes on this historical memory to his daughter.

Unlike the novels discussed thus far, *Libertad* by Alma Fullerton takes place during the postwar era and affirms Roddy Brett's claim that "wars formally end and combatants lay down their weapons, yet what follows rarely amounts to a clear-cut, unambiguous 'peace.' Rather, societies are habitually post-accord and peaceless" (1). Fullerton dedicates her YA novel "to all of the children who have successfully made their own journey; to those children who have come so far only to be turned back; and especially to those children who have died along the way." In her author's note, Fullerton declares that although the story is fiction, "*Libertad* is based on the journey of a real boy named Mariano, combined with other children's actual experiences" (213).

Libertad highlights how "structural violence afflicts the lives of the poorest and most marginalised, above all those of indigenous origin" (Brett 3). I read this YA novel as denouncing the white supremacist view of impoverished Indigenous children as disposable youth that was weaponized during the civil conflicts and has continued into the current exploitative neoliberal system. *Libertad* embodies Henry Giroux's assertion in *Youth in a Suspect Society* that, "as the logic of the market fosters a narrow sense of responsibility, agency, and public values, it reinforces a politics of disposability in which diverse individuals and populations are not only considered redundant and disposable but barely acknowledged to be human beings" (171). Having already migrated from his highland village where soldiers hid "behind masked faces, rattling rifles slung over their shoulders" (10), Libertad lives on the margins of Guatemala City. He is twelve years old and works in a garbage dump with his mother to help support Julio, his seven-year-old brother. Their father migrated to work in the United States five years ago, when Libertad was Julio's age. His mother dreams that one day he will return for them and then they will be free. Meanwhile, to survive, Libertad competes with vultures for food and shares what he finds with Julio, "so Death doesn't knock at their door" (14). He also competes with many others to collect sellable garbage, cardboard, and plastic bags. He is fearful of gangs of men, teens, and children who "lurk around the dump, ready to jump on us like vultures, just because they can. I avoid them, weaving through piles of garbage, taking the long way home" (24). The family lives in a tin-roof shack just outside the dump and away from the gangs, "but we have more harassment from the police. To them we're the enemies, and their job is to protect society from us" (25). Here Fullerton acknowledges that the police serve elite capitalist interests by criminalizing and racializing the poor.

As Ana Patricia Rodríguez contends with reference to other literary works, "The image of *garbage* or *waste* surfaces as the metaphor of Central American nations attempting to rebuild themselves from the rubble of armed conflict, while at the same time confronting the disruptive fallout of global capital" ("Wasted Opportunities," 230). Similarly, Deborah T. Levenson refers to stigmatized *mareros,* or gang members, of the postwar period as "part of the heritage of war, and they portend the permanency of the war in everyday life. Neither rebels nor conformists, they are orphans of the world, not only of Guatemala" (98). In this postwar context, the neoliberal cycle of exploitation and repressive power marks Libertad and gang members as undesirables, reminiscent of the way the army killed people during the war while protecting the interests of the capitalist class.

Despite his precariousness, Libertad exercises agency by making decisions to improve his brother's life. When their mother is tragically buried alive under an enormous pile of rotting garbage, the unaccompanied children must set off on a journey to cross the Guatemalan border into Mexico in hopes of reuniting with their father in the United States. Along the way, Libertad is beaten by a policeman for stealing an apple but interprets finding a ten-quetzal bill as a sign of good luck since it covers their bus fare on a chicken bus heading north. When the brothers reach the colonial city of Antigua, they play the marimba for tourists to gather money for fruit and a series of bus rides to the Mexican border. When the journey and responsibility become overwhelming, Libertad succumbs to the desire to numb his fear, trauma, and grief by joining a group of glue-sniffing street kids. Little Julio persuades him to persevere with their audacious plan, and when they finally reach the river that takes them to Texas, a compassionate woman connects them with their father, fulfilling their mother's dream of family reunification. Despite the oversimplified ending, the representation of Guatemala's postwar violence, drugs, gangs, and forced migration set the stage for harsh realities that other YA novels take up, where youth agency and resilience are challenged as protagonists risk life and limb to defy death and reach safety.

Representing Mayan Girlhood's Coming of Age(ncy) during Guatemalan Genocide

From death of family in the rural male escape narratives to the targeted death of entire Mayan communities, a second set of YA novels underscores acts of genocide and gendered violence in Guatemala's highland villages during the armed conflict but for different ends. As the bearers of culture, the Indigenous adolescent female protagonists embrace their identities by proudly speaking their Mayan languages, wearing hand-woven *traje*, respecting community traditions, and holding on to their dreams despite being surrounded by violence and death.

At first glance, these narratives might seem to portray Mayan girlhood in the Guatemalan highlands in stereotypical fashion—as rural, poor, and powerless—but upon closer inspection, as genocide survivors, the girls become empowered protagonists who denounce injustice to the rest of the world. By framing their coming-of-age(ncy) stories through the critical lens of testimonio, which has deep roots in Latin America and Guatemala in particular, I study these texts as survival narratives that denounce unresolved injustices from Central America's wars and subsequent forced migration.

One of only two authors in this corpus born in Guatemala, Omar S. Castañeda moved to the United States as a child, and his YA novels *Among the Volcanoes* (1991) and its compelling sequel, *Imagining Isabel* (1994), are also the first to appear chronologically. In fact, they were published during Guatemala's civil conflict, which officially ended with the signing of peace accords in 1996. Ben Mikaelson's *Tree Girl* (2004) and Marge Pellegrino's *Journey of Dreams* (2009) depict the need to flee targeted violence in highland villages. Ann Cameron's *Colibrí* (2003) takes place in the postconflict era and points to the deep roots of racialized and gendered violence that have endured throughout the country's history due to impunity for genocide and human rights abuses that continue to shape life in Guatemala, driving migration. For this reason, I include these texts to visibilize indigeneity in Latinx YA, weaving my analysis with a consciousness of Victoria Sanford's admonition that when we fail to consider the Maya as actors in their own history, we commit a discursive silencing of human agency: We "compound the terror of La Violencia by not taking into account the voices of the survivors—in effect, [we] silence them. Thus, however unwittingly, [we] compound the political, social, cultural, physical, and material violence with discursive violence" (*Buried Secrets* 71). In chilling detail, these YA novels set in the Guatemalan highlands condemn the horrors of US-supported war.

Castañeda's novels portray the fear that penetrates all aspects of daily life during the period known as La Violencia. The oppressive impact of militarization in Indigenous communities and divisive distrust looms over Isabel Pacay's lakeside village in *Among the Volcanoes* and *Imagining Isabel.* At first glance, life develops around family, school, church, and a cooperative, with occasional travel to the neighboring towns of Santiago Atitlán and San Lucas Tolimán for goods they don't produce themselves. Isabel's friendships and romantic relationship, however, reveal deeper community fears and tensions just below the surface of a town immersed in Cold War–era military conflict.

Surrounded by volcanoes in the majestic Lake Atitlán area, life in Isabel's village of Chuuí Chopaló is eerily similar to Linda Green's ethnographic description of a pervasive atmosphere of fear and repression in villages due to the constant presence of civil patrollers and soldiers. In *Fear as a Way of Life: Mayan Widows in Rural Guatemala* (1999), Green underscores the lasting impact of state-sponsored atrocities: "The silences that permeate everyday life, the innumerable clandestine cemeteries that only now are being excavated, the blood on people's hands—both literally and figuratively—and the half secrets about what was done to whom and by whom" (5). Unbeknownst to Isabel, her relationship with Lucas Choy unfolds within a similar atmosphere of secrets and manipulations. Although she is in love, she dreams of postponing marriage to pursue her studies and become a teacher, thus putting her personal aspirations in conflict with others who feel vulnerable and fearful of provoking the army's wrath.

Interestingly, Isabel's desire for an education also clashes against gendered and racialized practices of caregiving. As the oldest child and a young woman, she is required to skip school to care for her sick mother. Racially structured poverty, gender roles, and class and ethnic expectations intersect when an elder inquires about her mother's health and admonishes Isabel that it's time to leave school. Castañeda expands on conflicting values around education in a subsequent scene: "To her, going to school was like gazing dreamily into a quiet pond and reflecting on the bewildering universe, or it was like flying high above everything and looking where others could not" (*Among the Volcanoes* 20). The desire for reflection and liberation is viewed as threatening or destabilizing to an Indigenous community under military rule because education traditionally enforces the will of the landowning class which historically has seen Indigenous people as inferior. Racialized class differences are upheld in the village of Chuuí Chopaló because "school was a luxury few could afford. The families of the Bird House people had been living and dying in the very same homes for a thousand years, and formal schooling was a relatively recent thing, which usually implied change. In Chuuí Chopaló, change always had something of fear housed within its bright skin" (21). For Isabel, becoming a teacher means connecting "with something important in the world; to feel a part of something larger and more necessary than a single person" (21). For the community, however, the idea of a young Indigenous girl seeking out new ideas in distant places disrupts the patriarchal hierarchy, as well as the ethnic, economic, and gendered structures that subordinate women.

Isabel is clearly attracted to Lucas, but her increased responsibilities at home and desire for an education puts her at odds with her boyfriend and community. To sway her toward maintaining traditions, a series of mysterious warnings appear at the entrance of her home as rumors spread about Isabel. These passive aggressive tactics are attempts to shame her into obeying the town's customs when the war threatens the social fabric of community life. Devastated by the militarization of the village and her inability to continue her studies, Isabel turns to her teacher, Maestro Xiloj, for support. Modeling agency for social change, he tells her that teachers have declared a strike to demand that the government allocate more money for education and pay rural teachers higher salaries. When he tells her of a teachers' strike that took place years ago, when he was jailed for three weeks and others disappeared forever, she is frightened for his safety. Aware of the stress at home and pressure to marry as well as frustration for not being able to pursue her studies, he encourages Isabel: "Trust yourself. . . . You *can* be different. . . . You don't have to do what everyone else says. It won't be easy for you, but you don't have to kill your hopes. And you may not be able to get what you want, but the worst thing is to live by lying to yourself, by never even trying. That's not living at all!" (*Among the Volcanoes* 168). This advice gives her the courage to speak her truth to Lucas. She learns that her friend Teresa has been lying to him and spreading rumors about her to keep them apart. Isabel affirms her love for Lucas, expressing her desire to be his wife as well as a teacher, so they vow to fulfill both dreams.

In the sequel *Imagining Isabel* (1994), Castañeda deepens the cultural and political context that is unique among the YA novels in this corpus. The political framework is apparent in the dedication: "To the slain and wounded heroes of the Massacre of Santiago Atitlán, 2 December 1990; and to the more than 220,000 slain or disappeared since the 1954 coup in Guatemala." The novel begins with Isabel's sick mother passing down the sacred Mayan bundle that has been in the family for generations. Despite her sickness and pain, she is happy that Isabel will finally marry Lucas. Isabel is given a rare opportunity when she receives a letter from the Commission of Education because, unbeknown to her, her teacher Andrés Xiloj recommended her for a rural teacher training program. After her mother's death and her wedding, a second letter arrives, informing her that she has been selected to enter the teachers' training program in Sololá and will receive a stipend for the eight-week program. Since her family needs these funds, they allow her to enroll. As it's her first time away from home, she feels insecure in the classroom among the strong personalities of Blanca, a girl with albinism who has always felt rejected by Guatemalan society and dreams of studying in the US, and Nina, who holds strong political opinions. After Lucas's weekend visit, Isabel takes a walk around town and encounters a man who gestures for her to follow him. From a distance, he signals that she must look in the bushes and when she does, she finds a man with multiple stab wounds. In a coming-of-age moment, she runs for help, then hides in the crowd because she is afraid of being questioned. Later when soldiers arrive at school to question her, she does not reveal anything about the wounded man or the stranger who guided her to him. In a turn of events, Isabel understands that she was being tested and the interrogators were not actually military soldiers but guerrillas dressed as army officers. They interpret her ability to keep silent about clandestine activities as a sign that she would be an asset in the counterinsurgency struggle against structural oppression. Lucas, however, wants her to return home to a traditional life and is surprised by Isabel's growing critical awareness and newfound ability to speak up for herself. After the Santiago massacre, he accompanies Isabel to a protest to demand justice, and she states that Indigenous people are not safe anywhere. Finding her voice, Isabel feels empowered to tell Lucas that she will complete the program, and he once again vows to shift his patriarchal stance to support her dreams for a better world.

As an example of Mayan girlhood coming into political consciousness, Isabel Pacay's agency sets the stage for delving into other YA novels that take place amid Guatemala's scorched-earth policies through the critical lens of testimonio to denounce injustice and break imposed silencing. As we will see in the portrayal of life in militarized highland villages, Mayan girls come of age by coming into *agency* and speaking back to power.

Ben Mikaelson's *Tree Girl* (2004) and Marge Pellegrino's *Journey of Dreams* (2009) depict Mayan girls' subtle resistance amid the atrocities of war. In Mikaelsen's YA novel, based on a true story, Gabriela Flores, or Gabi, is nicknamed Laj Ali Re Jayub (Tree Girl) in Quiché at age fourteen because of her passion for climbing trees. Her mother encourages her to hold on to her dreams as tightly as she grips onto the tree branches she climbs. Like Isabel, Gabi loves school and dreams of becoming a teacher. As she weaves her traditional huipil in preparation for her quinceañera, her fifteenth birthday celebration, her parents try to prepare her for the changes taking place in their community. Noting increased militarization, Gabi is critical of the fact that soldiers and guerrillas use the same rhetoric when questioning them: "Both sides used the same words—You must not help the enemy. If you do then you are also the enemy. We learned to say nothing" (15). Her father, however, dares to voice his critical views at home: "Her father says the guerrillas and the soldiers just use us to get food and information. I don't think they truly fight for us" (35). Voicing these opinions is dangerous because people are disappeared from their homes in the middle of the night. When her brother is forcibly recruited, Gabi's teacher Manuel accompanies her to the military post in a brave act of solidarity to ask if they are holding him. He tells her that the soldiers' new rifles were provided by the United States, where the comandantes were trained. Given their education and ability to speak the colonizer's language, Manuel warns Gabi that the authorities see them as threats: "Manuel says 'war has come to our country, and Spanish is the language the cantons will use to communicate when they need to fight their enemies. The soldiers know this, and already they're killing Indios who can speak Spanish. You and I are among those they wish to kill. Knowing Spanish places us in great danger" (41). As the fear tactics worsen, she grows critical of the historical collusion between the military and Ladino landowners when a column of twenty soldiers march into the village demanding to see land titles. If residents can't prove that they own their land, they are given thirty days to leave: "This country was our home long before the Latinos [*sic*] came from a different land to claim what wasn't theirs to claim" (58). As in *Caminar* and Castañeda's novels, *Tree Girl* depicts how rumors and distrust tear the community apart: "A person could simply say that someone they disliked had helped the soldiers or the guerrillas, and often that someone would soon be taken away in the middle of the night. Living with this constant fear made my own stomach knot up and turn at night" (61). The oppression continues when soldiers take away the men's machetes, leaving them to work the fields with their bare hands, defenseless and dehumanized: "We were like a bunch of sheep surrounded by mad dogs" (63). Gabi's social consciousness grows more critical after her mother's death and her teacher's public torture: "Most of the people in our canton had never heard of the words communism, democracy, socialism, and capitalism. We wished only to be left alone to live the ways of our ancestors. Why should that make us someone's enemy?" (70).

Gabi's critique of state violence voices a critical perspective that goes beyond the personal. As a witness, Gabi embodies the tenets of testimonio as her community's memory keeper, or Tree Girl. When she returns home from the market, she encounters dead bodies and homes burning; her father and siblings are among the massacred. She digs a shallow grave for them, knowing that she must flee to Mexico. When she reaches the next town, soldiers begin shooting, so she saves herself by climbing a nearby tree. From this precarious vantage point, she witnesses people shot in cold blood; she sees adults and children forcibly separated and tortured. Using sexual violence as a weapon of war, soldiers take turns raping a woman in the plaza. The last soldier shoots the woman and drags her body into the fire. Gabi testifies to the traumatic horror:

> My body trembled as if the tree were shaking. Tears blurred my vision, and I swallowed back desperate screams. I needed to throw up but didn't dare. For many long minutes I clung to the branches, gasping with anger and fear. . . . Another woman is raped. For hours I watched from the machichi tree as bodies were thrown into the flames. Soldiers used their knives to pry gold-filled teeth from the corpses before they were dumped into the hungry fire. I wanted desperately to close my eyes, but I feared being spotted or falling. I tried instead to cover my ears, but I couldn't block out the desperate screams and cries of pain. Many different Mayan languages filled the air with screams and cries that day, but the laughter and joking of the soldiers knew only one language, Spanish.

Here Mikaelson underscores a linguistic hierarchy as government soldiers violently protect capitalist interests with impunity. Matilde González Izás asserts that, through rape, "the army and civil-patrol commanders also sought to denigrate the women and destroy them physically and mentally. In this way, they assured the silence of these women" (405). Moreover, sexual violence also ensured the silencing of the entire community: "For the army and its allies, the mass rape represented the dance of the victors, the spectacle of shame through which the entire community became accomplices to war crimes. . . . No one remained untouched, no one would have the moral solvency to judge, much less denounce what had happened" (González Izás 407). Traumatized, Gabi hides in the tree all night, but the morning brings new horrors: "Children were brought out from the schoolhouse to watch their parents being tortured and raped. And throughout the atrocities, the sadistic evil laughter of the soldiers echoed among the buildings and up through the branches of the tree" (Mikaelsen, *Tree Girl* 133). This scene resonates with the dehumanizing terror recorded in the military's Plan Sofia. According to Victoria Sanford, Ixil women were referred to "as 'cockroaches' and Ixil children as 'chocolates.' In this idiom, forced displacement, the organized rape of women and girls, systematic slaughter of unarmed men, women, and children, and the burning of hundreds of villages all boil down to a simple order: 'Kill the cockroaches and leave no chocolates'" ("Command" 87). From the hidden shelter of the tree,

Gabi resolves to remember and denounce this spectacle of death and structural silencing: "After all I had seen, what reason was there to continue living? But my anger burned as hot as the flames in the plaza. My revenge would be to stay alive and someday speak of what I witnessed" (Mikaelsen, *Tree Girl* 135). As the sole survivor, she is overcome with survivor's guilt and feelings of complicity after hiding for two days. Although she feels like a coward, she exercises agency by climbing the tree, witnessing the atrocities, and surviving in order to denounce the genocidal acts.

Fleeing for her life, she reaches a refugee camp on the Mexican border, where she reflects on all the deaths she has witnessed and struggles to survive in this new precarious reality. Here she gains a deeper political consciousness and agency as a genocide survivor, which prompts her to reach out to other grieving orphans. Her testimony and solidarity with other displaced children initiate a much-needed personal and collective healing process.

Like Castañeda's and Mikaelsen's YA novels, Pellegrino's *Journey of Dreams* takes place during the period known as La Violencia. When the army storms into Tomasa's K'iche' village in the highlands in 1984, she is prevented from gathering with the community or attending school. Although she obeys the new restrictions, she resists the army's characterization of Maya villagers as guerrillas in her drawings and dreams: "Surely the soldiers will see that we are not the guerrillas who, they say, cause trouble. They must understand we are just people from the village who are on our way to the market to sell what we grow and weave, what we gather and cook and build" (18). By countering the army's portrayal of the Maya as "subversives," *Tree Girl* and *Journey of Dreams* denounce the state's scorched-earth tactics and genocide against the Ixil people. These valuable YA novels introduce young readers to Guatemalan survivor testimonies, illustrating that the army's goal was the destruction of the social fabric of collective Indigenous life, which aligns with Judith Butler's theorization of how easily human life is annulled (xvii). In *Precarious Life*, Butler asks, "Who counts as human? Whose lives count as lives? And finally, what makes for a grievable life?" (20). Based on Guatemala's Truth Commission findings, Beatriz Manz states that what threatened the army and elites was the "mind and actions of the Mayan peasantry. Therefore, they went after that population to bring them, dead or alive, under army control, and then they attempted to defeat the hearts and minds of the survivors" ("Reflections" 315). Moreover, the Truth Commission Report declared that the purpose of the terror "was to intimidate and silence society as a whole, in order to destroy the will for transformation, both in the short and long term" (CEH 1999, 27, cited in Manz, "Terror" 294). Together, Isabel's, Gabi's, and Tomasa's survival narratives counter targeted silencing to offer readers chilling insight into Maya resistance as they embody dignity as genocide survivors with agency to work for social change.

In Tomasa's village, soldiers fire shots, detonate explosives, and set fire to the church and several homes as part of the government's scorched-earth strategy of terror. After her grandmother dies during an army attack that also destroys their home, Tomasa must support her father by taking care of her younger siblings. The family is forced to separate when the army comes for her fourteen-year-old brother, Carlos, and Tomasa's mother receives anonymous death threats for speaking out against the local growers' use of pesticides that harm the community's health. Given that the army's role is to protect the growers' economic interests, they enact state violence by driving the population away to take their land, through killings, intimidation leading to displacement and forced migration, or enlisting boys as young as ten years old in military service or civil patrols.[2]

Tomasa manages to escape with her father and two younger siblings, but as they flee she begins to understand why there are no boys to dance with at local celebrations: they have been "forced into the army, spirited away to fight with the guerrillas, or who have fled north to escape, or just gone—disappeared" (Pellegrino 75). As she observes her surroundings, she gains critical consciousness and comes into agency. Fleeing toward the Mexican border, she resolves, like Santiago in *Red Midnight,* to remember the horror she witnesses along the journey until it is safe to disinter the memories.

Fortunately for the family, a Ladina or non-Maya woman gives them food, shelter, shoes, and Western clothing so they can mask their Indigenous identity, which would put them in danger of deportation upon crossing the Suchiate River into Mexico. When Tomasa manages to cross the river, a body of water that is weaponized as a political boundary between Guatemala and Mexico, she must hide her Indigenous identity. Like Rosa Xuncax in the film *El Norte* (1983), who flees her Mayan village with her brother Enrique after soldiers kill their father and take their mother away, Gabriela in *Tree Girl* and Tomasa in *Journey of Dreams* must remove their Indigenous *traje* to pass as Mexican. Mayan anthropologist Irma Alicia Velásquez Nimatuj explains the

2. See Diana M. Nelson, "Reckoning the After/math of War in Guatemala," for a discussion of controversial state reparations to survivors and paramilitaries that carried out massacres. She notes, "Yet participation in the patrols was complex for many men. Some did fear the guerrillas, or at least the effects of their presence (even the suspicion of support could lead to an army massacre), and not only individuals but also collectives were brutally punished by the army if even a few people refused to serve" (92). She asks, "Can we account for the unsettling double state these men inhabit? Can accounting's promise of zero balance reckon with the peculiarity of being (willing and unwillingly) 'agents of the State of Guatemala,' being both victim and victimizer?" (93).

cultural and political significance of wearing *traje*: "Whenever we are seen in regional traje, the ruling classes are reminded of the failure of their efforts to make us disappear, which have ranged from genocide to ideological coercion. Five centuries of humiliation have not succeeded in bringing the Maya people to their knees" (526). She views wearing *traje* as a means to challenge the "imaginary Guatemala" that has been socially constructed by a small economic elite with power and control over the State. As an Indigenous girl, Gabi admits her fear: "I hid my terror . . . of the soldiers who eat at my country as squirming maggots eat the carcass of a dead deer" (Mikaelsen, *Tree Girl* 125). The simile of the maggots not only responds to the army's use of "cockroaches" but also positions the authorities as "vultures" who threaten Libertad's survival in the garbage dump. These images of death emphasize the state's power to prey on the vulnerable amid a culture of silence and impunity.

Not surprisingly, in *Journey of Dreams*, the refugee camp Tomasa and her family eventually reach on the Guatemalan-Mexican border is full of children who speak Quiché, Mam, Tzutujil, and Spanish. Later, when they reach the shelter Casa del Peregrino in Mexico City, they meet a nun who informs them that their mother and brother have made it safely to Phoenix, Arizona. She promises to share the family's testimony with other solidarity workers so that they can hopefully be reunited. The threatening letters they received in Guatemala, which her father sewed into his trousers, and Tomasa's drawings of her village on fire with the helicopter and bloodied dead people are entered into evidence in their asylum case. Although the Sanctuary volunteers could face arrest, they help the family continue the journey north on crowded buses and trains. In "Sanctuary and Women," activist Renny Golden writes that drawing on scriptural tradition, scores of religious communities sheltered undocumented refugees in defiance of the US government's interpretation of the Immigration and Nationality Act of 1980: "Sanctuary has become one of the first acts of authentic solidarity for the North American religious community—a solidarity of defiant love" (132). This alludes to the defiance of US policy by various churches during the Sanctuary movement of the 1980s that stood in solidarity with Central American refugees and disseminated counterhegemonic testimonies like Gabi's and Tomasa's to bring attention to the horror that was taking place with US funding. Tomasa's prayers are answered when they make it across the Sonoran Desert through Tohono O'odham lands to reunite with her mother and brother. Tomasa hopes her dreams will become more restful in the United States so she can build a new life far from the nightmares of the Guatemalan army's genocidal terror.

The theme of children fleeing death and state violence prompts readers—presumably of the same age as the protagonists and subsequent generations of the Central America diaspora—to reflect on the legacy of US involvement in past conflict alongside the humanitarian response of activists. These YA novels challenge us to think historically about the risks that Central American unaccompanied minors have endured for decades, since the US-backed civil wars, in addition to the militarization of borders in the postwar era. YA novels such as *Among the Volcanoes, Imagining Isabel, Tree Girl,* and *Journey of Dreams* emphasize that systemic terror must be reckoned with in order to truly heal.

Like *Libertad* by Alma Fullerton, Ann Cameron's *Colibrí* (2003) is particularly tragic because the young Mayan protagonist experiences gendered and racialized postwar violence after the signing of the peace accords in 1996 officially ended Guatemala's thirty-six-year civil conflict. This novel is illuminating for its portrayal of an ex-soldier's power to oppress and cause traumatic harm, in addition to highlighting testimonio's power for healing justice. Colibrí, the protagonist, is a Maya girl who does not even know her real age because she was kidnapped from her parents by an ex-soldier. As a Ladino, the ex-soldier holds a command over her that underscores structural violence that is gendered, racialized, and never legally brought to justice—from the time of Spanish colonization to the current postwar era. Cecilia Menjívar explains, "The term *ladino* is complex, and it refers to Guatemalans who do not identify as Indigenous, are largely monolingual Spanish speakers, and do not adopt cultural practices associated with Indigenous groups. In the Guatemalan racial hierarchy, they occupy a position between whites and Indigenous and Afro descendants" (131). Although her Mayan name is Tzunún Chumil, which means Colibrí in Spanish, or hummingbird, and is a sign of peace, she is invisibilized as an Indigenous girl when she is abducted at four years old by a Ladino kidnapper, who renames her Rosa García. Throughout her captivity, she holds on to her given name Tzunún as a secret she had almost forgotten. The man she calls "uncle" stole her from her parents to sell her into adoption, but his plan fails because foreigners are only interested in babies. Instead, this highly trained Kaibil exploits her as they wander throughout the Ixil area of the Western highlands, forcing her to beg and steal to provide for them. His power as a Kaibil is paramount since the Kaibiles were elite special forces of the Guatemalan army, trained in counterinsurgency tactics (Green, *Fear* 31). Due to her isolation and itinerant life, she is illiterate and has mostly forgotten how to speak Kaqchikel during her eight years of captivity.

When they reach Nebaj in El Quiché, her captor pretends to be disabled to take advantage of people's sympathy. Her job is to assist him when he begs or uses counterfeit bills to swindle vendors. Forced to steal to support him, she is robbed of her history, language, and cultural identity. As they move from place to place, she gathers that there was a "big war here in Guatemala before I was born. Back then a lot of people who said the wrong thing in front of the wrong stranger died. In many places people still don't like to talk much to strangers" (27). But she gains clarity and ultimately finds her voice when she meets Doña Celestina Tuc, a Day Keeper, or fortune teller. This wise elder sees through the kidnapper's lies and knows that he has many debts, particularly because of his past actions during the war. As a sacred knowledge keeper, Doña Celestina recognizes Colibrí's captor, who goes by false names, when he inquires about his luck. He denies knowing her or being at La Hortensia. Later, in an act of testimonio, she describes her husband's killing to Colibrí. He was burned alive by soldiers at La Hortensia twenty years before. Retelling this tragedy becomes in itself an act of resistance for historical memory and collective liberation. This testimony of state violence and death is rooted in the value of passing on a silenced collective history to the younger generation. Their bond underscores that testimonio is a transgression "against accepted norms of social hierarchies, conventional modes of literary production, and hegemonic constructions of knowledge. . . . At once personal and political, testimonio seeks to convey lived reality as perceived by those who do not have control over the official manufacturing of recorded history" (Bolt 266). Armed with this new consciousness, Colibrí feels empowered for the first time and resolves to take action—another fundamental component of testimonio. When she overhears her captor reminiscing with a fellow soldier about the atrocities they committed to prove their fierceness, she finally has the capacity to envision fleeing. Their barbaric acts and human rights violations against civilians during the conflict point to the impunity that has shielded them from justice in the postwar era. With Doña Celestina's guidance, she begins to heal and reconnects with her Mayan culture and language, in the end reuniting with her parents. In effect, this testimonial relationship liberates her from a legacy of fear and shame, highlighting that Colibrí's story, like the male escape narratives, are ultimately acts of resistance for finding one's voice to denounce injustice.

In sum, this group of YA novels representing gendered escape narratives and Mayan girlhood testimonies eloquently connect today's youth to the violence of the past while raising awareness about the need for healing justice as a roadmap for future action. By exposing the impact of structural terror and injustice in El Salvador and Guatemala, these YA novels acknowledge the invisibilized legacies of war as root causes for migration. As we will see in subsequent chapters, postwar globalized neoliberal policies in Central America and Mexico have generated more inequality and social exclusion, unleashing a cycle that results in more violence and forced migration.

The death-defying journeys of these resilient Indigenous protagonists denounce racialized capitalism's politics of disposability, for which testimonio offers a vehicle for self-expression and agency. Like testimonio, these YA novels record state-sponsored violence including gendered violence and genocide "so that future generations may be aware" and never allow it to be repeated. Based on a truth-telling call for justice, these YA novels empower coming-of-age(ncy) survival narratives wherein children who were once viewed as "the seed that has to be eliminated" during the Salvadoran and Guatemalan political conflicts instead embody hope for the future. While acknowledging survivors' pain and trauma, this literature for youth offers vital "windows, mirrors, and sliding glass doors" (Bishop, "Mirrors"), highlighting the need for greater critical awareness of past harms that continue to drive migration.

CHAPTER 2

The Adolescent Migrant Journey through Mexico

Neoliberal Disposability in Latinx YA

In this chapter, I study an array of middle-grade and YA novels published in English for a US youth audience that feature the clandestine migrant journeys of Guatemalan and Mexican adolescents as they attempt to cross the US-Mexican border. With gripping detail, these works of fiction, published between the 1980s and 2023, follow unaccompanied youth risking their lives in transit through Mexico, venturing across the Sonoran Desert, and battling the strong currents of the Río Bravo / Río Grande to reach the United States. To accomplish their goal of crossing the militarized border, the protagonists endure a series of physical risks and emotional traumas. Along the way, they navigate terrifying encounters with smugglers, gangs, border patrol agents, and corrupt officials. Most importantly, as they come of age during this dangerous journey, they gain critical consciousness that prompts them to exert agency despite their fears. Viewing their journeys through the lens of racialized capitalism, I argue that their migration is a form of resistance against neoliberal disposability and that as mirrors and windows, the YA novels challenge readers of all ages to question the white supremacist narrative that criminalizes migrants for fleeing poverty created by a long history of US interventionist policies.

Like Sciurba et al., I believe these stories can serve as tools to elevate critical consciousness among young readers. As in the previous chapter, I include YA novels by non-Latinx authors because they enrich the chronology of Latinx

YA literature. Collectively, *Lupita Mañana* (1981) by Patricia Beatty, *La Línea* (1985) by Ann Jaramillo, *Crossing* (1998) by Manuel Luis Martinez, *Crossing the Wire* (2006) by Will Hobbs, *The Only Road* (2016) by Alexandra Diaz, *We Are Not from Here* (2020) by Jenny Torres Sanchez, and *Borderless* (2023) by Jennifer De Leon offer readers vital insight into the conditions of poverty and violence in Guatemala and Mexico while asserting the dignity of the protagonists by humanizing the harrowing border-crossing experience. Ultimately, they exercise agency to survive—whether in making the decision to flee, searching for a trustworthy coyote or guide, navigating violent encounters with gangs or Mexican authorities seeking to take advantage of their vulnerability in transit, taking precautions to minimize the risk of sexual violence for girls, facing death on the infamous freight train known as La Bestia, finding temporary respite in migrant shelters, or risking the river or dessert crossing. These coming-of-age(ncy) stories matter because by humanizing moments of vulnerability and solidarity, they resist neoliberal disposability, thus inviting readers to grow in understanding and empathy, hopefully unlearning harmful stereotypes along the journey (Cummins, "Border"; Sciurba et al. 2021; Rodriguez and Braden).

Youth Fleeing Poverty: Representing Precariousness on the Mexican Migrant Trail

A common thread that unites this literature is the need to cross the border into the United States to flee poverty and violence. Using the concepts of precarity and neoliberal disposability, I examine how the unaccompanied adolescent migrants experience vulnerability and death during three key moments of their journey: when fleeing gang violence, riding the cargo train known as La Bestia, and crossing the desert to reach the United States.

As the earliest YA novel in this corpus, Patricia Beatty's *Lupita Mañana*, published in 1981, depicts youth precarity along the dangerous route to the border.[1] The protagonist, Lupita Torres, is a thin thirteen-year-old Mexican girl nicknamed Lupita Mañana because of her optimistic stance that tomorrow will always be a better day. Her cheerful outlook is challenged on a hot, windy day in Ensenada, Baja California, when her father is lost at sea while working on a tuna boat during a storm. To complicate matters, her fifteen-

1. Beatty was awarded the Jane Addams Children's Book award for *Lupita Mañana* in 1972. According to her obituary published in the *Los Angeles Times* on 13 July 1991, she began writing children's books when she was a librarian and described her characters as self-reliant.

year-old brother Salvador has been secretly dating the captain's daughter, so he is reluctant to demand his father's wages, which the family desperately needs. Unlike Salvador, Lupita worries about how they and four younger siblings will survive on their mother's low wages as a hotel housekeeper. Although Lupita contributes to the household by running errands for neighbors, losing her father devastates the family emotionally and financially, signaling that poverty leaves the lower class in Mexico with few options for subsistence other than migrating north. The loss of the family breadwinner in *Lupita Mañana* coincides with Linda Green's view that "migration is one of the few remaining survival strategies for many. At the same time, migration has exacerbated economic and social divisions further eroding any sense of collective solidarity or possibility of struggle" ("Nobodies" 362). To help the family, Lupita puts her dream of becoming a teacher aside when she and Salvador quit school, but they can't find work in town. When the siblings decide to migrate, their mother borrows from a money lender so they can cross the border to reach their aunt Consuelo, who has lived in Indio, California, for twenty years. Their goal is to find work so that they can send money back to provide for the family. As an outsider author, Patricia Beatty's dated and problematic language, such as "pocho" and "yanqui," points to racialized differences that indicate to Salvador that "the gringos don't want them to live and work there without special papers. They will be breaking the law" (35). This reference to "legal violence" (Menjívar and Abrego) or illegality offers young readers a glimpse into the language of "othering" that constructs migrants as undesirable.

Like *Lupita Mañana,* Ann Jaramillo's *La Línea* highlights poverty as a root cause of migration from Mexico by connecting the economic and environmental devastation left by drought and neoliberalism's impact on a market flooded by cheap, foreign corn as factors that spur migration. The town of San Jacinto, for example, epitomizes gendered migration because it has been emptied of young boys, who are looking elsewhere for jobs. Soon fifteen-year-old Miguel, the protagonist, will be one more boy who leaves town. On his fifteenth birthday, Miguel receives news that it is now time for him to join his parents in California. For Miguel, migrating marks his coming of age. Curiously, the opportunity to reunite with his father, who he hasn't seen in seven years, and mother, who he last saw three years ago, is not extended to his thirteen-year-old sister Elena. She shows agency of her own by disguising herself in order to accompany him.

Due to his young age, the dangers of the migrant journey are withheld from Miguel but shared with the reader. During his small going-away party, people share border-crossing stories but purposely withhold examples of extreme violence or death so as not to frighten or discourage him: "Fátima didn't tell how her brother Eleuterio left suddenly one day, only to be found two weeks later, suffocated to death, stuffed into an abandoned tractor trailer one mile north of la línea, or the death with twenty-six others" (28). Carlo doesn't mention how his father was robbed, beaten, and left for dead in the desert, nor does he disclose that he returned deaf in one ear and missing the fingers of his right hand. The information that the community withholds from Miguel communicates the imminent danger of the journey to the reader, ranging from a long, cruel death at the hands of unscrupulous coyotes to kidnapping or abandonment in the desert.

For Victor Flores, Hobbs's protagonist and first-person narrator in *Crossing the Wire,* the factors that lead him to migrate are extreme poverty and the dream of providing for his mother and five younger siblings. While fifteen-year-old Victor works the fields on an empty stomach, his best friend Rico Rivera shows him the "coyote money" his brother in the US has secretly sent him so he can cross the border.[2] Unlike Rico, Victor does not want to leave Mexico or abandon his family. In fact, he should have the right not to migrate, but as the breadwinner, he has "adultified" responsibilities toward his loved ones. As in *Lupita Mañana,* Victor mourns the loss of his father, who was killed on the job in South Carolina four years earlier, along with his own premature "coming of age." He reflects, "My childhood had ended when my father died, when I left the village school and began to work in the fields. Rico's ended when this idea had taken root in his mind" (10). Even though Victor is afraid of leaving home, he sets out on the journey to provide for his family.

In the novels, death and the threat of deportation of the family breadwinners are emotionally and financially devastating. This painful reality underscores the relationship between migration and neoliberalism, "as both an economic model and a mode of domination" (Gilly 2005, cited in Green, "Nobodies" 367). As "disposable people," Green states that they are quite literally redundant: "At the same time, these 'nobodies' are reworked into 'illegals' after crossing the Mexico-Arizona border. . . . As a cheap yet expendable source of labor and profit, whether as workers or detainees, they become crucial to shore up the floundering American economy" (367). Clearly, legal, structural, and gendered violence are at play, as noted in the following sections.

---

2. As an example of the ever increasing cost of the migrant journey, Heidbrink reports that the cost of irregular migration from Guatemala to the United States spiked from $1,000 in the 1990s to $12,500 in 2019, a "reaction to an increasingly militarized response to migration management since the 1990s and early 2000s" (59).

The Only Choice: Fleeing Guatemalan Gangs and Gendered Violence

Besides representing youth fleeing poverty, the YA novels *The Only Road, We Are Not from Here,* and *Borderless* portray agency in deciding to undertake the dangerous migrant journey to escape gang violence in Guatemala. As the daughter of Cuban refugees, Alexandra Diaz acknowledges that for many Central Americans, fleeing may be the only option for survival. Diaz's solidarity in giving visibility to a Central American migration story is significant because in the last decade, they have made up the majority of immigrants despite being conflated with Mexicans in the US popular imaginary (Rodríguez and Campos, "Book Review: *We Are Not*"). As noted in the previous chapter, Guatemala's thirty-six-year internal war officially ended in 1996 with the signing of the peace accords. But by design, according to Green, the accords "did little to redress the marked social inequalities that permeate Guatemalan society and the virulent racism directed against the Maya people—the two central underpinnings of both the insurgency and popular movement demands for social justice" (*Fear* 321). Furthermore, as an arrangement between the business elite, the military, and guerrilla leadership, the peace accords espoused two instruments of violence wagered against the poor—impunity and free market capitalism, with the backing of the World Bank, US Agency for International Development, and US military (Green, "Nobodies" 371). As Rodríguez and Campos rightly point out, Central American migrants are fleeing violence created by US imperialism. Bridging the past and the present, the fear and suspicion that divided Maya communities in the previous chapter play out in similar ways decades later in *The Only Road, We Are Not from Here,* and *Borderless* when gangs, with an abundance of drugs, weapons, and police complicity, prey upon vulnerable youth.

When Jaime Rivera in *The Only Road* hears a piercing scream and wailing, he immediately feels guilty for staying home sick with a fever instead of walking to school with his twelve-year-old cousin and best friend Miguel. The local gang, known as the Alphas, surrounded Miguel and beat him to death. How is it possible that Miguel's dreams of pursuing an education were so violently cut short? "He was ecstatic over his scholarship into the exclusive science prevocational school in the city twenty kilometers away: he had always wanted to be an engineer" (8). The stark contrast between Miguel's educational plans and the violence with which the gang gains money and power by illegal means sets up a troubling opposition: the worthy subject who dreams about academic excellence on the one hand and the criminal gang banger on the other. In my view, it's important to name the differences that separate their lived realities as structural violence so that the circumstances that divide them are viewed within a larger socioeconomic context, something that is rarely acknowledged in the media.

Sociologist Steven Osuna traces the emergence of gangs or *maras* to the global capitalist system of the 1980s and the development of neoliberalism in Central America, along with the impact of US law and order policies. He discusses MS-13 as a "transnational moral panic" because "moral panics serve to obfuscate the social relations of exploitation in capitalist society, which in the first instance create the conditions of poverty, degradation, misery and the justification for a punitive populism" ("Transnational" 3). In the 1990s, postwar El Salvador and Guatemala embraced neoliberal policies such as structural adjustment, which subsequently "abandoned a whole generation of youth whose families either were murdered or disappeared, fled during the war, or were living in extreme poverty" (10). After passing the Illegal Immigration Reform and Immigration Responsibility Act of 1996, the US began mass deportations of Salvadorans: "Between 1998 and 2007, more than 74,000 Salvadorans were deported, many of whom were youth or young adults who were refugees during the armed conflict and had been raised in cities such as Los Angeles" (10). Likewise, the US deported thousands of gang members from Southern California to Guatemala in the early 1990s. Unfortunately, the postwar era has been marked by increased violence and economic instability, with femicide as an alarming cause of death for women because they are women.

There is abundant documentation of the impact of US deportation policies in the creation of transnational criminal gangs in postwar Central America, but without a critical context, it is easy to demonize gangs as the embodiment of everything that is wrong in Central America, as the media often proclaims. Right-wing politicians often point to gang violence to justify exponentially increasing police and military budgets while suppressing civil liberties and refusing to address increasing poverty and inequality. Osuna underscores that "what continues to be neglected is that the violence of poverty, in the form of femicide, police repression and gang violence that Central American families and children are fleeing, is rooted in past and present capitalist relations of exploitation, all of which are exacerbated by neoliberalism and punitive populism. In El Salvador and Central America, the maras are neoliberalism's greatest contradiction" ("Transnational" 20). Recalling Osuna's use of moral panic, anthropologist Wendy Vogt notes that moral and individualized discourses are used to blame gangs for violence, obscuring the historical and structural roots of their formation (*Lives* 43), along with the state's failure to protect its citizenry, since it's often complicit in and sometimes a perpetrator of criminal violence (47). Likewise, Néstor Rodríguez et al. point out, "But these gangs do not have an independent existence; they developed from changing institutional conditions in society that could no longer support an adequate social incorporation of youth, a situation exacerbated by US deportations of thousands of youth, including gang members, to the northern countries of Central America" (219). As reflected in Latinx YA, this is a crucial context for understanding the root causes driving migration.

These often-unacknowledged structural factors impact Jaime's and Miguel's dangerous surroundings in *The Only Road* as their parents are very poor and barely make enough to keep the family fed and sheltered. Given the poverty in the area and the lack of state protection, the gang's strong presence looms over surrounding villages by extorting shopkeepers, coercing them to pay for "protection," and forcibly recruiting boys like Miguel and Jaime to join their ranks. Although he was violently targeted by the gang, Miguel's death is declared an unfortunate accident by the police because "money meant more than morals and justice to the force. It also didn't help that the police chief's drug habit funded many of the gang's operations" (12). Diaz's critique of police collusion with local gangs highlights that impunity and corruption are embedded in structural violence, leaving the poor extremely vulnerable. To make matters worse, after Miguel's funeral, his fifteen-year-old sister Angela is threatened by the Alphas. Feeling helpless and guilty, Jaime thinks about the dangers he would face if he dared to cross the border. He remembers two villagers who attempted to make the journey but were never heard from again, as well as a young woman named Marcela who was still missing and was assumed to have been sold as a sex slave. Fortunately for Jaime, his older brother Tomás works legally on a cattle ranch in New Mexico, so he and Angela plan their escape there: "If he and Angela stayed, they could end up dead; if they left, they might end up dead. Either way, life was never again going to be the same" (24). They have no choice but to flee Guatemala.

Similarly, in *We Are Not from Here*, fifteen-year-old Pulga, his best friend Chico, and Pequeña are forced to flee Puerto Barrios, Guatemala, due to gang violence. Given their violent surroundings and overt displays of toxic hypermasculinity, Pulga internalizes the belief that to be a man means to be hard: "What I need is a heart of steel, a heart that is cold and hard and numb to the thorny pricks of pain, the slashes of tragedy" (Torres Sanchez 6). Pulga tries to teach his best friend Chico to be hard, to curse and insult as survival skills, but deep down, they are both sensitive, artistically creative boys who must hide their true selves to survive. Their bond is strong because Chico has lived with Pulga and his mother ever since his own mother was shot and killed in front of him. The police did nothing to protect or save her since she was forced into prostitution.

The gang forces Pulga and Chico to drop off drugs in backpacks but they don't want any part of that violent lifestyle. Early in the novel, their friend

Pequeña, who was raped by Rey, the local gang leader, delivers a baby boy she refuses to look at or touch. By rejecting him, she fears repeating a vicious cycle: "I see he needs to be loved. And I don't think I can love this baby. So he will grow up unloved—become just like Rey. And that fills me with shame and fear" (Torres Sanchez 72). It's hinted that Pequeña, feeling trapped, attempted to kill herself after she was raped by Rey, who was deported to Guatemala after serving a few years in a US prison. Since his return, he has become a feared gang leader, with an intimidating scar from his right cheekbone to his chin. When the boys witness Rey kill a neighborhood store owner who pleads for more time to pay the extortion that the Alphas demand, they know he won't be held accountable since the police are in cahoots with gangs. Traumatized and fearing forced recruitment, Pulga and Chico know that their only option is to flee.

Clearly, gangs and gendered violence intersect on the migrant trail due to heteropatriarchal power, since sexual violence is carried out based on preexisting social hierarchies like gender and racial inequality (Vogt, *Lives* 69). Hypermasculinity is legitimized along what Vogt refers to as the "arterial border," increasing insecurity for both migrants and local residents. Without access to protection or justice, the cycle of violence and impunity reigns. Forced to leave home because of extreme poverty and gang violence, the young protagonists in both novels set out on the long journey exposed to multiple dangers, including many of the perils they faced in their communities, such as threats and extortion from criminal gangs, robbery, and assaults. For boy characters, facing their fear of leaving home is an important coming-of-age milestone to manhood. Girl protagonists, however, are doubly victimized when they face gendered violence, so the young women cut off their hair to disguise themselves as boys to lessen the chances of sexual abuse. This survival strategy simultaneously illustrates their gendered vulnerability and agency. In *Lives in Transit,* Wendy Vogt underscores, "Gendered violence, like much of the violence experienced along the journey, is not just the work of bad individuals, but rather produced at the nexus of state and structural forms of violence that permeate the lives of migrants at home, during their journey, and once they reach their destinations" (19). She states, "In reality, the 'bad guys' blamed for violence are actors maneuvering within the constraints of the structures of global capitalism and state enforcement where there is profit to be made from the mobility of unauthorized people (*Lives* 4). Bordering Guatemala in Tapachula, Chiapas, Jaime and Angela in *The Only Road* encounter the violence of state enforcement with the Mexican migra, known for their corruption and abusive power: "Everything seemed worse than what they had left behind. Except here there seemed to be a greater variety of ways to die. . . . They were going through places more corrupt than his village, running from gangs more violent than the Alphas" (Diaz 41). This quote signals layers of state violence in which migrants are routinely victimized. Regrettably, abuse of state power and corruption extend all across the migrant journey through Mexico, which serves as gatekeeper to the US border. US Central American scholar Yajaira Padilla rightfully critiques "Mexico's active role as part of a broader US-Mexico interstate regime focused on immigration regulation and (US) national security that renders the lives of undocumented Central Americans expendable while also deeming these migrants as undesirable citizen-subjects of the United States prior to their arrival" (*From Threatening* 91). Sadly, to escape danger at home, the young protagonists must endure precariousness and deadly risks on the migrant trail.

"Move or Die": Danger, Death, and Neoliberalism's Politics of Disposability on La Bestia

By portraying the danger that migrants face throughout the journey across Mexico in what Cristina Rhodes calls "unapologetically realistic" terms ("Book Review"), exercising agency as resistance becomes all the riskier. In terms of the graphic scenes on the cargo train, where migrants risk being devoured or dismembered if they fall off the train, Lauren Heidbrink states that La Bestia itself has become emblematic of a shared trauma of Central American migrants, "a known reality that dehumanizes migrants while simultaneously offering a promise of a different future" (64). In effect, for the unaccompanied protagonists, one of the most precarious moments on the migrant route is when they jump onto La Bestia because every minute on board is a struggle to survive. As their only means of crossing Mexico, La Bestia marks them as a replaceable, surplus population, valued for their cheap labor by an exploitative system that disenfranchises them from social or political power. Critics such as Giorgio Agamben have referred to this kind of precarity as "bare life," to dictate how some people live and how some die.

For example, in *La Línea,* after Miguel and Elena are robbed, they can no longer afford to hire a coyote as they had originally planned, so they are forced to risk their lives on the Bestia freight train, called the *mata gente* or "people killer" in the novel. Fortunately for the siblings, they meet silver-haired Javier from El Salvador, who left behind a wife and two children. Javi is a loving father, and he helps Miguel and Elena navigate the cargo train and migrant journey. Once they all jump on the train, however, they witness an all-too-common horrific scene. They see a boy fall silently off the train "like a leaf" and an old man who tripped as he tried to hop on and then "disappeared without a sound beneath the grinding wheels" (Jaramillo 67). When

Javi, Miguel, and Elena climb to the top of the train, Javi cries quietly, and they hold hands to comfort each other from the unspeakable, traumatizing deaths. As they ride on the train's exposed rooftop, they cannot rest since they must be vigilant of sudden raids by Mexican officials or roaming gangs out to rob them, in addition to low-hanging tree branches that could knock them to their deaths. Though they are exhausted and hungry, the threat of death is momentarily countered when a group of people in solidarity with migrants throw food and water up to them on the moving train. Miguel reflects, "The people knew we were looking for our padres and madres. There must be trainload after trainload of niños, all of them headed north, searching for their families" (71). This soul-stirring scene evokes the humanitarian work of the Patronas, Mexican women who show solidarity and a culture of care, as opposed to the dehumanization the migrants experience throughout their long journey to the border. Montes and Pombo describe Las Patronas as a group of defenders of migrants' human rights that was formed by women volunteers from the community of La Patrona in the state of Veracruz. Since they began in 1995, they have fed thousands of migrants traveling on top of La Bestia attempting to reach the US-Mexico border.[3]

Sadly, there is no solidarity to be found in *Crossing* by Manuel Luis Martinez. Since the book's publication in 1998, crossing the border has become exponentially more costly and deadly. Based on a true story, *Crossing* relates the death of a group of migrants who are abandoned by their coyote and left to suffocate inside a locked railroad car in the northern desert. According to Guadalupe Correa-Cabrera, these types of smuggling operations are in greater demand because of the difficulty of crossing by any other means. She views them as unintended consequences "of enhanced border enforcement and security measures. Further enhancing border security puts migrants under greater risk and strengthens transnational human smuggling networks" (Montgomery et al.).[4] Given this deadly cycle, youth agency in these circumstances is all the more remarkable.

---

3. To witness the inspiring solidarity of Las Patronas, see the documentaries *De Nadie* (Dirdamal 2005), *Llévate mis amores* (Arturo González Villaseñor 2015), and *La cocina de las Patronas* (Torre García 2016).

4. Fatal incidents involving tractor-trailers carrying migrant adults and children are routinely reported in the media, such as the tragic incident in San Antonio in June 2022 where fifty people perished and in a Walmart parking lot in 2017, where thirty-nine abandoned people were locked inside a trailer. Jorge Ramos's *Morir en el intento: La peor tragedia de inmigrantes en la historia de Estados Unidos* (2005), translated as *Dying to Cross: The Worst Immigrant Tragedy in American History* (HarperCollins, 2005), tells the story of migrants trapped inside an unventilated trailer of a semi-truck. Of the seventy-three migrants in the trailer, nineteen died of asphyxiation, dehydration, and heat exposure.

Martinez's first novel, *Crossing* was selected as one of the ten best books by the PEN American Center in 1999. Told in the first person by Luis, a sixteen-year-old Mexican boy, the novel is a heart-wrenching story that refuses to gloss over the drawn-out suffering seldom acknowledged in YA migration fiction. Responding to Frederick Luis Aldama's comment that "There's a lot of pain and suffering in your so-called YA and adult novels," Martinez states, "Youth is where the trauma starts. It's when you experience identity formation, confront trauma, survival, powerlessness, and alienation. . . . The issues don't change. It's our ability to deal with trauma and turmoil that changes, to grow through the ugly" (Aldama 122).

Voicing the idea of coming of age(ncy) as growing "through the ugly," *Crossing* is framed by an epigraph from Ernesto Galarza's *Merchants of Labor* (1964), which hints at the multilayered trauma resulting from devastating climate change, economic injustice, and violence as interrelated root causes for leaving Mexico: "Migration is the failure of roots. . . . Nature and man, separately or together, lay down the choice: move or die." Manuel Luis Martinez's YA novel gives the reader a nightmarish view of migrants locked in a dark freight car, faced with the choice of migrating or dying, through Luis's perspective. As a young boy among adult strangers, Luis fearfully observes fellow migrants near the railroad stop at a slaughterhouse in Monterrey: "There were twelve, besides me. Many of them looked like criminals. They were dirty, seeming to me the kind of men who stayed at the cantinas all night drinking and causing trouble. I didn't want to talk to them, so I sat away from them, watching" (Martinez 1). Clearly he is distrustful, so he physically distances himself, but why does he immediately subscribe to the dominant narrative that equates fellow migrants with dirty criminals? Vogt unpacks the notion of undocumented migrants as "dirty others," along with the idea that the US outsources immigration enforcement to Mexico to do the "dirty work." She explains, "Constructions of dirt and dirtiness are central to anti-immigrant sentiment, which in turn influences immigration and transit policy targeting unauthorized Central Americans in both the United States and Mexico" ("Dirty" 54). Like the racial slur "dirty Mexicans" used in the US, Vogt points to the derogatory slang term *cachuco* for Central Americans often used in southern Mexico. In Oaxaca and Chiapas, Vogt observed that *cachuco* was used to signify "dirty pig" or "dirty Central American," conflated with "dirty smugglers" and "dirty criminals." For Vogt, "Such constructions can be read as codes for deeper social hierarchies and anxieties based on class, race, nationality, and gender" (55). Similar to Osuna's framing of MS-13 as a "moral panic," Vogt underscores that in Mexico's violent context, "migrants become easy and visible scapegoats to blame, while the structural causes of such violence are rendered invisible" (56). Unlike most YA novels, *Crossing* offers the reader valuable insight into the reasons why migrants would pay to be hidden, locked up, and transported on a railway. Without overtly pointing to neoliberal policies and practices that displace people from their traditional livelihood strategies, the novel illustrates the deadly consequences of weakening the social safety net, minimizing worker protections, and forcing many into the informal sector or to migrate (Vogt, *Lives* 42).

Luis, for example, hands over two hundred thousand pesos to a labor contractor, with the understanding that he will work off the rest of the debt when he reaches the United States. As a link in the exploitative chain, the contractor warns Luis about difficult conditions he will have to endure once the cargo door is shut and padlocked from the outside. His warning of deadly conditions and demand for payment upfront reveals that for the labor contractor and coyotes, migrants are simply cargo or commodities to profit from, in line with what educator Henry Giroux refers to as a neoliberal "politics of disposability." In *Youth in a Suspect Society,* Giroux asserts, "as the logic of the market fosters a narrow sense of responsibility, agency, and public values, it reinforces a politics of disposability in which diverse individuals and populations are not only considered redundant and disposable but barely acknowledged to be human beings" (117). As if responding to Judith Butler's piercing questions in *Precarious Life,* "Who counts as human? Whose lives count as lives? And finally, what makes for a grievable life?" (20), *Crossing* depicts a long, torturous, and collective death; it is a tragically vivid tale of the consequences of neoliberal policies deliberately endangering migrants.

When the migrants are locked into the wooden boxcar, Luis reflects on the fact that because his mother did not want him to leave, he took off at night without her permission. When his friend told him about a man who would provide a job and transportation to Texas, Luis began to save and secretly plan for his freedom away from his village. As the unbearable heat within the train car begins to physically affect him, he sweats profusely, becoming dehydrated, and he dreams of his father, who died when he fell repairing a roof, leaving him as the man of the house. Like memories of home, the railway car moves in short bursts then stops altogether in the desert, where the blazing heat and dehydration become the migrants' victimizers. Throughout their confinement they experience hallucinations and turn on each other out of fear and desperation. A fight breaks out between a Guatemalan and a small man called Chico who launches the racialized slur "Indio cabrón": "Give me that cup. I don't want your Indian mouth to pollute the water. . . . You pinche Guatemalteco. You don't even belong here. You people take everything when you come and leave nothing. You shouldn't be here" (18). This hateful slur not only reinforces a nationalist, hierarchical divide between Mexicans and "illegalized" Guatemalan migrants as unwanted; it points to an added layer of racialized discrimination based on his indigeneity (Menjívar, "Guatemalan-Origin" 97). Hearing the social construct of "dirty others" launched against a fellow migrant as they are all trapped and dying, Luis chooses to distance himself again for his own protection. His silence, however, echoes Green's warning that migration exacerbates divisions, further eroding collective solidarity. Without water, they resort to drinking their own urine; the heat is overpowering and the smell becomes unbearable. Unable to tell how many people have died, Luis feels discarded, giving voice to the haunting power of neoliberal disposability. *Crossing* and other YA novels feature La Bestia, a train meant strictly for cargo, not people, as a salient dehumanizing trope of migration literature.

We find another powerful example of dehumanizing conditions on the migrant trail in *Crossing the Wire* by Will Hobbs. As a displaced Indigenous person from Chiapas, Victor, the protagonist, knows that he doesn't have any safe options for reaching the border: "This was the way I was going to have to travel now, like an outlaw in my own country" (Hobbs 44). This quote mirrors Vogt's assertion that "while in transit, migrants may be valued in various combinations of cargo to smuggle, gendered bodies to sell, labor to exploit, organs to traffic, and lives to exchange for cash. Migrants may both gain and lose value during their journeys in material and embodied ways through their dismemberment, disappearance, and death" ("Crossing Mexico" 765).

In contrast to the gruesome details in *Crossing,* Jaime and Angela are ordered into a boxcar attached to other cargo cars in *The Only Road.* The Guatemalan cousins are "locked in a pitch-black train car with no way of getting out, prisoners in their escape for freedom" (Diaz 138). As the heat level rises, they are drenched in sweat and suffer from a lack of oxygen, compounded by the bad smell of their own urine. Jaime feels like he is in a caged oven and falls into a heat-induced slumber. When the door finally opens in Lechería, a borough of Mexico City, they run away from armed immigration officers and see graffiti and bad words calling them "centroamericano scum" (158). As they flee, they see "a mangled foot inside a shoe along the train tracks, an unidentified person chopped to bits by the train. He'd died by himself, in a strange country, and his family would never know" (187). Later, Jaime and Angela have to hop onto another moving train heading to Ciudad Juárez. They meet two Guatemalan brothers who explain the "rules" of riding the trains, but later the brothers steal their backpacks when Jaime, who was supposed to keep watch, falls asleep.

Relatedly, in *Beast Rider: A Boy's Journey beyond the Border* (2019), Tony Johnston and María Elena Fontanot de Rhoads collaborate to create a middle-grade novel that tells the story of twelve-year-old Manuel Flores, who migrates to Los Angeles from the village of San Juan, Oaxaca.[5] As a Mexican psychotherapist and translator, María Elena Fontanot de Rhoads adds valuable insight "into the psychological trauma produced by the Beast experience" (Johnston and Rhoads 180).

Due to the drought and the family's struggles to make ends meet with their small plot of corn, Manuel migrates to join his older brother Toño, who sends remittances from Los Angeles, California. Toño, who works cleaning toilets and doing other odd jobs, left Oaxaca four years ago and is now nineteen. Manuel turns thirteen on the Beast, well aware of the danger but nevertheless feeling a sense of camaraderie with fellow riders: "The Beast is racing fast like a panther. The brotherhood of Beast Riders is lifting me in a huge hum of instructions, with great ferocity of purpose, with a kind of love new to me. Love that says Stranger, we are in this together" (26). Wisely, Manuel prays for safety and protection from "the brotherhood of rateros or thieves, swarming The Beast like rats" (26). Although he views fellow migrants in dehumanizing terms, he also witnesses solidarity. Along the way, he meets a kind man and wisely decides to work for him for a year before continuing the journey. Later, when Manuel resumes the journey, he tries to jump onto the train, but he is ambushed and dragged away by a brutal gang who works for the police for privileges, such as stealing from Beast Riders with impunity. Cruelly, they brand him like an animal with a hot iron until he can smell his own flesh melting. Robbed of his savings and emotionally broken, his hair turns white from the physical and psychological trauma. His eye droops permanently from the beating and he walks with a limp, but thankfully people help him, including Las Patronas, who he refers to as Warrior Women, and who nickname him El Chavo Viejo, The Old Kid.

After three years of suffering on the migrant trail, he finally makes it to the Río Bravo / Río Grande, where someone helps him contact Toño, who pays a coyote to get him across. Once he reunites with his brother, he acknowledges the trauma he's endured. His long trek across Mexico has awakened his critical consciousness as he has come of age(ncy) with a sharpened capacity for reflection. Eventually, he decides to return to his family in Mexico. Comprehensibly, the trauma that Manuel and other protagonists endure on the migrant trail is legally, socially, and politically produced violence, so their agency ensures their survival. As political scientist Raymond Rocco asserts, "The debilitating and corrosive sense of disposability is not merely a byproduct of neoliberalism

5. According to the text, "Tony Johnston has written over one hundred books for children. She lived in Mexico for fifteen years. . . . Her children were born and raised in Mexico. They return when they can. Mexico is their second home" (179).

but is inherent in the contradictions at the root of the economic, cultural and political processes and structures that have characterized the domestic neoliberal regime that required the development of racialized modes of containment of marginalized Latino immigrants" (115). Building on Vogt and Rocco, I maintain that the characters' experiences of mobility embody their agency and, when viewed within a larger racialized context, help us see how young migrants journey on the edge of disposability while discovering a sense of self. The bloodied limbs scattered throughout Mexico in these works of fiction, mirroring reality, are not accidents—they are the result of larger structural processes of inequality and deadly violence.

Danger and Death as Deterrence: The Desert as a Neoliberal Militarized Border

Just as several YA novels in this corpus portray fleeing from Guatemala and Mexico due to poverty, gang recruitment, and gendered violence, *La Línea, Crossing the Wire,* and *We Are Not from Here* stand out for their representation of the dangerous desert crossing. In *La Línea,* Miguel eventually finds Don Clemente's connection, who crosses him and Elena through the desert during the hottest time of the year. They soon become aware that the natural elements of the desert become "a whole new set of enemies" (Jaramillo 95)—the sun, heat, animals, la migra, and white supremacist militia across the border. Feeling afraid and disheartened, Miguel questions, "Why bother with fences or la migra or militias? The heat, the cold, the snakes, the evil cholla spurs—they all conspired to keep us out or slow us down or outright kill us" (108). Experiencing excruciating pain and extreme thirst, Miguel and Elena come across a dead woman's body holding a dead small child in the desert. Later, a blinding sandstorm strikes and they try to take shelter. When the storm passes, the siblings discover that Javier, their Salvadoran companion, is gone. They mourn his loss along with countless other anonymous deaths in the desert, and recognize that in solidarity, he made the ultimate sacrifice for them, leaving his water for their survival. Thanks to Javier's gift of water, they make it across *la línea* and reunite with their parents. The novel ends with a phone call between Miguel and Elena years later, after he's graduated from college with a degree in English and she's returned to Mexico, having completed high school in the United States. He admits to Elena that it took him years to come to terms with the aching childhood feeling that his father had abandoned him. As is typical of many children separated from their parents due to migration, Miguel had to grapple with the understanding that his father went to the US out of love for the family, as a sacrifice, to provide for them so they would not have to depend on dangerous traffickers like Don Clemente, who ruled over San Jacinto in the absence of the Mexican state. We gather that Miguel is still undocumented based on his tenuous situation on the northern side of *la línea*, as opposed to the privileges that his younger twin sisters enjoy as US-born citizens, for whom there is no geopolitical dividing line.

When Victor Flores, in *Crossing the Wire* by Will Hobbs, eventually reaches the border city of Nogales, he is overwhelmed by the border industrial complex. Equipped with night goggles, motion sensors, hidden cameras, and heat sensors, border patrol agents work to keep migrants like Victor out. In effect, the border wall "makes state power explicit and creates spaces of enclosure and violence, rupture and transgression" (McGuire and Van Dyke 42). As a violent extension of state power, the young protagonists experience the militarized border as the deadly "Prevention through Deterrence" policy. Locked inside Mexico by the impenetrable wall, Victor feels betrayed when he discovers that Rico lied to him, since the border-crossing arrangement requires them to serve as drug mules through the Arizona desert. Victor survives the unbearable heat and a snake bite and shows agency by escaping, fearing he will be killed by the head trafficker. Thankfully, a white man finds him and gives him a ride, and Victor ultimately finds work in Washington harvesting asparagus, which enables him to wire his mother $250. After everything he endured on the migrant trail, he reflects, "All I knew was, I had to survive here, so that my family could survive at home. It might be many long years before I saw them again" (214). The remittances he sends will help his loved ones while also spurring others to undertake the same journey.

Jenny Torres Sanchez's *We Are Not from Here* brings together several important elements of the coming-of-age(ncy) journey, including the US Prevention through Deterrence strategy that deliberately channels migrants into the desert so that nature and the hundred-degree desert can serve as enforcers. Crossing on rural, desolate routes with limited access to food or water not only places migrants in mortal danger; it makes it easier for law enforcement to monitor them. For example, after Chico's death, Pulga and Pequeña almost die in the desert. To signal her coming of age and new critical awareness gained on the migrant trail, Pequeña embraces her given name Flor as a refusal to make herself small to accommodate others. Exerting agency, she sells the ring that Rey gave her to pay for a coyote to take them across the border. They are warned that they will walk for three days and nights, from sundown to sunrise, and must keep up because the coyote will not wait for anyone. They endure cold desert nights, the debilitating heat of the day, blisters burning with each step, and the constant fear of dying. When they can no longer continue, a border patrol officer finds them, but Flor manages to run away while the agent attends to Pulga after he collapses. While Pulga is taken into detention, Flor finds spiritual strength in La Bruja, who has accompanied her all along: "I become her. And I am all the women who are leading me through the land of the dead. I feel all of their spirits inside me. I hear their voices, from inside my head. I see their faces flickering in my mind, all their faces. I feel their spirits entering my body. Filling me with some kind of strength, with some kind of will" (327). In resistance, she declares, "We are specks that don't matter to this world. Our lives, our dreams, our families don't matter to this world. All it wants to do is crush us" (330).[6] As if emphasizing collectivity and community, two women help her contact her mother, who reaches out to Pulga's parents so that he can be released to his aunt, to begin the healing journey. Flor's agency and acknowledgment of the spirits' and ancestors' guidance point to collective liberation as resistance to a politics of disposability (see chapter 5).

Viewed together, this corpus of Latinx YA novels represent the harsh realities of the migrant journey and affirm the power of fiction to speak back to dehumanizing policies by providing compelling stories from the migrants' perspectives. As mirrors and windows, they can generate empathy by reflecting humanity and dignity. As educators and scholar-activists, we too can exert agency by calling attention to the structural causes inherent in unjust economic systems driving the dangerous journey. A critical intersectional lens not only challenges white supremacist notions of illegality but also the racialized capitalist model that depends on the cheap labor of lives considered disposable commodities.

The Journey from Vulnerability to Youth Agency and Solidarity

Complementing these texts, Jennifer De Leon's *Borderless* represents the creative agency of sixteen-year-old Maya Luz Silva, who lives with her mother in a rough part of Guatemala City and commutes to her all-girls private school in Zone 10, an upscale neighborhood. A gifted designer, she attends the Salomé

6. Reinforcing the fact that they absolutely do matter, Jenny Torres Sanchez names the seven Mayan children who died in ICE custody in her dedication to *We Are Not from Here*. She also dedicates her YA novel to "all the children who also suffered and died in US custody while seeking refuge. For the children lost along the journey, the ones caught in between, guided only by their fragile hope, whose ghosts roam the borders and deserts of countries that failed them. You deserved so much more. You deserved help. You deserved to dream. You deserved to live."

Fashion Institute on a scholarship. If she wins the school's fashion contest with her "trashion" designs, the prize money will allow them to move to a safer neighborhood. *Borderless* holds a noteworthy place in this corpus because it depicts the need to flee an urban setting during neoliberalism's "peace time." It's also unique in that Maya is of mixed heritage since her mother is Ladina and her father, who was shot when her mother was six months pregnant with her, was a Mayan activist. Her life takes a sudden turn when her best friend Lisbeth introduces her to Oscar, her boyfriend who belongs to a local gang, and his recently deported cousin Sebastian. When she witnesses Oscar shooting a neighbor dead, Maya and her mother manage to escape with Sebastian's help, but without any of their belongings.

Maya experiences a range of traumatizing emotions, particularly because Sebastian, who she's developed feelings for, was involved in the gang incident in which her mother was held at gunpoint. Knowing that he'll be killed for helping them escape, Sebastian flees with Maya and her mother. Like other novels discussed in this chapter, *Borderless* depicts Mexico as a danger zone, yet her mother's ex-boyfriend, who has experience crossing, drives them from Guatemala to the border, where he delivers them to a coyote he trusts. Walking through the desert proves to be a harrowing experience, as Maya struggles to make it across the river while witnessing a fellow migrant drown. Once they make it into the US, border patrol arrives and arrests Maya and her mother. They are taken to a detention center where they experience dehumanizing conditions in the freezing cold *hielera*. Her mother is deported but Maya is allowed to seek asylum.

Keeping in mind that Thompson et al. define agency as "an individual's intrinsic capacity for intentional behavior developed within the individual's environment(s) and subject to environmental influences" (236), it's encouraging to see Latinx YA novels lift up migrants' resourcefulness and decision-making skills. For them, migration is a conscious decision that exemplifies agency, particularly when their personal survival or their families' well-being is at stake. Most importantly, the protagonists counter the violence that surrounds them by openly expressing empathy and solidarity with people they encounter along the migrant trail, demonstrating that a more humane and dignified path is possible.

In my view, reframing youth migration as an expression of agency in the larger context of structural violence is necessary so that socioeconomic and political conditions that force children to flee are brought to light, rather than invisibilized or normalized. Swanson and Torres assert, "as long as violence is considered normal, natural—oppressive structures and practices will be perpetuated at the expense of those most marginalized and disadvantaged" (27).

Likewise, Sciurba et al. note that "hearing the otherwise silenced voices of young people, telling their own stories, is vital to the unlearning of harmful stereotypes" (425). Rodriguez and Braden argue that these books can serve as tools for understanding immigration and "can help disperse the clouds of fear that many of our students experience" (58). Cultivating a sense of agency in young readers can help build empathy as they question unjust structures that force people to undertake the harrowing journey and inspire them to break down hateful borders by challenging ideas of "illegality" and "disposability."

CHAPTER 3

Fleeing Mexican Narcoviolence

Coming of Age(ncy) in Latinx YA

On the day Donald Trump announced his candidacy for president in 2015, he asked and professed, "When do we beat Mexico at the border? They're laughing at us, at our stupidity. . . . They are not our friend, believe me" (Graizbord 88). Scholar and literary critic Ignacio M. Sánchez Prado refutes that claim in "Mexico: The Essential Neighbor," stressing that in fact,

> Mexico is a faithful friend, the source of the largest population of immigrants in the US, and a trade and cultural partner. Yet Americans are often unable or unwilling to understand their southern neighbor in all of its complexity. . . . Americans often see Mexico with a patronizing gaze. . . . The mutual knowledge of our nationals has become a political and intellectual obligation.

Building on the literary representation of Mexico as a danger zone for migrants examined in the previous chapter and taking to heart Sánchez Prado's characterization of our southern neighbor as an often-misunderstood friend, this chapter examines the portrayal of the coming-of-age(ncy) journey in the drug war context. First, I study how violence is depicted as a root cause for migration during the so-called War on Drugs in *Diego's Crossing* (2015) by Robert Hough, *Playing for the Devil's Fire* (2016) by Phillippe Diederich, *Saint Death* (2016) by Marcus Sedgwick, *Disappeared* (2017) by Francisco X. Stork, and *The*

Border (2017) by Steve Schafer. Second, I examine young women's coming of age(ncy) in *The Everything I Have Lost* (2020) by Sylvia Zéleny, *Thirty Talks Weird Love* (2021) by Alessandra Narváez Varela, and *Brighter than the Sun* (2023) by Daniel Aleman as cross-border mirror and window texts. And third, I offer a brief reflection on the literary marketing of drug war violence and the debate about who has the right to tell certain stories. By focusing on the fictional lives of youth immersed in drug war violence, I also tackle the larger matter of how US readers and the publishing industry can deepen their awareness of Mexico as an "essential neighbor" while rejecting a patronizing gaze.

This chapter builds on the analysis of the internal armed conflicts that took place in Central America during the 1980s and 1990s (chapter 1) because sadly, as noted in chapter 2, postwar impunity and corruption are intrinsic to the drug war as a continuation of state-sponsored violence. Since the beginning of Mexico's war on drugs, an estimated two hundred thousand have been killed, and tens of thousands have disappeared. Canadian journalist and sociologist Dawn Paley masterfully connects Central America's past civil conflicts and the contemporary drug war taking place across the hemisphere:

> The war on drugs in Mexico, Central America, and South America is a twenty-first century reboot of the wars that pitted national militaries and police against communists and so-called "internal enemies" in the second half of the twentieth century—from Argentina all the way to Central America. Today, the drug war provides an updated formula to usher in systemic economic and political change and ensure social control through terror, all to the benefit of transnational capital. ("Response" 142)

I borrow Paley's bold claim as a framework for this chapter to take up Sánchez Prado's call for "mutual knowledge of our nationals" as a "political and intellectual obligation." My own view is that US popular culture in general and the white literary publishing industry in particular have stereotypical views of Mexico and immigration, so I specifically examine the depiction of the Mexican drug war in Latinx YA literature since the sensationalized topic and genre appeal to youth and adults alike.

Additionally, this chapter digs deeper into the image of Mexico as a danger zone because, as noted in the previous chapter, NAFTA, neoliberalism, and the Prevention through Deterrence policy of the 1990s had devastating effects on impoverished Mexicans and forced many youth to embark on the dangerous migration journey across Mexico to reach the United States as undocumented, unaccompanied minors. Taken together, these novels depict narcoviolence and violence against women as root causes for either forced displacement within Mexico or clandestine, unauthorized youth migration to the United States. Although the novels do not explicitly critique how forced migration and drug war politics benefit transnational capital, I argue that situating them within the larger theoretical context of neoliberalism's politics of disposability, which places economic profits over human dignity, helps us move beyond a stereotypical patronizing gaze, to see the complexities of migration and violence as transnational issues. To be sure, the publishing industry's marketing of these stories of extreme cruelty and trauma to a US youth audience echoes education scholar Henry Giroux's assertion that "today, a predatory mode of politics and its accompanying representations, images, and discourses are constitutive of how American society has increasingly come not only to privilege death over life but also to view death as a form of entertainment" (593). I insert Paley's and Giroux's claims into this discussion of YA to stress that the stereotypical view of Mexico's "bad hombres" allows the US popular imaginary to ignore the role that global capitalism and neoliberal policies play in that violence. My aim in situating the representation of drug war violence in this larger critical context is to support educators' antiracist pedagogy and culturally relevant teaching that activates adolescent students' lived experience and prior knowledge of Mexico, thus encouraging Latinx youth in particular to question one-dimensional representations of life across the border and counter white supremacy's patronizing gaze.

"I Own You. And Now It's Time to Die": "Bad Hombres" in YA Coming-of-Age(ncy) Narco Narratives

Donald J. Trump launched his first presidential campaign in 2015 referring to Mexico's "bad hombres," who he accused of bringing crime and drugs into the United States as rapists, though he assumed that some "are good people" (Graizbord 88). By denigrating Mexican migrants as narcotraffickers and rapists, Trump purposefully stoked stereotypical fears about the spread of brutal narcoviolence into the US. His anti-Mexican rhetoric reinforced his promise to build a wall across the two-thousand-mile US-Mexican border. Boasting that he would make Mexico pay for that border wall, he unmasked the historically unequal economic and political relationship between the United States and Mexico. Additionally, his politicization of Mexican drug violence, much like his gratuitous references to the Salvadoran gang MS-13, relied on anti-immigrant and anti-Mexican rhetoric centering Mexican masculinity as "bad hombres." In their content analysis of 206 news stories, Vanessa Bravo and María De Moya found that the terms Trump used most in his speeches and public appearances referred to Mexican migrants as "bad hombres," "a threat" to public safety, and "a problem," followed by designations such as "criminals," "illegal immigrants," "rapists," and "criminal aliens," in order of prevalence (64). By repeatedly using these inflammatory terms, he construed a fear of outsiders to call for the deportation of more than eleven million undocumented immigrants. Noting the conflation of immigrants with dangerous others—criminals, smugglers, and delinquents—Wendy Vogt upholds, "in such a violent context, migrants become easy and visible scapegoats to blame, while the structural causes of such violence are rendered invisible" ("Dirty Work" 56). In this vein, I examine a body of YA realistic fiction that uses narco tropes to represent violence in Mexico during the so-called War on Drugs that forces youth to flee to the United States. Following Vogt, I study the portrayal of narcoviolence while underscoring the structural causes that the literary genre, larger publishing industry, and popular culture invisibilize.

Admittedly, the YA novels *Diego's Crossing* by Robert Hough, *Playing for the Devil's Fire* by Phillippe Diederich, *Saint Death* by Marcus Sedgwick, *Disappeared* by Francisco X. Stork, and *The Border* by Steve Schafer have their share of "bad hombres," if we take this term to stand for men involved in narcotrafficking who commit acts of heinous violence for economic profit. Conversely, the protagonists are upstanding adolescent Mexican boys and young men who live in the northern borderlands or in the central state of Mexico. Although they have strong friendships and close family ties, their lives are marked by poverty and violence as they come of age(ncy) immersed in the drug war due to outside forces, not of their own choosing.

I refer to these texts as YA narco narratives because they contain explicit examples of necroviolence marketed to US youth. In *The Land of Open Graves,* anthropologist Jason De León defines *necroviolence* as "violence performed through a specific treatment of corpses" in ways that are offensive (69). The term *necroviolence* resonates with Michel Foucault's notion of biopolitics, Giorgio Agamben's theorization of bare life, or *homo sacer,* and Judith Butler's writing on precarious life. In reference to border matters, De León notes that necroviolence can be aimed at the living by horrifying them while also enabling the powerful to deny responsibility for death. I argue that these YA novels do both—they captivate and horrify the reader with descriptions of forced disappearances, targeted massacres, beheadings, and bodies hanging from bridges as well as dismembered body parts displayed in prominent places for all to see. Equally revolting is the fact that nobody is ever held accountable for these crimes. Although the authors themselves do not label these horrific acts as necroviolence, I assert that this term helps us center structural violence since there is no reliable system of justice for accountability, thus echoing

Paley's ("Response") contention that the drug war implements social control through terror. By connecting these drug war narratives to neoliberalism's biopolitics of disposability, I make a larger argument about how our individualistic culture criminalizes immigration and refuses to take responsibility for it as a result of global capitalism's inherent inequality. Furthermore, I maintain that youth in the US would benefit from discussions about how the impoverished Mexican protagonists are painfully aware of the facts that the Mexican police are not there to protect them and that seeking justice from the Mexican judicial system is not an option. Given the contexts of mass shootings and youth activism for racial justice in the US, I posit that YA readers of color in particular are acutely able to understand that the objective behind what journalist John Gibler calls an "extractive industry of death" is to instill fear, trauma, and a climate of terror to silence a population in resistance. Although the young men and women protagonists of these novels feel despair due to the violence they witness, they nevertheless find ways to exert agency as resistance.

Corruption and complicity between state officials and organized crime, along with impunity for their crimes, are key components of necroviolence evident in these narco narratives. *Playing for the Devil's Fire* and *Saint Death* are structured around the theme of life and death in Mexico as a game of chance. The title *Playing for the Devil's Fire* refers to a game of marbles that Liborio, the book's protagonist and first-person narrator, plays with his friends Mosca and Pepino. Liborio's nickname is Boli, short for "bolillo," or a white bread roll, because his parents own a bakery in their hometown of Izayoc, in the State of Mexico. In Nahuatl, the name of their town means "place of tears." Boli and his friends play marbles and shine shoes for money, but the sudden influx of outsiders make them painfully aware of their precarity and helplessness when Izayoc is overtaken by violence. Edwin Contreras, called Zopilote or Vulture, looks down on the measly amount of cash the boys earn shining shoes. As a seventeen-year-old, he distinguishes himself from the younger boys because he is "making friends in important places" (Diederich 13). Boli admits that he would like to make more money to attract the attention of beautiful girls, but the appearance of a brand-new truck with California plates implies that Zopilote's new friends earn their wealth by illegal means.

Like Diederich's premise of life as a game of marbles, *Saint Death* by British author Marcus Sedgwick is centered around Calavera ("skull"), a high-stakes card game. The protagonist, Arturo Silva, must save his friend Faustino's life by playing against powerful men in a bar full of narcotraffickers. This YA novel is one of several texts that takes place in the border city of Ciudad Juárez, Chihuahua. Arturo lives on the outskirts of Colonia de Anapra, which is described as "a little less than a shanty town, trying hard to be a little bit more than a slum, poorest of all the poor colonias of Juárez" (Sedgwick 4). The city of Juárez is described as "the fulminating beast of violence and of the vastly unequal wielding of power; where the only true currencies are drugs, guns, and violence. Juárez is a new monster in an old land: Juárez is the laboratory of our future" (4). As we see in Boli's hijacked town of Izayoc and Arturo's shanty town in Ciudad Juárez, in these YA novels Mexico becomes a site of terror, injustice, and necroviolence for the protagonists and their communities. Seemingly overnight, Boli's town becomes a place "where drugs are run and bodies are hanged from telegraph poles . . . where people vanish in the night" (Diederich 4). Boli is a vulnerable adolescent who struggles to make sense of the violence while trying to maintain hope and a sense of self. His story begins with a graphic scene of necroviolence: "It was a hot Sunday morning when we discovered the severed head of Enrique Quintanilla propped on the ledge of one of the cement planters in the plaza" (7). Boli recalls, "Except for the big black flies buzzing and crawling into his nostrils and ears and his open mouth, he looked just like when he was alive. He looked sad" (10). The warning "He talked too much" is placed on his teacher's body. Was Professor Quintanilla speaking out against corruption and abuse of power? Who had the power to silence him forever? Captain Pineda, the authority in town, is called immediately but doesn't answer—implying that the absence of the state leaves the door wide open for narcotraffickers, or worse, as Boli begins to suspect, that local authorities work in collusion with organized crime. Unfortunately, the teacher's death is only the first of several graphic killings in the novel.

Beheadings and an anonymous warning also appear in the opening scene of *Diego's Crossing* by Canadian author Robert Hough. The seventeen-year-old protagonist, Diego Hernández, lives in northern Mexico in a town called Corazón de la Fuente, in the border state of Coahuila. Hough's novel begins with an important coming-of-age rite of passage—Diego's driving lesson in his father's ancient Datsun on the highway toward Nuevo Laredo. Diego and his father are shocked to see a *narcomanta,* or long white banner, that warns, "This is what happens to those who offend the double letter" (Hough 7). Joining day laborers gathered around, they see five headless men on the roadway with their hands tied behind their backs. Stunned by this necroviolence, Diego stares at "their bloody neck stumps buzzing with flies" (8) and throws up. Horrified by what he witnesses, Diego nevertheless makes an assumption about the men that subscribes to the dominant "War on Drugs" narrative about "bad hombres" involved in the drug trade and therefore deserving of their fate: "Three are obviously cartel members because they're wearing baggy jeans and their arms are covered in tattoos, while the other two look like regular people—they could be our neighbors back down in Corazón de la Fuente" (8). Diego's presumption signals that he has bought into the mass media's depiction of certain clothing and tattoos as indicators of involvement in organized crime, while others could be campesinos struggling to make ends meet.

As they leave this grotesque scene to return home, Diego's father expresses a critical view that contests the drug war narrative by directly implicating the United States in this necroviolence. Pointing across the border to the US, he exclaims, "None of this would happen if that country didn't like drugs so much" (10). This critique stands out among the YA novels discussed in this chapter by openly pointing to the US as a key market for drugs and as the policymaker for the "War on Drugs." Just two weeks later, a local newspaper headline announces, "Massive Tunnel Found!" and police say that "a few million dollars' worth of drugs were confiscated, just waiting to find their way into the States" (12). Deeply distressed by this drug war violence, the barrage of sensationalized stories leave him feeling depressed and powerless.

Having recently graduated from high school, Diego and his friends have few economic options in their small town so they refer to themselves as "ninis"; appropriating the undesirable term for "a young male who doesn't study or work" (15). *Abecedario de Juárez* provides the following definition and context for *ninis*:

> A widely used derogatory term for young people (generally aged fifteen to twenty-nine) who do not study or work; Juárez teens from low-income families who have few legal paths to self support. These young people cannot afford to pay for books, transportation, and other expenses required to attend high schools or universities. Potential employers often suspect them of delinquency and refuse to hire them. Their limited options lead some to use and sell illegal drugs. (Cardona and Briggs 158)

By not continuing his studies or working, Diego stands in stark contrast to his older brother Ernesto, who makes a grand entrance into town driving a new customized truck and sporting a tattoo of two C's linked together to stand for the Coahuilan Cartel, referenced in the narco banner on the highway. As if the tattoo and new vehicle weren't enough to visually mark Ernesto as a member of the drug trade, he has a diamond set into his front tooth that shines in the sunlight and wears a hairnet along with "baggy gangster pants" (Hough 22). Diego knows that Ernesto could not possibly pay for these luxury items with his supposed construction job. When he confronts him, Ernesto admits, "It's not what you think. I'm an errand boy, nothing more. Strictly low level. I'll be rich in a year or two and then I'll get out of it" (26). Ernesto's easy access to money by illegal means upsets the family dynamic because when he gives his mother money for household expenses, he emasculates his father, who is unemployed like Diego. Sadly, the economic disparity within the family communicates to the reader that the only way to make money in border towns like Corazón de la Fuente is in the drug trade.

After Ernest crashes his new truck and comes home with a concussion, he asks Diego to make an important delivery for him across the border in Nuevo Laredo. Knowing that his brother's life is in danger if the delivery isn't made as planned, Diego uses Ernesto's fake passport and driver's license and borrows his father's old car to complete the drug transaction. He arrives at El Tranquilo's middle-class home and notes that the man is recovering from plastic surgery.[1] El Tranquilo orders a secret compartment installed in the car for four bricks of uncut black tar heroin, stamped with a pair of linked C's. Diego's mission is to cross the border to deliver the four kilos to Crazy J in San Antonio and return to Mexico with the money. This transaction affirms William Avilés's statement: "The reality is that the vast majority of drugs trafficked into the United States are smuggled through legal ports of entry—concealed in passenger vehicles and legitimate merchandise" (299). Diego is nervous about driving across the border but makes it across safely, even noting the same poverty and geographic terrain on both sides.

When Diego arrives in San Antonio, Crazy J gives him a bag filled with cash in exchange for the drugs. Shockingly, Diego experiences a second grotesque scene of necroviolence on the US side of the border. He witnesses four African American men and one white woman being used as human guinea pigs to test the quality of the drugs—they are given needles, bent spoons, and lighters. When the woman faints, falling to the ground from the power of the heroin, Diego is complemented: "You done good, dope boy. You're a natural" (Hough 108). This dehumanizing testing of the drugs' potency on a woman and Black men echoes Paley's claim that the drug war prioritizes the economic flow of transnational capital over peoples' lives; what matters is the quality of the product for financial gain. Diego knows that if he manages to deliver the money to El Tranquilo in Mexico, he and his family will be allowed to live.

After completing the deal, Diego feels overwhelmed by the sudden changes in his life. In shock, he physically shakes when he returns to the old Datsun: "It comes on suddenly, like a bracing chill. I can't help it. I'm picturing the

1. Curiously, plastic surgery is another narco trope. In 1997 Mexican cartel boss Amado Carrillo Fuentes, known as "The Lord of the Skies," died after extensive plastic surgery to alter his appearance. His story is featured in Mexican telenovelas and Netflix's *Narcos: Mexico*. He was best known for chartering private planes to transport Colombian cocaine to Mexico and the United States.

white woman in Crazy J's drug den, the way the froth bubbled up from the corner of her mouth, and then I'm seeing those corpses out on the highway next to Corazón, and then I hear the buzzing of flies in my ears" (109). When the Datsun breaks down in the middle of nowhere, he walks through a cotton field with the bag holding $100,000 in cash. Paradoxically, as a "dope boy," Diego now confirms Trump's claim about Mexicans bringing drugs into the US, although he does it to save his family from harm. After delivering the cash to El Tranquilo, he receives his commission, minus what Ernesto owed on the new truck, totaling $5,000. Pleased with his work, El Tranquilo asks Diego if he would like to stay on, starting debt free with $30,000 as his cut, and assures Diego that most of the Mexican police work for him. His plan to diversify his business by controlling the flow of peppers, avocados, plantains, coffee beans, and pineapples into the US requires smart guys like Diego who don't attract attention. El Tranquilo no longer needs flashy "bad hombres" like Ernesto who are as disposable as the addicts that Crazy J used in San Antonio. With two days to think about this life-altering decision and just weeks away from his eighteenth birthday, Diego ponders, "My days as a nini could be over. With one simple decision, I could be a rich man" (147). *Diego's Crossing* is unique among the novels discussed in this chapter because it specifically points to US demand for drugs along with easy access to high-powered weapons, and also inserts race into the plot, which is important since African American and Latino youth in the US make up the bulk of the more than two million incarcerated due to drug violations (Amaya). Moreover, it portrays Diego's limited agency within a drug war context of neoliberal impoverishment and lack of legitimate economic opportunities.

Like Diego in *Diego's Crossing*, the male protagonist in Francisco X. Stork's YA novel *Disappeared* must also make a life-and-death choice between staying true to his values or getting his hands dirty in the narco business. Like *Saint Death, Disappeared* also takes place along the border, in Ciudad Juárez. Storks's novel alternates between Emiliano Zapata's perspective and his older sister Sara's story as an investigative journalist, which I discuss in the next section. Emiliano's feels resentment toward his father, who migrated to the US. Like many migrants, Mr. Zapata had planned to work temporarily in the US to save money then return to his family. Regrettably, he felt that to get ahead financially in Mexico he would have to work in the drug business, which he refused to do. After divorcing Emiliano's mother, his father marries a white woman in a Chicago suburb and starts another family. The lack of lawful financial mobility for the Mexican working class is a consistent theme throughout the novels. But unlike the others, Stork's novel establishes an important connection between Mexico's wealthy business class and narcotrafficking. When

Emiliano develops feelings for Perla Rubi, who is as upper class as her name implies, he must make a similar ethical choice as his father. As an entrepreneur with a small folk craft business, he does a couple of small jobs for a man connected to the drug trade, who suggests expanding his piñata production. If Emiliano agrees to load drugs into the piñatas when they are made and sell them in airport stores in the US, he could net thirty thousand pesos a week. He feels the need to earn much more money when he attends a party at Perla's home, immediately perceiving the economic divide between them as he feels "shabbily dressed" and "stands paralyzed, dazed by the opulence" (Stork 79) To further complicate things, Perla's father admonishes, "There's no way to be successful in Mexico without getting dirty. The best one can do is control the degree of the dirt" (93). As a lawyer and successful businessman, Perla's father believes corruption is inevitable. His outlook points to the financial divide between lawful, low-paying employment in Mexico versus profitably "getting dirty" in the illegal underground economy. These references to "dirt" relate back to Trump's racialized accusation of Mexicans as "bad hombres" and Vogt's references to doing the "dirty work" of smuggling drugs into the US for American consumption.

Unfortunately, the male protagonists have little support when external forces submerge them in narco- and necroviolence. Shortly after the teacher's beheading, Boli overhears his parents thinking of how to get outside help for their community. They believe that "the whole country is infected" (Sedgwick 26) and that they must stomp out the criminals they consider vermin because of their corruption and illicit activities. Although they seek social change, their dehumanizing language echoes racial slurs used in the US to refer to Mexican immigrants as a pest "infestation." Boli and his older sister worry when days go by and their parents don't return. They seek help from Pineda's office, but nobody investigates. Paley defines these enforced disappearances as "situations where the state is either directly responsible for or complicit in disappearance" ("Mexican Disappearance"). In effect, Boli's community experiences what Marcos Mendoza refers to as the tyranny of narco power, which he defines as "a tyrannical political force exercised over everyday life" (411) that involves limited governance and armed social control. The collusion between the state governor who constructs a highway and attracts a Walmart to the area with ineffective local police, along with corruption within the church and business owners mirrors what Oswaldo Zavala highlights in *Drug Cartels Do Not Exist,* where he asserts that "the cartel wars most likely hide the federal government's strategy to facilitate the illegal appropriation of territories of the county rich in natural resources now open for the exploitation by transnational companies with acquiescence of various political and business interest groups in Mexico" (154). Given the unsustainable living conditions, it's no wonder that Boli feels disempowered when he notices people leaving town, fewer students attending school, and people staying home at night with a self-imposed curfew as safety measures. Unsure of how to cope, he reflects, "Who didn't want to be like them, with money and power and guns? They could do whatever they wanted. I could do nothing" (Diederich 99). Boli's feelings of powerlessness mirror Paley's clarification: "Confusion is a known outcome of terror; together with fear, it is a key part of what keeps people submissive" ("Response" 141). This context of fear through terror necessarily limits the protagonists' coming of age(ncy), yet they find subtle ways of bringing about change.

When the festival comes to town, Boli tries to break free of the oppressive powerlessness by cheering for the lucha libre masked wrestler known as El Chicano Estrada, who he considers an underdog and "an undiscovered hero" (Diederich 106). According to Janina Mobius, "Other than soccer, no other spectacle is as deeply rooted in the Mexican working class as lucha libre. Day by day, in wrestling arenas around Mexico, the country's less privileged folk are constructing a world of their own, a counter-world to the one taken over by the upper echelons of society" (72). El Chicano Estrada's arrival boosts Boli's faith for social change amid the violence. When more people are found hanging from the pedestrian overpass and two naked men hang from a bridge, Boli asks El Chicano to take them down, and people cheer when he does: "It was as if they had been released from a spell" (Diederich 156). Boli believes his new hero can fight whoever is destroying the town, but El Chicano challenges him to think more critically because "Strength is an illusion" (160). Like Boli's parents, El Chicano believes the town is infected "like the rest of the fucking country. This shit's everywhere. There's no way to fix it. . . . We are a country built on lies. . . . Listen, forget the illusion that the world is a good place. It's not" (172, 173). Although lucha libre wrestlers never reveal their identities, El Chicano shares his difficult past with Boli so that he won't put him on a pedestal. He reveals that because he lost his mother when he was eight years old and his father was a drunk, he grew up on the rough streets of Tepito in Mexico City and got by as a pickpocket. He never made it past third grade, and he stole cars, did drugs, sniffed glue, served a year in prison, and even raped a woman. He confesses he was a lost cause until he walked into the Nuevo Jordan gym, where he trained as a wrestler and turned his life around. Although he's not proud of his past, El Chicano's story offers Boli an example of exercising agency despite injustice and structural violence.

Other horrific scenes of necroviolence follow to discourage Boli from searching for his disappeared parents, yet they are depoliticized, meaning that they repeat the dominant narco narrative about the War on Drugs without a critical connection to state authorities or business elites who maintain the status quo with their complicity. El Chicano, however, points out the local priest's corruption, who he considers "as dirty as Pineda," when a new shrine is dedicated to Jesús Malverde, the patron saint of bandits. Malverde's shrine signals that the sacred space of the church where the community gathers for comfort has itself been co-opted by drug dealers. This realization sparks Boli's critical consciousness and agency as he understands that silence is complicity: "The people in town had killed my parents. Their silence was their confession. Everyone who shook their heads, and turned away, everyone who kept silent, everyone who told me not to worry, everyone who left Izayoc. They were guilty of killing them" (231). The final straw resembles the opening scene of *Diego's Crossing*—Boli approaches a crowd and witnesses the body of his hero, El Chicano Estrada, hung by the neck with a rope tied to a giant white cross. After this injustice, Boli abandons the town with his sister, grandmother, and her caregiver. Forced to flee the only home he has ever known, Boli vows to use his agency to create a new life for himself, and, inspired by his hero, to become a luchador.

The grotesque image of El Chicano Estrada stung up on a cross resonates with Arturo Silva's precarious existence on the outskirts of Ciudad Juárez in Marcus Sedgwick's *Saint Death*. He lives alone in a shack on Isla de Sacrificios on a hill known as Mount Cristo Rey, where Christ on the cross blends in with other victims overpowered by guns and drugs. Like the other YA novels, *Saint Death* depicts Ciudad Juárez as a place where bodies are hung from telegraph poles and "people vanish in the night" (Sedgwick 4). Although people believe in Cristo Rey, they also express strong devotion to La Santa Muerte or Saint Death who is associated with the criminal underworld of narcoviolence. In the opening scene, Arturo witnesses a red pickup truck with tinted windows pull up to the center of town to beat and drag away a shop owner who begs for more time to pay the extortion. When he sees four men with tattoo markings of a local narco gang pull up just as the police drive away, he interprets this as a sign that the police are in cahoots with gangs like M-33, leaving the townspeople on their own. One gang member with a tattooed face points a finger gun at Arturo, shooting the imaginary trigger. Why does he threaten the protagonist in this way at the beginning of the novel? Is Arturo next in line to be dragged off?

After witnessing the shop owner being dragged away and hearing the cries of his family, Arturo returns to his shack and is surprised to see his old friend Faustino, who has changed so much. Despite their poverty, Arturo's parents took in Faustino when he was a boy, so the two grew up as brothers. Faustino's story as an orphaned Guatemalan boy resembles the YA novel *Libertad* analyzed in chapter 1 because "back home in Guatemala, his family survived in La Limonada, picking scraps from the garbage dumps, reselling what they could, along with 60,000 other people crammed into the teetering ravine that cuts almost to the heart of Guate" (Sedgwick 34). He and his parents fled Guatemala's poverty, frequent murders, and corrupt police. On the perilous migrant journey discussed in chapter 2, Faustino and his parents hitched a ride to the Mexican border, paying to cross the Suchiate River at Tecún Umán on a makeshift raft, then hopped onto the infamous Bestia. On Faustino's seventh birthday, a gang of armed robbers took his mother away and shot his father dead. As an unaccompanied child migrant continuing the journey, he slipped while attempting to jump onto the next train; his right foot was sliced in half under the wheel and he was taken to a shelter, unconscious from the pain. At age ten, he met Arturo in Anapra, and they became best friends.

Faustino left town over a year before without saying a word, so there is tension between them because Arturo feels abandoned. When they wrestle as they did when they were boys, Faustino's gun falls onto the dirt floor and he confesses that his life is in danger because he's been recruited as a lookout spy for the Libertadores. He is responsible for overseeing other kids who are also lookouts, reporting any suspicious activity to his boss, El Carnero. He has returned to ask for Arturo's help because he has taken one thousand dollars from El Carnero's stash to send his girlfriend and infant son across the border with a coyote, and must repay it. As a seasoned Calavera player, Arturo knows that Faustino has played "an unbeatable card." Since Arturo can't cover the full amount demanded for the crossing, his girlfriend will have to serve as a drug mule, running additional risks as she carries drugs and a child across the desert. Unlike the other works, this YA novel makes a noteworthy attempt to dig deeper into the high-stakes border-crossing business: "It costs a lot because the borders are controlled, not just by Migra, not just by the American border patrol. There are other forces controlling who crosses the desert, and you either pay them and be safe, or you take your chances" (Sedgwick 45). He wants to send his young family away to safety because Los Libertadores work for Barrio Azteca, a cartel that has people everywhere, "as far away as Chicago" (46).

Given the severity of the situation, Arturo promises to help but before embarking on the mission, Faustino wants to pray for La Santa Muerte's blessing since she is considered "a saint of the people" (56). According to Jungwon Park, folk saints signal a perceived lack of care and attention from the government and the official Catholic church. La Santa Muerte highlights the absence of the state as a defender of the population, so it's "no coincidence that those in marginalized sectors seek care and protection that they cannot find in the official system" (Park 253). The fact that these YA novels feature the need for help from an antihero such as El Chicano Estrada, Jesús Malverde, or La Santa Muerte underscores structural injustice and heightened insecurity due to state collusion with narcoviolence in the broader context of neoliberalism's economic violence. Laura Roush frames her study of the Santa Muerte as a politics of survival, referencing frustration over the lack of access to the law or protection from the injustices of institutions as well as from violent people. Her discussion of the Santa Muerte cult in Mexico City's Tepito neighborhood opens a space for thinking about who protects whom, and from what. Roush asserts that Santa Muerte devotion is used to talk and think about experiences of extreme abandonment given factors such as the economic crisis, the crisis of the rule of law, the crisis of faith in the national future, and inadequate access to justice in Mexico. Likewise, Park attests that Santa Muerte devotees are "those cast aside in the neoliberal transformation and excluded from the official system." As the novels reflect, the protagonists' survival depends on a stroke of serendipity in a marble or card game, yet these are subtle acts of agency taken at great risk among larger deadly forces.

As in other YA narco novels exposing state collusion, Arturo finds it "hard to tell just where the gangs stop and the cops start" (Sedgwick 62), yet unlike other works, *Saint Death* voices a scathing critique of the economic divide heightened by the so-called War on Drugs. By listing people last in an assembly line of cheap commodities, the novel emphasizes neoliberalism's politics of disposability. Arturo must play for his friend's life under these deadly conditions while fearing for himself because earlier, in desperation, he stole money from the Santa Muerte shrine. After a short winning streak, he loses almost everything and makes the problematic choice of borrowing from El Carnero, so now he needs to earn five thousand dollars by the following night. He begs El Carnero to understand that these are impossible odds. He seeks help from friends, but there is little they can do, except pronounce another sharp critique against the wall built by the following bricks: "the drug gangs, the police of Mexico and of America, Migra, the DEA, the government and politicians of these two countries. The biggest brick of all: companies; these giant corporations that are more powerful than anything, more powerful even than the countries where they operate" (153). It's no coincidence that local bar owners Siggy and Carlos, a queer couple, express a critical view of their patriarchal society that sustains economic injustice and structural violence in Mexico. As Arturo reflects on his in-betweenness, on the border between childhood and adulthood, Siggy urges him to be strong: "You are at the hardest point of all. You are not a kid. You are not a man. You are somewhere in the middle. You are walking over a bridge between the two, and you know how dangerous bridges are. In Juárez we all know how dangerous bridges are, right?" (158). Out of options, El Carnero says he never expected Arturo to come up with the money, so he offers him the opportunity of working for him. Arturo refuses on the spot, so he is beaten with a hammer and knifed to death, then he is thrown in a pickup. Although other YA characters such as Diego and Emiliano consider joining the narcos out of desperation, Arturo is the only one who is killed for refusing. In a final act of solidarity, self-sacrifice, and youth agency as resistance, Arturo had given the thousand dollars he gathered to Faustino so he could escape to the US with his girlfriend and son.

Like *Saint Death,* Schafer's *The Border* portrays the deadly consequences of getting involved with Mexican narcotraffickers. The novel opens with Pato, the first-person narrator, noticing a suspicious-looking car outside of his cousin's quinceañera; he later regrets not reporting it at the family gathering. While sixteen-year-old cousins and best friends Pato and Arbo secretly smoke outside with nineteen-year-old Marcos and his fifteen-year-old sister Gladys, gunmen emerge from the suspicious car to storm the party. Hearing the shots, Arbo runs into the house while one of the gunmen is still inside. As the gunman is about to shoot Arbo, Marcos kills him. With precision, Schafer opens a window and sliding glass door for the reader: "Bodies. Everywhere. Some lie together, embracing each other as though they went down mid-dance. Some lie alone" (15). Pato vomits on himself, sobbing, "My mother and father lie somewhere. I don't search for them. I don't want to. I can't. I break" (15). In shock, the teens know they must run for their lives. As Pato and Arbo flee across the Sonoran Desert with Marco and Gladys, they learn that La Frontera is offering a reward for each of them, dead or alive. As they are pursued in the desert, they realize that their fathers, who owned a construction company, were targeted along with family and friends because of their involvement with the wrong people. They "did projects for the gangs, construction work to hide drugs, secret rooms and things like that. They got paid not to ask questions and not to talk" (205). Unbeknownst to the boys, their fathers provided for the family by doing "dirty work" for "bad hombres."

As the youth run out of water in the desert, the novel ends with alarming intensity. From a safe distance, they follow a coyote, but they are recognized by tattooed men. There is a shootout and Gladys, who Pato was developing feelings for and kissed, is shot and dies. The gunmen from the party show up with high-powered weapons, and one melodramatically declares, "I own you. And now it's time to die" (308). As border patrol swarms in, the boys escape in the chaos and are saved by an American couple out riding mountain bikes in the desert who give them water and drop them off at a motel in Phoenix with forty dollars. Pato and his cousin Arbo vow to start new lives but their future as traumatized, undocumented youth in the US could be as uncertain as in Mexico.

"A Girl Is a Human": Coming of Age(ncy) by Writing as Resistance in Latinx YA

Although drug war violence is a recurring theme in the cross-border journeys examined in this chapter, the following novels, featuring young women's voices, eschew sensationalist descriptions of narcoviolence to focus on the need for trauma healing and justice in the border zone. Another difference is that these authors identify as Latinx and write in what was previously referred to as "own voices" because their identities match those of the protagonists. Francisco X. Stork, for example, was born in Monterrey, Mexico, and grew up in El Paso. Sylvia Zéleny was born in Hermosillo, Sonora. Alessandra Narváez Varela was born and raised in Ciudad Juárez. Sara Zapata's story in *Disappeared* (2017), *The Everything I Have Lost* (2020) by Sylvia Zéleny, and Alessandra Narváez Varela's *Thirty Talks Weird Love* (2021) take place in Ciudad Juárez during the 1990s, when NAFTA, neoliberalism, the global maquiladora industry, and femicide converged along the border.

As Gabriela Polit-Dueñas attests, Ciudad Juárez has become a global fetish during the last two decades: "a cherished vehicle for describing the nefarious effects of neoliberalism in the region, violence against women, and the War on Drugs" (78). Reminiscent of Sánchez Prado's statement that the US often views Mexico with a patronizing gaze, Polit-Dueñas astutely remarks that most representations highlight one aspect of Ciudad Juárez's violence without understanding the complexity of the whole, and this tends to alienate "foreigners and locals alike, impeding them from understanding the complexities of local violence and limiting ways of relating to it" (87). My reading of the representations of coming of age(ncy) in these novels is informed by a critique of neoliberalism given the interrelationship between maquilas, embodied gendered violence, and border politics.

For Sara Zapata in *Disappeared,* Julia in *Everything I Have Lost,* and Anamaría in *Thirty Talks Weird Love,* journalism and journaling are tools of resistance and reflection with which to exert agency in their violent surroundings. Sara is well aware of the kidnapping and killing of girls and women taking place in the city, so she resents the assignment to write about a new mall for *El Sol.* She knows she must investigate the disappearance of her best friend Linda to shed light on the larger issue of impunity for violence against women. Rosa

Fregoso and Cynthia Bejarano define femicide as a crime against humanity "that is both public and private, implicating both the state (directly and indirectly) and individual perpetrators (private or state actors); it thus encompasses systematic, widespread, and everyday interpersonal violence" (5). Similarly, Victoria Sanford uses the term "feminicide" to refer to "the murder of women by men because they are women and also points to state responsibility for these murders whether through commission of the actual killing, toleration of the perpetrators' acts of violence, or omission of State responsibility to ensure the safety of its female citizens" (*Textures* 14). Moreover, she considers femicide a form of social cleansing. In the context of Guatemala, Sanford highlights "the ways military structures of the past have morphed into and overlap with contemporary structures of violence: gangs, drug traffickers, and organized crime" (16). These definitions are fundamental because they explain the interrelationship between the importance that *El Sol* places on the city's business ties and the lack of concern for how the economic sector benefits from exploiting women under neoliberalism. Sara's hopes of finding Linda and locating information on the disappearances converge when she receives an emailed photograph of a girl with an older man passed out at a nightclub, sent with a code word that only she and Linda know. She suspects that Leopoldo Hinojosa, the head of the Public Security and Crime Prevention Unit of the state police, is involved. Not knowing who to trust at work but understanding that Mexico is "the deadliest country in the world for journalists, and that most of the crimes against them remain unsolved" (Polit-Dueñas 78), Sara begins to link the abduction of girls to sex trafficking. Because she doesn't know anyone trustworthy in law enforcement, she turns to hackers and an American FBI agent to gather evidence that implicates the powerful. When her mentor jeopardizes Sara's privacy, her home is destroyed by high-powered gunfire, compelling the family to flee for their lives. Their mother relocates to León but insists that Sara and her younger brother Emiliano go live with their father in the United States. Due to his estrangement from his father and his infatuation with Perla Rubi, Emiliano refuses to leave Mexico, but he agrees to help Sara cross the desert to ask for asylum.

During the desert crossing, Sara's investigation converges with Emiliano's prospective business ties. Two armed men find them and take the cell phone Sara carries with proof of the disappearances. This forces Emiliano to finally confront reality: "There is no more denying the truth. Perla Rubi is the reason they were found. His sister was almost raped and killed because of Perla, or her father, or both. . . . It's like a spiderweb. Every thread is connected" (Stork 297, 298). He comes of age when he realizes that they want to kill Sara for investigating, yet he is protected because of his connections. Feeling remorse, he accepts he's dying of dehydration, but fortunately, he wakes up later in the home of an older couple, who tend to his injuries. He learns that Sara was taken to a detention center but has a good lawyer for her asylum case and that Bob Zapata, their father, wants him to join him in Chicago.[2] In my view, Stork's *Disappeared* challenges the hegemonic War on Drugs narrative by exposing the connections between the Mexican business elite and narcotrafficking, along with the fact that law enforcement officials have historically served the interests of the politically and economically powerful to maintain the status quo.

Like Sara, Julia in *Everything I Have Lost* and Anamaría in *Thirty Talks Weird Love* are acutely aware of the femicides in Ciudad Juárez. In my estimation, these novels stand out among the narco narratives in this chapter because they depict the psychological impact that the drug war and impunity leave on borderlands girlhood. This echoes Johan Galtung's claim that "a violent structure leaves marks not only on the human body but also on the mind and the spirit" (cited in Menjívar 2011). As a way of coping with the uncertainty at home and shuttling back and forth across the border between Ciudad Juárez and El Paso, thirteen-year-old Julia creates a sense of stability for herself by recording her observations in her diary. She reflects on her fraught relationship with her parents along with extensive caretaking responsibilities for her younger brother and great-grandmother with dementia. Surrounded by normalized violence and unpredictability, she lacks a supportive community to process the precariousness she experiences. She shows agency by journaling as a way of making meaning of her surroundings, on the journey from adolescence to young adulthood.

Julia unleashes her judgment of her dysfunctional home in her diary. She writes about her father's long absences and sudden access to weapons and large amounts of money. When he gets a job with El Gringo, they move into a house that feels like a fortress. In this confined environment, her critical awareness grows, and she resists the normalization of violence: "Every other day we either hear shootings or hear about shootings all over town. That's not normal. Just the other day there was a massive shootout downtown. Bad news, we live in a town that is all bad news" (Zéleny 68). She exerts agency by pushing back against powerlessness, precisely because power dynamics affecting gendered and racialized bodies are invisibilized. According to Rosa Linda Fregoso, "We should consider feminicide in Ciudad Juárez a part of the scenario of state-sponsored terrorism. . . . A tool of political repression

2. I examine the continuation of Sara's story in chapter 5. In *Illegal*, Stork's sequel, Sara fights for asylum as a targeted Mexican journalist during her confinement in a US detention center. Emiliano continues the investigation from a suburb of Chicago.

sanctioned by an undemocratic patriarchal state in its crusade against poor and racialized citizens" ("Complexities" 132, 133). With sensitivity, Sylvia Zéleny's YA novel offers a much-needed mirror and window into vulnerability and agency as resistance amid gendered violence.

Slowly, Julia starts to piece her father's story together as a "bad hombre" in Ciudad Juárez. When he returns home, she notices how much he has changed: "He is different. Skinnier, grumpier. He sleeps all day long, doesn't talk, and whispers. He smokes a lot. He gets mad at every little thing" (Zéleny 117). Given the violence, she stops attending school but journals about a car bomb, narco *fossas* (mass graves where victims of violence are disposed of), protests about elections, and a menacing army presence in Juárez. When they suddenly move again, leaving all their belongings behind, Julia is devastated without her diary: "I have lost my life, I have lost everything and no one seems to care, so no more writing for me, no more diary for me" (161). Fortunately, her aunt gives her a new diary and empowers her to express herself. Her suspicion is confirmed when her father is hospitalized in a vegetative state and a newspaper photo identifies him as "La Comadreja's hitman" (203). She notes that nobody attended his funeral, signaling that as a "bad hombre," he was disposable.

Alessandra Narváez Varela's *Thirty Talks Weird Love* takes place in Ciudad Juárez in 1999 when Anamaría Aragón Sosa is thirteen years old. Situating the storyline at this moment in time places Anamaría's coming of age(ncy) on the frontlines of femicide within NAFTA's neoliberalism, which she experiences while living close to the city's first Walmart. The uncovered sewer and maquiladoras within view reveal that private businesses are prioritized while city officials refuse to invest in infrastructure and safety for its citizens. This problem is magnified in the school setting, because she attends a highly competitive private school where she experiences bullying and suffers from severe anxiety and depression due to a debilitating fear of femicides. She has nightmares about monster men who drag her away by her feet. Although her father tells her not to be afraid because his job as the family patriarch is to always protect her, she grasps that the underlying message is actually the opposite: "Be afraid, something could happen to you" (Narváez Varela 27). She also dreams of hurting herself by taking a knife to her wrists. Her parents try to support her emotionally, but they are unaware of what she is really experiencing. To fill this void with agency and wisdom, her thirty-year-old self visits her from the future to encourage her to love herself as she struggles to cope with trauma.

Thirty, her older self, walks with a limp and is a poet and a teacher, which explains why Anamaría feels most comfortable expressing her poetic voice in free verse vignettes. She gives Anamaría a notebook so that she can write down the many thoughts she can't express out loud about feeling pimply and fat as she binges and secretly throws up. She tells her, "I know you're not . . . well. . . . We're the same. Inside. For now, just love you, sí? Loving you could mean loving at least one part of your body. . . . You are not your grades. . . . You're not well" (29, 33, 46). Thirty also encourages her thirteen-year-old self to express how she feels about the femicides. She is aware of how gender intersects with class and race, since mostly poor, dark-skinned girls are taken. As Anamaría listens to the music of Juan Gabriel, "our sweet prince of sung borderlove," she prays, "Save all of us girls. Save Ciudad Juárez" (71) because she considers the city "a second mami" (72), but she also expresses, "It hurts to love you, Ciudad Juárez! You're a red cruel beautiful mother beast" (147). These reflections help Anamaría express resistance to dehumanizing structural violence that views her as disposable. Exerting agency for herself and others, she declares: "A girl is a human" (159). When Anamaría is hospitalized, she finally tells her parents that she is depressed, and they promise to find another school and get her help. Her clashing conversations with Thirty start to make sense when she lets go of denial: "Wait . . . Does loving you mean loving that you're alive, flaws and all? Can it be that simple?" (181; ellipsis in original).

In "Notes from the Author," Alessandra Narváez Varela identifies as a Mexican American woman and native of Ciudad Juárez who feels the responsibility of bearing witness to the trauma caused by femicides. She writes about her own depression and suicidal thoughts, leaving medical school and seeking help. With the author's firsthand experience, Narváez Varela's novel offers an inviting mirror and window for social awareness and trauma healing.

In sum, *Disappeared, The Everything I Have Lost* and *Thirty Talks Weird Love* connect coming-of-age experiences that denounce the drug war as a war on women and youth and depict characters exerting agency by writing for survival and resistance against neoliberalism's biopolitics of disposability. Their writing is a form of witnessing that seeks healing justice and social change. The agency that Sara, Julia, and Anamaría exert in their reporting and journaling serves as an important critique of impunity and neoliberalism's politics of disposability, which values profits over human dignity.

Reflecting on the Representation of Mexican Narcoviolence and Who Can Tell This Story

Given the gruesome depictions of necroviolence and femicide featured in the Latinx YA novels studied in this chapter, I want to briefly consider the larger implications of how narco narratives portray Mexican drug war violence and who can tell this story. Much has been written about the controversy that ensued over the marketing attention that Jeanine Cummins's best seller *American Dirt* (2020) received as opposed to the "own voices" work of Latinx authors.[3] As a window book, Cummins's action-packed use of narco tropes is exactly what makes her novel so compelling. As we've seen, narco narratives give readers a window into Mexican necropolitics with recognizable tropes, reflected in Oprah's endorsement of *American Dirt,* which contributed to the uproar that ensued on social media and in print when Latinx authors spoke out against the lack of visibility of writers of color by the publishing industry, let alone Cummins's seven-figure advance and the book's first print run of five hundred thousand copies, unheard of for most Black and Brown authors. Oprah praised the novel because it helped her form a "newfound perspective about the migration process." She explains: "I really appreciated that book, and it helped me to see immigrants and the whole migration process differently than I had before. . . . So it opened up a space in me, allowed me to see things differently, and I appreciated that from the author and I thought the story was well told" (Aquilina and Wang). Her video endorsement to Oprah's Book Club is emblematic of what Bishop identified as an inviting "sliding glass door": "From the first sentence, I was *in.* I was opened, I was shook up, it woke me up, and I feel that everybody who reads this book is actually going to be immersed in the experience of what it means to be a migrant on the run for freedom." But these same tropes prompt others to call the book "stereotypical" and "appropriative" and to accuse Cummins of parasitically engaging in "brownface" (Alter). Given the controversy over the attention awarded to *American Dirt,* I believe it's important to briefly reflect on similarities and differences noted above with other non-Latinx authors.

Cummins used some of the same identifiable narco tropes as Robert Hough, Philippe Diederich, Marcus Sedgwick, and Steve Schafer to perpetuate the "bad Mexican" stereotype. Their fiction features ruthless assassins, life-risking rides on La Bestia, traitorous coyotes, and corrupt Mexican officials in collusion with narcotraffickers. My position is that it is highly problematic to give this one-dimensional representation of Mexico without a critical context. In my view, a portrayal centered solely on "bad hombres" depoliticizes and

3. Chicanx author Myriam Gurba denounces Cummins's novel as "trauma porn" in her blistering review of *American Dirt* titled "Pendeja, You Ain't Steinbeck: My Bronca with Fake-Ass Social Justice Literature." In her *New York Times* opinion piece, novelist Reyna Grande, who was born and raised in Guerrero, where Acapulco is located, and crossed the desert as an undocumented child, highlights the border walls that the publishing industry puts up for Latinx writers with lived experience, such as herself.

invisibilizes institutional violence and global capitalism's biopolitics of disposability. Without a larger theorization, the violence we witness in these narco narratives seems like random acts of cruelty during a chaotic drug war rather than a means of "social control through terror, all to the benefit of transnational capital" (Paley, "Response"). Clearly, the majority-white publishing industry profits from marketing extreme cruelty across the border devoid of a critical context that implicates US white supremacy and racialized capitalism. Lacking this nuance and the complexities of border politics, authors risk centering whiteness and individualizing ruthlessness rather than challenging the reader to reflect on how structural violence implicates power on both sides of the US-Mexico divide.

While I take issue with "single story" representations of Mexican narcoviolence that lack a critical context, I believe that we need more gripping novels about the War on Drugs from well-informed authors who offer critical, nuanced perspectives, especially in YA literature. As educators, it is our responsibility to provide a historical and sociopolitical context to our students and challenge them to read critically. Riveting fiction by outsider authors and introspective accounts by Latinx voices can spark discussions on the fraught relationship between drug war violence in Mexico and anti-Mexican racism in the United States, which often go unacknowledged in representations of immigration and cartel narratives. While I uphold the importance of Latinx representation with movements such as #DignidadLiteraria, #OwnVoices, and We Need Diverse Books, rather than policing who gets to tell the narco story, I prefer to focus on how the US and Mexico enable and profit from drug war violence and the lack of accountability on both sides of the border. As Paley remarks, it's typical to focus on the violence, "But the political and economic interests behind the violence have been largely ignored, masked by drug war discourses, and because of the scale of the social emergency generated through state-directed terror. . . . Part of the struggle for a better world is to make sense of the structures of violence and domination that are active all around us" ("Response" 140, 141). As we see in these post-NAFTA drug war narratives, the young protagonists endure economic precarity, which makes them more vulnerable to insecurity and violence. In this context, we also see that literary allusions to dirt and dirtiness are marketable ways of expressing otherness, which uphold anti-immigrant sentiment.

Although the representation of Mexican social realities in YA leaves much to be desired, this resonates with a similar situation that professor of education Rudine Sims Bishop pointed to in 1983, in an article about the predominantly "all-white world" of children's books, signaling that "we are no longer where we once were, but we are not yet where we ought to be" ("What Has

Happened" 653). Her words ring true in terms of the publishing industry, especially with respect to Central American, Mexican, and Latinx representation. As the book *Nerds, Goths, Geeks, and Freaks* makes evident, youth readers comprise one of the fastest-growing demographics in the US: "As the Latinx population in the US approaches becoming the majority by 2043, the need for scholarship centered on Latinx children's and YA coping has become more pressing" (Boffone and Herrera 5). What is more, given the scarcity of "mirror" books, I fear that the lack of well-informed, contextualized representation can negatively impact how Latinx readers view themselves. My goal in framing Mexican narcoviolence and migration within neoliberalism's politics of disposability is to enable educators to support readers' critical reflections about the drug war and its effects on youth. While kidnappings, forced disappearances, femicide, violence against journalists, corruption and impunity for the powerful are certainly mature issues, the intentions behind the neoliberal drug war impacting youth are deadly. "That youth and especially young men have been the hardest hit by violence in Mexico is not a coincidence or a natural occurrence," Paley observes. "Rather, it is indicative of a state at war with those it fears the most: young people with the capacity to rebel" (Paley, "Cold War" 157). In *Drug War Capitalism*, she states, "The image of the benevolent state against the bad drug traffickers provides a frame through which governments can justify rising military spending and attacks on unarmed civilians as necessary for national security" (220). Recalling Sánchez Prado's call for acknowledging Mexico's complexities, the YA novels discussed in this chapter present compelling stories of fleeing and staying put while writing as a brave act of agency and resistance. Together, these stories invite us to reject the traditional patronizing gaze so that we may grow in mutual understanding as neighbors.

In the following chapter, I focus on how the adolescent protagonists who survive the migrant journey from Central America and Mexico grow in mutual understanding as they develop friendships and romantic ties in the United States. Just like the YA novels studied thus far, their compelling stories teach us that their lives and voices matter.

CHAPTER 4

Cross-Racial Solidarity in the Coming-of-Age(ncy) Journey

Navigating Undocumented Teen Romance in Latinx YA

Building on the notion that readers are hungry for "mirror" books that make them feel seen as well as "window" stories about those with different life experiences from their own (Bishop "Mirrors"), in this chapter I study YA novels that portray undocumented Central American and Mexican teen romances, bringing white supremacy to the forefront. Taking place in Illinois, Missouri, Arizona, New Mexico, California, Texas, Georgia, Massachusetts, Vermont, and New York, these novels give voice to the anxiety of growing up without legal authorization and fears of family separation due to the ever-expanding detention and deportation regimes. Viewed through the critical lens of neoliberal racialized capitalism, these YA novels challenge us to reflect on how migration intersects with gendered structures of violence and white supremacy.

The novels represent the end goal of the migrant journey for those who have survived the arduous trek across multiple geopolitical borders: reaching the US. As undocumented migrants, refugees and asylum seekers, or US citizens in mixed-status households, the protagonists grow to see themselves as agents of change who model empathy and dignity while resisting purposefully cruel immigration policies as racialized others. I argue that by bringing visibility to characters rarely depicted as having agency, this burgeoning body of YA literature challenges us to denounce repressive policies of exclusion. Given the sizable quantity of texts, my argument unfolds in two distinct but interrelated parts.

First, I examine how YA novels *Journey of the Sparrows* (1991) by Fran Leeper Buss and Daisy Cubias and *Red Glass* (2007) by Laura Resau depict traumatic experiences from the Salvadoran and Guatemalan civil wars in a US context, and how the protagonists use their agency to create spaces of solidarity and sanctuary for healing justice. Then, through a larger set of YA novels that depict how undocumented teens negotiate their first cross-racial friendships and romantic relationships in the US, I assert that under the guise of teen romance, *Return to Sender* (2009) by Julia Alvarez, *Dark Water* (2010) by Laura McNeal, *Dream Things True* (2015) and *The Radius of Us* (2016) by Marie Marquardt, *Don't Ask Me Where I'm From* (2020) by Jennifer De Leon, and *Where I Belong* (2021) by Marcia Argueta Mickelson draw readers into the excitement of first love while portraying the fears of undocumented youth in the shadows of a white supremacist immigration system. I stress that like all immigrants, these narratives' protagonists bring with them an array of strengths that empower them to exert agency.

I argue that the portrayal of Central American and Mexican coming-of-age(ncy) experiences alongside those of US-born teens can serve as important mirror and window texts and meet antiracist teaching goals by raising awareness about the undocumented experience. As readers identify with or feel empathy for the characters, they might feel compelled to ask how they can be allies and raise their own voices to speak back to white supremacy. Whether these texts are read as part of an immigration unit or social justice curriculum in school, or read at home for pleasure, I believe they can empower immigrant youth to author their own stories in equally creative and liberatory ways as the protagonists—through storytelling, letter writing, or journaling. As Latinx YA literature, these diverse texts are critical tools with which to question the unjust economic and geopolitical forces driving migration, and they serve as important models for responding to hateful rhetoric that erroneously conflate a lack of authorized documentation with illegality.[1]

Sparrows and Quetzales: US Central American Solidarity and Sanctuary

Journey of the Sparrows by Fran Leeper Buss and Salvadoran poet Daisy Cubias and *Red Glass* by Laura Resau evoke the contradictory roles that the

1. I agree with Harald Bauder that language matters. He proposes the adoption of the term "illegalized" because it draws attention to the institutional and political processes rendering people illegal. The term "shifts the emphasis away from the individual and towards a societal process that situates people in positions of precariousness and illegality" (328).

US has historically played in El Salvador and Guatemala as a political and economic destabilizing force and as a space of solidarity and sanctuary when grassroots activists dare to defy repressive US policy. Fran Leeper Buss is an award-winning oral historian of poor and working-class women of diverse ethnic and racial backgrounds. According to the novel's biographical blurb, Daisy Cubias "is a poet and activist who left El Salvador as a young woman to come to work in the United States. Her brother, brother-in-law, and sister were all murdered in El Salvador, leaving orphaned children behind." Both books serve as mirrors and windows that humanize the migrant journey.

In line with YA novels studied in chapter 1, *Journey of the Sparrows* tells the story of Salvadoran siblings who flee the US-supported war and suffer family separation and deportation. María Acosta is the fifteen-year-old first-person narrator who fled El Salvador with her mother, her pregnant older sister Julia, her six-year-old brother Oscar, and her baby sister Teresa. After enduring the migrant journey from El Salvador to Mexico, María's mother and Teresa are too sick to continue on to the US, so they remain in the border city of Tijuana. The siblings and a Salvadoran boy named Tomás are nailed into a crate of onions and tomatoes and snuck across the US border, then transported on to Chicago. Given their vulnerability, the coyote's voice sounded "like the voices of the government soldiers, the Guardias, who had come to our home months before" (Buss 1). Memories of home haunt María throughout the novel because as discussed in chapter 1, the Salvadoran Civil War lasted twelve years (1980–92), left an estimated seventy-five thousand dead, and displaced roughly a quarter of the country's population. María's family has no choice but to flee because the Guardias stormed into their home, killed their father and Julia's husband, and raped Julia. Their father was targeted for trying to bring education and health resources to the community. Like the majority of Salvadorans at the time, they were very poor; four brothers and one sister had already died due to undernourishment. From the confined space of the crate, to calm their fears as they yearn for their own liberation, María uses her agency to quietly recount the story of when she freed a quetzal from a cage. This is a key story to tell because the quetzal cannot survive in captivity. Barillas Chón relates the flight of the quetzal to Maya peoples' migration: "Maya peoples migrate to exist. This migration is done in defiance of systems designed for their displacement and erasure" ("When Children" 292).

María's agency as a storyteller and an eyewitness to the killings in El Salvador embody testimonio, the Latin American genre that denounces injustice discussed in chapter 1. Traumatized by the war, the illegalized siblings are triggered by Chicago police sirens, so María comforts them by recounting a story their father used to tell them about a little sparrow that protects them from harm, including by soldiers. As undocumented Central Americans, they know "we'd have to be invisible, never complain, never get anybody to notice us. Because we wouldn't have papers" (14). This understanding mirrors the way Indigenous protagonists in chapter 1 had to flee Guatemala during the war, remove their *traje*, and try to pass as Mexicans so they could make their way across the border.

María displays agency as she reins in her fears to look for work to pay for the family's reunification with their mother and youngest sister. When she finds a job in a sewing factory, her boss touches her inappropriately, taking advantage of her age and status. When he puts his hands on her body, she has a flashback of the soldiers' abuse in El Salvador that equips her to fight back:

> The man laughed and grabbed me by my shoulders, and as I twisted to get away from him, he snarled, "You're illegal. I can do anything." He laughed again, and I smelled the Guardias and saw the blood as he reached for my breast. I screamed, "Stop! Don't!" and swung out hard with my fist, smashing him in the nose. He slapped me across the face, but I twisted away and kicked him in the leg and screamed, "Stay away!" (53)

This gendered, racialized, and economic abuse blurs the borders between El Salvador and Chicago for María, as the scene exposes how capitalism's patriarchal abuse is rooted in colonial legacies and white supremacy. Salvadoran American art historian Kency Cornejo posits, "U.S. imperialism is built on the idea that racialized peoples do not matter—not their lands, their cultures, their ways of being, or their existence. They are deemed sacrificial and expendable for the greater good of white domination" (195). The employer's harassment heightens María's fear because back home, she heard villagers whisper that the *norteamericanos*, "the people up here, had helped our leaders hurt us, that the guns they used came from the United States" (39). This implicates US economic policy in the militarized oppression of Salvadorans like María's father, who was killed for advocating for basic needs such as a school. Given its Cold War mindset, the Reagan administration sent $82 million in aid to the military-run Salvadoran government. Elizabeth Barnet writes, "By 1982, the tiny country became the fourth-highest recipient of US aid dollars. The Salvadoran military, instructed in counterinsurgency tactics by the United States, sought to isolate the FMLN from the social base that sustained it, using a 'scorched earth policy' that deliberately targeted unarmed civilians in rural El Salvador" (3). Cold War logic and the United States' role in the violence had a devastating impact on migrants and asylum seekers like the Acostas. Lloyd

D. Barba and Tatyana Castillo-Ramos explain, "Because of Cold War politics and the role that the US played in causing this mass exodus, US officials decided to systematically deny asylum to nearly all Salvadorans and Guatemalans. The inadequate response of immigration courts and border enforcement officers led many to decry the US for both its role in Central America and how it attempted to deny entry and asylum to these refugees who were fleeing violent civil wars. They would later be labeled 'economic migrants' by the Reagan administration" (7).

Importantly, María's coming of age(ncy) transpires alongside Salvadorans and Americans who worked clandestinely with religious communities to support the organizing work of committed laypeople. When María, deemed an "economic migrant," climbs a fence to steal a loaf of bread from a Catholic church, she learns of an opposing view of using agency to offer sanctuary to Central Americans fleeing US-supported wars. Instead of punishing her for breaking in and stealing, Father Jonathan surprises María by explaining, "Not everyone here agrees with Immigration. Or backs the Guardias. Some of us are trying to change things. To make it legal for people like you" (Buss 80). By giving her food and a job cleaning the church, where she will also be allowed to sell her drawings of saints to provide for her family with dignity, he upholds the tenets of the Central American Sanctuary movement to work for social change. María tears up when she sees a poster in downtown Chicago demanding "Justice for the Salvadoran refugees." A woman who speaks Spanish and is handing out flyers explains, "We're part of a movement. . . . We're helping people without documents, those who have come here secretly because of killings in their lands. . . . We're trying to change the laws" (121). This activism and advocacy points to the grassroots Sanctuary movement that took place in the 1980s, calling attention to human rights abuses by lifting up survivors' testimonies while demanding accountability for US intervention in Central America. Susan Coutin reminds us that the term *sanctuary* dates back to the medieval custom of granting refuge to fugitives and that "solidarity activists accompanied Central American communities at risk of political violence, pursued changes in refugee and immigration law and policy, and opposed interventionist foreign policies" (27). They also sent delegations to Central America to accompany communities in harm's way, hoping that their international presence could offer some protection. Because the US supported the repression in Guatemala and El Salvador, in 1984, less than 3 percent of the asylum claims filed by Guatemalans and Salvadorans were granted (Coutin 29).

I find it compelling that María's coming of age(ncy) takes place within the larger context of the solidarity work of Central Americans, US-born Latina mothers, and Father Jonathan, because the narrative of the Sanctuary movement is often whitewashed by limiting it to middle-class faith-based groups such as the work of Quaker rancher Jim Cornett and pastor John Fife in the Southwest. Barba and Castillo-Ramos call attention to other voices that have been silenced along with gender and racial disparities in the rendering of the movement.[2]

Despite these acts of agency and solidarity, *Journey of the Sparrows* also depicts abusive incidents that reinforce the connection between economic exploitation coupled with anti-immigrant sentiment in the US and political violence in Central America against the poor, shining light on policies of exclusion on both sides of the border. During María's shift in the garment factory, for example, chaos breaks out during a violent immigration raid:

> Suddenly, the door slammed open and uniformed men jumped inside. "Immigration! Immigration! Stay where you are!" they shouted. . . . The screaming, crashing of tables, and sounds of fighting turned to hysterical sobbing, like at home, when the Guardias took away friends and relatives. I heard a woman cry in Spanish, "No, no. Don't take me. I've got kids." (Buss 69)

Hidden under a table, María is transported via her trauma back to the cruelty she witnessed in El Salvador, reinforcing the connection between the state-sponsored violence she fled and economic injustice she experiences in Chicago's neoliberal labor market: "Today was pay day. The boss had planned the raid so he wouldn't have to pay us. Tears scalded my cheeks, and I burned with fury" (69). As William D. Lopez exposes in *Separated* (2019), immigration raids are designed to be startling, confusing, and violent (156). Regrettably, many people swept up by the immigration regime would be deported back toward the killings. This economic exploitation of people deemed "disposable" under neoliberal capitalism mirrors the brutality committed by the Guardia to protect the privileges of the Salvadoran business elite and US transnational capital. Just as she experienced back home, María must silently bear witness to legal violence and injustice, which have no borders.

Amid this cruel economic and legal violence, María receives unexpected kindness that helps her heal from internalized oppression she experienced

---

2. Nathan Ellstrand underscores the role of the sanctuary movement in Chicago. See also *Strangers No Longer: Latino Belonging and Faith in Twentieth-Century Wisconsin* by Sergio M. González, *Sanctuary People: Faith-Based Organizing in Latina/o Communities* by Gina M. Pérez, and "Visualizing Imperial Encounters: PLACA and US-Central American Solidarity Murals in San Francisco's Mission District" by Mauricio Ernest Ramírez, *Latino Studies*, vol. 22, 2024, pp. 429–51.

back home and empowers her to see her inherent beauty and dignity. Tomás teaches her English, takes her to churches for clothing and soup kitchens, and gives her a present that she cherishes—a small gold locket in the shape of a heart on a chain so that she can take consolation in something pretty. She also receives supportive wisdom and validation from Doña Elena, a midwife from New Mexico who reassures her, "The goodness you had before, it can't ever really go away. It's all inside of you. Your family, your home, your land, before the killings began. You can keep those things living inside" (Buss 96). These offerings empower her to come into her agency.

When the Acostas receive news that their mother was deported but little Teresa remains in Tijuana, María knows she must make the reverse journey back to Mexico to find her sister. On the bus to the border, she gains consciousness of her coming of age(ncy): "The angle of light had changed in the window, and I saw the reflection of my face. The childhood smoothness of my cheeks and chin had vanished, and I saw a woman with dark shadows beneath her eyes" (123). This window and mirror imagery reflect the importance of seeing oneself and feeling seen, which US Central American readers particularly crave within Latinx YA.

Traumatic memories of home trigger her once again when she conflates armed highway patrol officers with the Salvadoran Guardias. She is so terrified that she throws up in front of them, so they let her go, fearing she has a contagious flu: "In my mind, I heard the guns at home and saw Papá and Ramón begin to fall. . . . I saw Mamá, Julia, Oscar, little Teresa, and me hiding in the gully behind our house as the Guardias returned in a jeep to kill us" (133). This episode serves as another example of how traumatizing treatment in the US mirrors the state-sponsored killings in El Salvador, reemphasizing how these violences are geopolitically connected. After receiving heartwarming acts of solidarity, at the end of the novel María exercises agency by successfully crossing the Río Grande with Teresa and, most importantly, escaping an immigration sweep by hiding in a bathroom. As illegalized youth, María and her siblings will have to continue hiding in the shadows of US society, which shows how agency within an anti-immigrant context is necessarily limited yet possible.

The theme of children coming into agency by hiding and fleeing death prompts readers, presumably of the same age as the protagonists, to reflect on the legacy of US involvement in Central American wars alongside the humanitarian response of activists—polarizing positions that continue to divide immigration politics. Like *Journey of the Sparrows'* depiction of the clandestine migrant journey from El Salvador to the US as an intended destination, *Red Glass* (2007) by Laura Resau illustrates that a fear of death continues to be a way of life in Guatemala during the postwar era, spurring migration to the US. Analogous to *Colibrí* and *Tree Girl* (chapter 1), *Red Glass* emphasizes that systemic terror in Guatemala must be reckoned with in order to truly heal from past violence.

Unlike the YA novels discussed thus far featuring Central American or Mexican protagonists, Laura Resau's *Red Glass* blends elements of the hero quest and the bildungsroman to tell the coming-of-age(ncy) migration story as seen through the eyes of a white sixteen-year-old whose family takes in a six year-old Indigenous Mixteco boy, Pablo, after his parents perish along with other migrants crossing the desert.[3] Sophie's awareness of the root causes of migration deepen when she meets Pablo, prompting her journey of self-discovery across the Mexican and Guatemalan borders.

Given that Sophie's Mexican stepfather crossed the desert in the 1980s and legalized his status by marrying Sophie's mother, the family often shows solidarity by offering sanctuary to migrants. Even though it's against the law, during emergencies they offer food and water and allow a group to rest temporarily on their land before continuing their journey.[4] Resau's novel is structured as Sophie's journey of self-discovery as she confronts her insecurities by opening up to others' war and gang violence traumas.

Interestingly, Pablo's border story of Indigenous migrant "disposability" unfolds alongside two refugee narratives. First, Sophie's great-aunt Dika, a recent Bosnian refugee from genocidal violence in the former Yugoslavia, seeks shelter with the family. Then, Dika befriends fellow refugees, Mr. Lorenzo and his son Angel, who crossed the Mexican desert fleeing Guatemala's postwar violence and gained asylum in the US. As Resau weaves these refugee stories through Sophie's coming-of-age(ncy) journey, we see that initially she holds biased, stereotypical views of Mexico and unconsciously practices white saviorism despite growing up along the border. When she first meets Pablo in the hospital, she infantilizes him as a victim and focuses on his trauma since he rarely speaks or smiles. She secretly hopes that after visiting his relatives in Mexico, he will decide to return to Tucson to be adopted by her parents so he can have a better life with access to education and health care. Her assumption of a "better life," however, is based on white supremacy and extends to Angel, who she barely remembers from a high school woodshop course during which they never spoke. As Sophie, her aunt, Angel, and his father drive Pablo to reunite with his family in Oaxaca, images of "bad Mexicans" come

3. Resau's two-year experience living in the Mixtec region of Oaxaca, in southern Mexico, as an English teacher and anthropologist informs this important mirror and window text for white readers to benefit from diverse literature.

4. For Reverend John Fife's valued perspective on the Sanctuary Movement in the Southwest, see Fife, "From the Sanctuary Movement."

to mind. Sophie notices Angel holding a box he carved and wonders, "Maybe it was drugs. What if it was drugs and we got caught and sent to a Mexican prison? I didn't know anything about this guy and his father. They could be drug dealers. I did some deep breathing and tried to act casual" (Resau 39). In line with the coming-of-age journey trope where the geographic trek also represents interior growth, Sophie and Angel get to know each other beyond racialized stereotypes—sparking attraction and intimacy, despite their differences. For example, he flirtatiously teases her about her fear of germs as a cultural outsider, calling her "Lime-girl" because she squeezes lime juice on all her food. As they cross Mexico, she grows from stereotypes to greater nuance of her understanding, and Sophie and Angel become attracted to each other as they become more intimate.

Shifting from apprehension to attraction, the time in Oaxaca with Pablo's family becomes a space that cultivates healing and agency. When father and son travel on to Guatemala, Angel is brutally attacked by gang members, who steal his money and passport. In solidarity, Sophie uses her agency and white privilege to rescue Angel: "For the first time in my life, I was taking a real risk. And yes, I felt fear, but it wasn't the endless loop of worries I'd grown used to. My thoughts shone clear and sharp as cut crystal. *This is the path I am taking. This is what I need to do*" (177, emphasis in original). By herself she crosses the infamous Guatemala-Mexico border, which Linda Green refers to as "the 1500-mile . . . corridor of death, crime, and corruption where drug cartels, gangs, and Mexican law enforcement officials commingle. Almost everyone who passes through becomes a victim of some combination of robbery, rape, assault, kidnapping or violent 'accident.' It is a particularly perilous passage for women" ("Nobodies" 372). Well aware of the physical dangers she faces as an outsider, several kind strangers accompany her, referring to Sophie as *gringa* or *gringuita,* marking her whiteness and class status in this danger zone. However, she comes into agency when she boards a crowded second-class bus:

> A few men offered me their seats, but I said no thanks. Plenty of other people were standing, and if they could do it, so could I. I felt glad I was standing, because I felt taller, as if my whole life, I'd let fear cram me into a small box, a space so tiny I was always curled over, my shoulders hunched, my back bent. That box had seemed too strong to break through, so I hadn't tried before. But maybe, all along, the box was just flimsy cardboard, and all I had to do was stand up, punch through the top, and climb out. (Resau 203)

Although Sophie's imaginative box contrasts with María Acosta's literal crate, she feels liberated from her self-doubt while gaining insight into how the open wounds of Guatemala's civil conflict, which killed Mr. Lorenzo's wife and left torture marks on his body, currently play out in "peacetime" gang violence, landing Angel in the hospital.

Continuing the undoing of stereotypes, Mercurio, one of the gang members who attacked Angel, must share a hospital room with him after a car accident. Countering one-dimensional images of gang members as savage criminals, Resau humanizes Mercurio when his Indigenous mother comes to the hospital and shares stories about their Mayan village, close to where Angel grew up. She describes the violence they suffered during the war and discloses that Mercurio was forcibly recruited by a gang that declared he was either with them or against them, so he joined to survive. Sophie admits, "the more she talked about her son, the more tenderness crept up on me. It's hard not to feel tenderness toward someone seen through his mother's eyes" (237). In my view, Resau's sensitivity in this scene is significant because mainstream society often refuses to see gang violence as a long-lasting effect of decades of structural violence such as war, poverty, racism, and an influx of weapons in postwar Central America. Resau admirably connects Guatemala's genocidal past to present levels of gang violence and forced migration, but *Red Glass* goes even further, depicting the boys' indigeneity while poignantly depicting Mercurio's remorsefulness for stealing Angel's life savings and attacking him. Their peacemaking gesture is significant for two reasons: first, because it counters the essentialization of "worthy refugee" and "bad gang member," and second, by including Indigenous characters who are often marginalized or erased altogether, assumed to be Guatemalan ladinos or mestizos in Mexican or Chicanx contexts. Moreover, it highlights storytelling's creative power to spark empathy as a window into another's social reality, modeling solidarity while cautioning readers about white saviorism.

Sophie's agency along with her caretaking of Pablo and attraction to Angel are bound up in a problematic self-focus from a privileged position, mirroring a US Central American critique of Chicanx solidarity fiction. Ana Patricia Rodríguez's analysis of *transfronterista* narratives asserts that "the act of solidarity begins in letting others produce their own narratives out of their particular pain, injury, and situations" ("Fictions," 218). Likewise, Gloria E. Chacón critiques the use of Indian characters while unwittingly privileging a US brand of mestizo identity ("Metamestizaje" 182). In "Indian Trouble" (2019), Chacón states, "The task before us is not to simply add the Mesoamerican Indian to Latinidad, but to account for how this Indian troubles Chicanxness, LatinX-ness, North American indigeneity, and immigrant/native dichotomies" (59). While essentializing or erasing Indigenous otherness is indeed a risk, Resau's text offers valuable insight into the power of witnessing survivors' trauma rooted in neoliberal violence and death, which ultimately facilitates Sophie's coming of age(ncy).

Sophie's decision to cross the Mexican and Guatemalan borders in solidarity with marginalized "others" illustrates her agency while simultaneously visibilizing the hypocrisy behind US legal discourse that turns displaced Indigenous youth into "illegals" or "nobodies." The death-defying journeys of resilient YA characters like María Acosta expose neoliberalism's politics of disposability, for which testimonio offers a vehicle for resistance and agency. Responding to the call for solidarity and praxis, fellow community members resist the forces of violence by making space for solidarity and recognizing the courage and human dignity of witnesses. The journeys of young migrants risking their lives across multiple borders in search of safety stress the importance of clarifying the past and advocating for the most vulnerable in our midst so that they are not dismissed as "nobodies" to be disappeared.

Angels or Trespassers? Undocumented Teen Romance and White Supremacy's Immigration Regime

As the budding romances of María and Tomás and Sophie and Angel illustrate, feeling seen and loved is a human need we all desire, particularly during adolescence, when the coming-of-age(ncy) journey and the quest for self-identity intertwine with a sense of connecting and belonging. In the novels discussed in the previous section, the function of romantic teen relationships was to work through trauma with solidarity. This next section examines texts where romantic teen relationships involving immigration are more politically charged within a context of white supremacy.[5] By questioning the white supremacist notion of illegality, the diverse characters illustrate that actively listening to each other's stories forges bonds of solidarity and fosters agency to reject a politics of exclusion that A. Naomi Paik refers to as "the United States' settler colonial project to exclude and remove the unwanted" (76).

Featuring themes of fear, shame, and exclusion, *Return to Sender* by acclaimed Dominican American author Julia Alvarez depicts how two very different twelve-year-olds forge a supportive friendship during the trauma of family separation and deportation. Situating the narrative from the summer of 2005 to 2006 is noteworthy because in May 2006, under the George W. Bush administration, ICE unleashed Operation Return to Sender, just weeks after nationwide May Day rallies for immigration reform. Within a month,

5. Incidentally, YA fiction and romance are widely read genres, and romance in particular, according to Anna Michelson, "is a billion-dollar industry that accounts for nearly a quarter of all fiction sales." Both generally provide an "emotionally satisfying and optimistic ending," marked by a belief that love and hope will make the world a better place. The Latinx novels I study, however, combine romance with real-world political issues such as immigration.

"the operation swept away nearly 2,200 immigrants in raids across more than thirty states; by April 2007, ICE had arrested almost 19,000 immigrants, the deportation terror rippling through communities that had demanded greater rights and equity" (Paik 94). Unlike Laura Resau's *Red Glass,* which exclusively privileges the perspective of a white protagonist regarding the migrant experiences of an Indigenous Mexican boy living in her family's care, Alvarez develops her storyline in alternating chapters. Also unlike Resau, Alvarez gives equal space to both characters' perspectives, but privileges Mari's voice as a Mexican immigrant over Tyler's white American perspective by writing hers in the more intimate and immediate first person and his in the more distancing third person. Together, Mari and Tyler confront their differences and defy racialized geopolitical borders.

Mari Cruz was born in Chiapas, Mexico, and crossed the border at the age of four with her parents, with the help of a coyote. As a prominent prize-winning author, Alvarez uses her platform to bring attention to the family's mixed status: Mari and her parents are undocumented, but her younger sisters are US-born citizens. Leisy Abrego defines mixed-status families as "household units with immigrant members with different legal statuses, that may include undocumented immigrants, DACA recipients, Temporary Protected Status (TPS) holders, Legal Permanent Residents, a number of humanitarian statuses, and US citizens" ("Relational" 4). Given her precarious status, Mari expresses her innermost thoughts only in her diary and in a series of letters that she is not allowed to mail for fear of drawing the attention of police or immigration authorities. We learn from her letters that her father recently moved the family from North Carolina to the Paquette dairy farm, where he works to save up for the ransom to rescue her mother, who was kidnapped after returning to Mexico to visit her own dying mother.

Like Resau's Sophie, as the dairy farmer's son, Tyler's initial view of the Mexican family as outsiders is informed by stereotypes—in this case, specifically the anti-immigrant political discourse and sentiments expressed in the media. At first, he views the Cruz family as trespassers on their land and admits that after the tragic events of September 11, 2001, he feels "a little scared of strangers from other countries who might be plotting to destroy the USA" (Alvarez 42). In addressing Tyler's fears, his parents challenge these anti-immigrant stereotypes and narratives, explaining that dairy farms across the country are suffering financially and that affordable hired help is hard to find.

Although they don't refer to neoliberal free trade agreements, they acknowledge that economic inequality is hurting people on both sides of the border but that undocumented migration from Mexico translates into cheap labor: "Lots of them are coming up here because they can't earn enough back home to live on. Many of them used to farm. They're separated from their families for years" (14). In fact, Tyler's parents explain that thanks to the lower cost of immigrant labor, these "trespassers" are actually "angels"; they are the reason the Paquette family can now dream of keeping the farm they feared losing. Tyler's father praises their work ethic and considers Mari's father and uncle "the best workers" who "put us all to shame" (14), glossing over questions about the legality of hiring undocumented workers as performative. Even though his mother considers them "our angels," Tyler feels guilty about breaking the law and wants to keep the Cruz family a secret, but since everyone is hiring unauthorized Mexicans, they're really not a secret. Mrs. Paquette debunks the weaponized rhetoric of exclusion by contrasting it to the morally just cause of welcoming strangers, as exemplified by the Sanctuary movement: "Many of us who still remember what it really means to be an American welcome outsiders, especially those who have come here to help us" (42). Tyler's initial fear of outsiders, however, is consistent with conservative media's characterization of immigrants as a national security problem, which scholar activist Susanne Jonas refutes. Jonas asserts that after September 11, immigrants, especially Latinos, became the target of repressive legislative measures under the guise of "national security": "Many thousands of Latino migrants have been subjected to arbitrary roundups, preventive detention and/or summary deportation, with no recourse to legal counsel or court appeals" (9). Seeing through this xenophobic politicized manipulation, Tyler's father questions the rhetoric around legality and justice by assuring Tyler that the situation is not wrong in God's eyes: "Sometimes, a country has these laws that have nothing to do with what's right or what's best for most of the people involved" (Alvarez 56). This conflict between the parents' nuanced view of immigrants and Tyler's stereotypical view is representative of the larger community's polarized views. Beyond the Paquette farm, the economic ties between the families are deemed shameful and illegal, so Tyler pays a price among his peers. On the school bus, boys tease Tyler about his "little Mexican girlfriend," while another declares, "Your dad's breaking the law! You should all be thrown out along with them!" (66). Given the conflicting views between his parents and peers, it's not surprising that Tyler is reluctant to get to know Mari when she joins his sixth grade class.

Like the Central American quetzal and sparrows in Fran Leeper Buss's YA novel, Alvarez's offers recurring images of swallows or *golondrinas* and monarch *mariposas* that travel freely between Mexico and the United States, marking the dairy farm as a space where migrants are welcome as angels instead of trespassers. Nonetheless, Alvarez acknowledges that outside the Paquette farm, the mood toward immigrants is actually quite hostile. At a town meeting, for example, Mr. Rossetti puts forward a motion that anyone who is not there legally needs to be rounded up (189). Although it's voted down almost unanimously, the community's hard-line opinions speak to what is often called a "crimmigration crisis" or the "immigrantization of criminal law" (Macías-Rojas 9). For Tyler, this acrimonious debate is a valuable civics lesson about the democratic process, but Mari, who is politically excluded yet personally affected by the hostility, cries when she hears their xenophobic views.

Despite the town's white supremacist conflation of Mexicans with illegality, Tyler and Mari's friendship flourishes through cross-racial dialogue as they both exercise agency. Tyler loans Mr. Cruz all of his savings to rescue Mrs. Cruz from smugglers in Texas. But after her release, an immigration raid amid the national Operation Return to Sender sweep tears the Paquette and Cruz families apart. Despite her fear, Mari testifies to Homeland Security on behalf of her parents. Inspired by Mari, her mother testifies against the human traffickers who kidnapped her and extorted her family so that they won't inflict suffering on others. In a telling gesture after the deportation, Tyler gifts Mari his telescope to underscore that they are not just patriots of a country but citizens of the planet who can stay connected through the stars, swallows, and letters, despite geopolitical borders.

The oppositional framing of undocumented migrant workers as angels or trespassers echoes Rosaura Sánchez's reading of xenophobic narratives: "This condition of being included through an exclusion, of being outside of membership and always in relation to something from which one is excluded, is in fact the global condition of the migrant, or undocumented workers, who are 'marginal' yet central, 'superfluous' yet needed, vilified yet undeniably key to the economic operations of the increasingly fluid and highly stratified economies of what used to be termed the 'first world,' now globally dispersed" (137). In voicing the angel/trespasser binary framing of undocumented migrant workers, Alvarez shows both the complexity and the divisiveness of the debates surrounding immigration politics and policies. But by voicing the perspective of the undocumented child, Alvarez provides a mirror for young migrants' experiences while opening a window or sliding glass door through which readers can identify with the migrant experience, thus moving beyond the flattened binary view toward a more nuanced understanding that would allow for better informed, heartfelt discussions.

Viewed together, these fictionalized experiences represent the fears of undocumented youth immersed in a dehumanizing post 9/11 context. They depict the vulnerability of the 1.5 generation like Mari, which Roberto Gonzales defines as young people born outside the US who began their American lives as children, culturally integrated but legally excluded. In *Lives in Limbo: Undocumented and Coming of Age in America,* he argues, "For undocumented members of the 1.5 generation, illegality extends far beyond legal boundaries. It reaches into the bodies, minds, and hearts. It saps their energy, consumes their dreams, and crushes their spirits" (206). *Return to Sender* is one of several YA novels where the protagonist resists by exercising agency, offering insight into the neoliberal cycle of emigration, immigration, and deportation (Golash-Boza 3).

Similar to *Red Glass,* McNeal's *Dark Water* is told from the perspective of white fifteen-year-old Pearl DeWitt, who lives with her mother temporarily on her uncle Hoyt's avocado ranch in Fallbrook, California. Echoing Rhodes's insightful scholarship on transformation ("Corporeal," "Processes"), the reviewer for the blog *Rhapsody in Books* (26 Sept. 2011) perceptively notes that Pearl stands on the brink of her own transformation yet is unsure of the right course of action. The tragic Agua Prieta fire divides her life into a before and after, embodied in the fact that she has one blue eye and one brown eye, reinforcing the coming-of-age lesson she learns: "You can only belong to one world at a time." Pearl learns this tragic lesson as a sophomore in high school in an agricultural area where illegalized migrants seek work. She meets the nearly nonspeaking Amiel de la Cruz Guerrero, who juggles and has a talent for mime, when he's hired as an undocumented laborer on her uncle's avocado farm.

Pearl is instantly smitten with seventeen-year-old Amiel. Though their verbal communication is limited given his damaged voice and her lack of Spanish, their physical attraction is undeniable: "Amiel was looking at me with the kind of interest that made my mouth dry up. I was Braille and his eyes were fingers" (McNeal 40). McNeal's erotic use of Braille here refers to an entirely different disability to describe Amiel's gaze, to help the reader feel how Pearl senses that his eyes are actually touching and reading her, giving him a moment of agency as someone who depends on nonverbal communication. Their increasing intimacy gives her a deepening understanding of his impoverishment since he doesn't earn enough for housing, so he squats on a nature preserve in Agua Prieta Creek. As María Acosta hides during the factory raid, Amiel enacts agency to hide from border patrol. As they grow closer, Pearl resists white, middle-class exclusionary perceptions of the undocumented while also ironically adopting a politics of color blindness, given her two eye colors. Rather than acknowledging her white privilege, she states: "'This is America,' I said, 'Right? In America, we're the same. Equal.' He turned then and walked back along the path the way he had come, and I had no choice but to go on my own way home" (172). Amiel's turning away from the colorblind mindset speaks volumes about his awareness of the racialized borders separating them, yet later when they meet they hold hands and kiss. Acknowledging her multiple eye colors, he observes, "Tú eres de dos mundos," because she can freely move between her privilege and his precarity, while he must stay clear of multiple checkpoints that restrict his mobility and agency.

Their relationship unfolds during the tragic Agua Prieta fire, so Pearl worries that Amiel might be unaware that the flames are coming his way since he has no access to technology. When she finds him, he's more afraid of the police and deportation orders than of the fire. With hindsight, Pearl reflects on her poor judgment, since she is rescued and he flees. After being hospitalized, she visits what remains of his shelter and finds Amiel's note: "Vuelvo a México. Recuérdeme" (276). Crying, she kneels in the ash and covers her blue eye. I read this as a coming-of-age acknowledgment that although there are multiple ways of seeing, with respect to Amiel she can only belong to one world at a time. Her choice to cover the blue eye is a gesture that recognizes her white privilege, just as Amiel's use of the formal *usted* form instead of the informal *tú* form reinforces a hierarchically racialized difference that always existed between them.

After graduation, Pearl studies Spanish at night and works to save up for a Spanish immersion program in Silao, Mexico, where she plans to ask if people know Amiel de la Cruz Guerrero. Amiel lacks a voice and agency in McNeal's *Dark Water.* The fact that Pearl plans to search for him in Mexico signifies that Amiel is a vehicle for Pearl's agency, and while this plotline is problematic, it gives us much to consider. As noted with *Red Glass,* focalizing a developing romance with a migrant through a privileged white female lens invites the reader to reflect on white saviorism. Theorist and activist Ann Russo asserts that the white savior complex is a "narrative logic well rehearsed through US imperial, white supremacist, patriarchal, and heteronormative history that has served to produce systemic oppression and violence that it then simultaneously claims to 'save' (others/women) from." In my estimation, however, *Red Glass* and *Dark Water,* while problematic, are valuable as mirror and window books for the way they raise awareness about white privilege and saviorism's possible objectification despite a desire for friendship, romance, and solidarity.

Marie Marquardt's *The Radius of Us* engages in a similar white savior dynamic. Marquardt alternates first-person perspectives to tell the stories of Gretchen Asher, who suffers from post-traumatic stress after being attacked by a Salvadoran gang member, and eighteen-year-old Salvadoran asylum seeker Phoenix Flores Flores, who also suffers from trauma and panic attacks caused by fleeing gang violence back home and violence endured during the migrant journey. As in *Return to Sender, Red Glass,* and *Dark Water,* Gretchen and

Phoenix face intersectional class, racial, and cultural differences in addition to legal status as they experience their first love while helping each other heal from past traumas.

As traumatized outsiders, Gretchen and Phoenix speak honestly about their fears in a way that they can't with others. But things get complicated when Phoenix reveals that he wears a monitored ankle bracelet and has strict orders to stay within a twenty-mile radius of home at all times because of his asylum case. Gretchen reacts exactly as he feared, stereotyping him and demanding an explanation: "'What did you do?' I hear her voice, asking me. Accusing me. Afraid of me" (Marquardt 95). The tattoo of a gnarled hand spread across his abdomen with two curled fingers reaching toward his heart marks him as a Salvadoran gang member, unfortunately compounding her stereotypical view of him. Additionally, it triggers her trauma response because her attacker had the same tattoo. Like Mercurio in *Red Glass,* Phoenix was forcibly jumped into the gang at thirteen years old; after he was forced to drink alcohol until he passed out, his body was branded with their signature tattoo, claiming him for life. Ashamed of his past, he feels unworthy of Gretchen's affection. As she works to overcome her own fears and biases in dialogue with Phoenix, she gains insight into the social stigma that criminalizes migrant youth and sees him for the inherently good person he truly is.

Marquardt's use of the tattoo correlates with agency since Phoenix's inner transformation is outwardly reflected when the forcibly imposed gang symbol on his body is artistically reworked as a phoenix that rises from the ashes. This relates back to Rhodes's suggestion that "individual transformation is tied to recognizing systemic oppression and confronting it within oneself then undoing systemic oppression which cannot occur until individual transformation has taken effect and the more the young character becomes familiar with system inequality, the more they realize the internal and external changes that need to be made" ("Processes" 475). Central American gang violence is a symptom of systemic oppression with roots in state-sponsored violence and US deportations. In this vein, Velásquez Estrada's term "racist warring masculinity," applies to Phoenix as a "trespasser," to refer back to Alvarez. They are easily criminalized and thus illegalized. Velásquez Estrada takes this a step further, noting that gang members can be cast in the role of "the internal enemy," a term that was used by the Guatemalan military during the war to justify the killing of Maya peoples' including children: "Through processes of differentiation and hierarchization, the gang member's body emerges as a nonhuman Other whose sexually predatory masculinity and criminal activity constitute a 'social plague' upon whom violence can be legally exercised and whose existence may be eliminated" (46). This connects the immigrant-as-trespasser trope with Velásquez Estrada's idea of "racist warring masculinity," which distinguishes between those who deserve justice and those Others who must be eliminated to attain "peace" (44).

Within this white supremacist immigration system, this cross-cultural couple finds agency in solidarity around processing trauma, specifically around the trauma represented for them both by Phoenix's tattoo. With this symbolic rebirth, Phoenix and Gretchen deepen their relationship as they plan on continuing their education. Although *The Radius of Us* ultimately leaves the status quo in place since gang members are depicted as undeserving and disposable while Phoenix is salvageable, I believe the depiction of white saviorism makes an important contribution to Latinx YA by shifting the problematic "savior" logic toward solidarity. According to Russo, solidarity demands an analysis that positions our lives and social conditions as intertwined with histories of inequality, colonialism, imperialism, and white supremacy that shape our relationships: "In other words, it requires that we recognize our locations within these systems, and how forging alliances across these divides requires that we relate in ways that do not reproduce these systems based in hierarchy and notions of superiority and inferiority, but rather foster relations of equality, accountability, and reciprocity" (242). The cross-racial romances reveal the white supremacist immigration system and the use of agency to act in solidarity. Although this solidarity is not unproblematic and contains elements of white saviorism, their relationships show that agency and solidarity are possible nonetheless. These YA narratives invite critical reflection, whether read independently or as part of an antiracist curriculum.

Fostering relations of equality, accountability and reciprocity is prioritized in YA novels *Dream Things True,* also by Marie Marquardt, *Don't Ask Me Where I'm From* by Jennifer De Leon, and *Where I Belong* by Marcia Argueta Mickelson. Together, they portray romantic relationships that develop between Latinas of different immigration statuses and white boys amid nativist anti-immigrant rhetoric rooted in white supremacy.[6] In *Don't Ask Me Where I'm From,* protagonist Liliana Cruz transfers from a public high school in the Boston area to a prestigious school's desegregation program twenty miles away in the suburbs. She lives with her younger twin brothers and undocumented Salvadoran mom, who struggles to find stable employment. Life is particularly

6. Award-winning author Marie Marquardt has also coauthored two nonfiction books on Latin American migration to the southern US. She is the lead author of *Living "Illegal": The Human Face of Unauthorized Immigration* (2011) and cochairs El Refugio, a nonprofit in Georgia that serves detained immigrants and their families. Marcia Argueta Mickelson was born in Guatemala and immigrated to the United States as an infant. Jennifer De Leon was born in Boston to Guatemalan parents. Their narratives take place in Georgia, Massachusetts, and Texas, respectively.

stressful for the family because Liliana's father was recently deported to Guatemala. Aware of her love of journaling and writing short stories, her parents placed her on a program's waitlist to give Liliana education opportunities they never had. Her Honduran best friend, Jade, is the only person who knows about her family's stressful situation, which Liliana trusts she will understand: Jade came to the US at age three, and her father was deported after a violent incident at home.

Don't Ask Me Where I'm From reveals the racist immigration system in Lilian's school environment and her romantic relationship. When she arrives at her new school as part of the Metropolitan Council for Educational Opportunity (METCO) program, she immediately notices that the students here are mostly white, whereas her public school serves mostly people of color. This makes Liliana question whether she belongs at this new school, but she remembers her father's words: "Don't ever let anyone make you feel like you don't belong in the world. Entiendes?" (De Leon 44). However, Liliana's METCO student mentor contradicts her father's message, warning, "Don't trust anyone. Especially the white boys. . . . Just stick with the METCO kids" (55) and "This school right here is like the world. You have to carry yourself a certain way—in order to get what you want, and what you need. . . . Here, it's actually an advantage to be different. Work it. Raise your hand in class. Speak up. You have to get involved. Join a club at least. Make the system work for you" (100). These messages from her recently deported Guatemalan father and her mentor empower Lili to assert agency while also being mindful of an inherently unequal system that stereotypes Latinxs as disposable others.

But Lili is instantly attracted to Dustin, an entitled junior on the soccer team who pulls the school's fire alarm so he can spend some time alone with her. He is part of the same racist system that has separated her family, as the novel's title reinforces. Steve, Dustin's racist friend, asks Liliana: "What are you? Where are you from?" When asked to pen her autobiography in six words, she asserts her voice by writing, "Don't ask me where I'm from." Steve's questions are meant to locate her as an outsider in a predominantly white institution, showing anti-immigrant bias common in the US and linked to policy and practice.

Reflecting on her father's deportation, she admits that she has much to learn about her Guatemalan father's need to migrate. She knows that her father's real parents "were killed in some war" (115) but doesn't know much about it because he rarely discussed it. His reluctance to talk about the civil war and migration journey underscore the need for these YA novels to function as mirrors, windows, and doors for a younger generation of US Central American and other Latinx readers. Many youth like Lili have questions that their parents or grandparents might not feel comfortable answering because they open unhealed wounds and trauma, or because they don't want their children to be afraid or feel different because of their immigration status.

Unfortunately, the discrimination at school escalates to the point where Lili ends her relationship with Dustin when he doesn't defend her from his friends' racist comments. Students post dehumanizing comments on social media, including images of her face cruelly photoshopped onto a piñata with the word "wetback." School administrators draw attention to their policy of nondiscrimination and equity but take no institutional action, unfairly placing the burden of countering racist attitudes on victimized students of color. To address the problem, Lili shows agency by organizing an assembly with her friends to pose the questions, "What is it that you want us to know about you in terms of race and culture? What is it that you never want to hear again? How can we be allies and assist you?" Modeling vulnerability, Lili shares the truth about her undocumented parents and her father's deportation, but some students interrupt her, chanting "white lives matter" and "build the wall." Besides hurling nativist insults, they throw things at her and spit on other people of color. Not backing down, the METCO students pose their questions on a wall made of paper, sparking the interest of a local reporter to write about how students of color tried to raise racial awareness. After these dehumanizing racialized incidents, Dustin apologizes to Liliana and turns in Steve for his racist behavior, who is suspended. Lili's demonstrations of agency can serve as a window, mirror, and door for readers, especially encouraging empowerment among Latinx readers to speak up against xenophobic hate speech. It can be an important reading in an antiracist classroom environment.

Marquardt's *Dream Things True* and *Where I Belong* by Marcia Argueta Mickelson dramatize the stories of two Latina teenagers whose white boyfriends' wealthy families exploit their immigration experiences for political gain. *Dream Things True*'s Alma Julia García-Menendez is a sixteen-year-old undocumented high school junior who falls in love with Evan Roland, a senior and star soccer player from a politically conservative family in Georgia. This novel uses their romance to expose the racist immigration system. Despite her prominent role in charities for the underprivileged, Evan's mother disapproves of his relationship with Alma, based on stereotyping and othering. Her charity work for the less fortunate is characteristic of philanthropy's privileged distancing between wealthy donors and the communities they serve. As the Roland family's landscaper, Alma's overprotective Mexican father also disapproves of their relationship. Beyond the obvious class and racial differences and the power imbalance between the families, the relationship reveals a white supremacist immigration system that simultaneously uses immigrants' labor yet considers them unworthy. Additionally, Evan and Alma's relationship is problematic because Evan's uncle is Senator Sexton Prentiss, whose conservative politics against the undocumented lead him to endorse controversial "catch and release" policies to win votes. After the senator's website celebrates the headline "Roundup of 200 illegal immigrants in Sexton Prentiss's hometown of Georgia protects 200 American jobs" (Marquardt 65), the Latinx community exercises agency by organizing rallies and distributing flyers to build awareness about family separations and deportations.

Like Dustin in *Don't Ask Me Where I'm From,* Evan does not openly confront his racist family or friends who are "classic 'prepnecks'—part khaki-pants wearing Southern preppy and part confederate-flag waving rednecks" (Marquardt 74). Here Marquardt calls attention to the xenophobic attitudes of Evan's family and friends and greater white supremacy, which resonates with Bishop's claim that if white children "see only reflections of themselves, they will grow up with an exaggerated sense of their own importance and value in the world—a dangerous ethnocentrism." While Evan's feelings for Alma may prompt him to reflect on his friends' views, he endorses their racism by silently fuming when his friend Conway yells at gardeners for laughs, ordering them to "go back to Mexico" (43). Evan plays golf at the club regularly with Logan, whose father is a sheriff who collaborates with ICE, mandating detention and deportation for nonviolent infractions. His privileged life is starkly different from Alma's, but sparks fly at their first encounter, so they maneuver around family and friends to see each other.

The novel's intended reader gets a glimpse into the larger economic structural context that profits from labor branded as "illegal." Given that the romance is used to reveal truths about the immigration system and undocumented experience, Evan's awareness begins to grow as his relationship with Alma develops. When he sees "a bunch of yahoos on the town square for some kind of protest" with "signs about illegal immigrants and some law" (Marquardt 95), Alma "schools him," taking on the emotional labor that Lili resents in De Leon's novel. She explains that a proposed state law, SB 529, is supposed to make Georgia "tough on immigration," which it clearly already is. Furthermore, she points out that supervisors love hiring Mexicans because they work hard for low wages and don't complain. When he asks, "But why didn't they just come legally?" (98), she explains the difference between using language such as "illegal" versus "undocumented," something he had never considered because he lives in an environment where "illegal" is normalized and where his privilege allows him to be unaware of its dehumanizing impact. She also breaks down the economic addiction to "migradollars": "Migration's like a bad drug habit: Once it gets started, it changes everything on both sides of the border. Americans are addicted to cheap labor, and Mexicans are addicted to the migradollars cheap laborers send back home" (100). To drive home this systemic economic injustice, she helps Evan see how he benefits daily from cheap labor: "Do you like tomatoes? . . . Do you eat boneless, skinless chicken breast? . . . Is your room carpeted?" (100). What is more, she nudges him to reflect on his white privilege. Although he contends that his life is not perfect since his parents have a broken marriage and he feels pressure to overcompensate because appearances are so important to his mother, the novel is showing that white privilege doesn't imply that his life is easy or perfect. Rather, this is an example of white fragility (DiAngelo 2018) since his comment is a way of deflecting the fact that the challenges he faces at home are not due to race. As a mirror, window, and door, the novel invites the reader to consider what the characters are feeling and experiencing.

Given the anti-immigrant hostility in Evan's family and friendships, Alma is nervous about disclosing her undocumented status to him, but when she finally does, he genuinely seeks to understand her situation. In sharing her story, Alma fears losing Evan, but he reaches out in support and she feels relieved, reinforcing that their romance is used to show the inner workings of the immigration system, and also how the relationship is a pathway toward agency and solidarity.

As an example of an inherently racist system, specifically stereotyping around criminality, Alma's father and brother Raúl are racially profiled while driving; they are arrested, sent to a detention center, then deported to Mexico. Their crime of driving while Brown and undocumented in Georgia coincides with Paik's assertion that "most deported immigrants pose no threat to public safety. They are deportable only because they lack documentation or because they committed a minor offense" (77). Without mincing words, Paik denounces this as "state sanctioned terror we inflict on our neighbors" (78).

Feeling pressure to embody the model immigrant narrative, Alma challenges the notion of "deservingness" by coming out publicly as undocumented. With this action, she not only puts a human face on the contentious immigration issue but also becomes a vehicle for everyone else's growth and awareness. Evan is simultaneously inspired by her bravery to come out of the shadows and outraged by an unjust white supremacist system that could label someone a criminal for a nonviolent offense and deport them. He is so enraged that he attends a protest at the women's detention center, unconcerned about his family's disapproval. Additionally, he visits Alma's father in detention and asks for her hand in marriage. To his dismay, she calls out his white savior complex by addressing not only race and documentation status but also gender when he proposes to her: "You seem to think that you and your perfect life can just come in and save me, swooping down like some knight in shining armor or something, this isn't a fairy tale, Evan[,] you're not my handsome prince, and I'm definitely not your charity case" (Marquardt 267). As noted with *The Radius of Us,* the white savior complex is rooted in a desire to alleviate suffering by being extraordinary, but it ultimately maintains the status quo because by placing oneself outside the problems of racism, the uneven power distribution, and examination of complicity, the system that led to the harm in the first place is left largely unexplored (Finnegan 623). Nigerian American writer Teju Cole insists, "The White Savior Industrial Complex is not about justice. It is about having a big emotional experience that validates white privilege. . . . There is much more to doing good work than 'making a difference.' . . . There is the idea that those who are being helped ought to be consulted over the matters that concern them" (quoted in Finnegan 619). To move past good intentions, Amy Finnegan encourages us to investigate US imperialistic interventions: "We ought to be asking, how have social conditions enabled this harm to occur? . . . How can our efforts to address suffering also dismantle root causes? How are we entangled in those root causes of oppression?" (631). YA romance narratives like these provide an ideal forum to reflect on these questions.

The young characters grow closer as they tackle similar questions with vulnerability and honesty and as they enact solidarity on the long journey toward social change. After honestly addressing their differences, Alma and Evan make up: "Alma told Evan of the fears and the memories that came to her in the dark of night, and Evan whispered the truths that his family held silent. With the touch of their hands and the sound of their voices, they explored each other's broken parts, and they coaxed each other back into the light of day" (Marquardt 316). As they express previously hidden fears and beliefs, their romance reveals the inherently racist system that would keep them apart, serving as a pathway toward solidarity and agency.

Like Alma in *Dream Things True,* Millie (short for Milagros) Vargas in Marcia Argueta Mickelson's *Where I Belong* (2021) was brought to the US as a baby. Her Guatemalan parents wanted her to have what they didn't have back home, but she feels the weight of her status now that she is eighteen years old and has been granted citizenship. Her hardworking father died of a heart attack three years earlier. There is a similar socioeconomic power dynamic in *Dream Things True* and *Where I Belong* because Millie's mother is the Wheeler family's babysitter and housekeeper in Corpus Christi, Texas, and Millie and Charlie Wheeler develop feelings for each other. This Latinx YA novel, like the others, uses teen romance to reveal the workings of a white supremacist immigration system. Millie's life takes a sudden turn when Charlie's father, who is running for senator, exposes her family's immigration story for political gain. This situation simultaneously critiques negative stereotypes about immigrants and white saviorism that believes it's helping but ultimately endangers the people it purports to help by hijacking their agency over their own lives and stories. When Mr. Wheeler is asked at a political event about immigration policy and amnesty, he upholds the Dreamer narrative: "They're coming here because they have no choice. They're simply seeking a safe place where they and their children can work hard, study hard, and contribute to society" (Mickelson 25). Although he questions the negative stereotypes and narratives about immigrants, he also engages in a different narrative that is equally limited and harmful. He offers the example of his housekeeper's undocumented family, who fled violence in Guatemala and received asylum. Then he crosses a line, revealing personal information about Millie, endorsing the model minority trope:

> And now, eighteen years later, their daughter is a U.S. citizen about to graduate from high school. A straight-A student, and she had her pick of universities. . . . Our country is better with them in it. . . . They're here to work. They're here to serve. And we need to let them do just that. (26, 27)

Millie feels ashamed and angry because Mr. Wheeler had no right to use her story for his political platform without permission. When Mr. Wheeler and Charlie apologize for using her as an embodiment of the Dreamer innocence narrative, Millie isn't free to express her true feelings because they pay her mother's salary. Furthermore, his apology is suspect because he doubles down on wanting to use her story, insisting that her "good immigrant" story can change the anti-immigrant narrative: "You demolish every single stereotype out there. People need to see that, to get a true picture of what immigrants do, what they can accomplish" (34). Her agency is limited because she can't voice her views, and she feels that the Wheelers are more concerned about gaining political power than they are about guaranteeing her safety.

Ultimately, Mr. Wheeler's use of her story endangers Millie and her family, revealing the same anti-immigrant stereotypes that sustain a racist immigration system as in the previous novels. An internet troll discloses her name and posts a video about calling ICE on her family, and a freelance journalist wants to interview her. Despite Millie's firm stance that she doesn't want to "be an issue" (45), her mother feels pressured by the Wheelers, so she in turn urges Millie to do the interview. Oscar Zambrano, the journalist, wants to frame her story within the larger context of Central Americans fleeing home, referencing migrant boys losing limbs while riding La Bestia to reach the border in addition to the deaths of people locked in freight trucks (chapter 2). He considers her Guatemalan parents heroes who sacrificed to give her an incredible gift: "People coming for the same damn reason the Pilgrims came—to make a better life for their families. . . . Those are the kinds of stories we need to tell if we're going to combat the fear, misinformation, and downright racist attitudes about people like you and your family. . . . You are the face of the young immigrants who will make this country even better" (52, 53, 54). Like Mr. Wheeler, Zambrano tries to use her story to change the narrative, at her expense. Simultaneously, media stories of people fleeing targeted gang violence overlap with images of appalling conditions in detention centers and news of parents being unable to find the children who were taken from them at the border. To counter these images, Millie's story is lifted up as "living proof that immigrants are not a threat to our country. They're an asset" (60). Exposing how the system works, Millie identifies with the unspoken burden of perfection that Liliana Cruz feels as a student of color in a predominantly white school and Alma experiences as an undocumented student in Georgia: "We have to be the hardest workers, the brightest students, the biggest achievers, if we want to belong here. We can't just be human beings who mean others no harm" (62). Although a teacher calls her a heroine for doing the interview, trolls write hurtful comments on her Instagram, and someone writes "go back to Mexico" on her locker. Charlie accompanies Millie to the principal's office because she feels unsafe at school, but she is mortified that he witnesses her humiliation. Their romance reveals the system's human impact as well as how white saviorism exposes Millie to harm for the family's political benefit. Her worst fear comes true when their small home is set on fire and "Go back to Mexico" is written again in black graffiti, this time on the sidewalk.

This hate crime and arson leave them without a place to live, so they have no choice but to accept the Wheelers' invitation to stay in their home, revealing the economic disparity between the families. Millie feels out of place and silenced in their million-dollar home as she reflects that she would still have a home "were it not for Mr. Wheeler's big mouth" (88). While she resents the pity, her friendship and attraction to Charlie deepens as they confide in each other. When she is asked to attend an immigration event "to add humanity" to the cause, which Charlie insists is worth fighting for, Millie finally uses her agency to remind him of his family's privilege that shields them from harm: "You and your dad can afford to speak out without any real consequences. You don't actually get hurt. . . . I'm sick of explaining why meaning well isn't always enough." Illustrating agency, Millie gains self-awareness about her own privilege as a naturalized citizen when she meets Susana, a young woman who comes out as undocumented and discloses that she came to the US from

Mexico at age four with her parents, with the help of a coyote.[7] She shows solidarity by promising Susana she will volunteer at the migrant resource shelter in Potrillo, since there are several border checkpoints in the area that she can safely cross as a citizen, unlike others who risk deportation. Relatedly, she shows agency by being true to herself in her relationship with Charlie, who volunteers with her as they express sadness for the trauma and harm so many endure on the migrant journey.

Upon reflection, Millie acknowledges that her Guatemalan father was a dreamer when he named her Milagros and journeyed a long way for his family. She asserts her agency by accepting the significance of her name: "While I still don't think that I am miraculous in any way, I'm ready to add my small voice, to say that we do belong here" (253). Millie's embracing her name ties back to Rhodes's assertion that transformation is an inherent aspect of Latinx youth and their literary works: "Latinx youth in literature transform not to align with the dominant powers or be more palatable to them, but to unearth their own inherent power and agency" ("Corporeal" 54). Indeed, as this array of characters illustrate, within themselves, they possess the instruments of radical transformation (54).

The Latinx YA novels in this chapter focus on "illegalized" characters who are rendered vulnerable and exploitable in factories, dairy farms, and poultry plants or as housekeepers and gardeners, and used for political gain. They draw attention to discrimination that overlooks or silences the reality that immigration is a far-reaching consequence of historical US intervention in Central America and Mexico. These works are critical mirror and window texts that model paths toward agency and solidarity and help readers develop awareness in order to speak out against injustice. The following chapter discusses characters in "own voices" Latinx YA novels who come of age(ncy) by exploring their identities and historical memory.

---

7. In "Coming Out of the Shadows and Undocuqueer" (2016) H. Seif states that the first rally where undocumented youth publicly used the linguistic and political strategy of "coming out" in the US was in 2010.

CHAPTER 5

"All Cages Must Break!"

Latinx YA Finds Its Quetzal Voice and Tells Its Own Story

In the children's picture book *Rebeldita the Fearless in Ogreland* (2021) by Honduran author and educator Oriel María Siu, the Afro-Indigenous protagonist Rebeldita joins forces with other youth to combat state-sponsored oppression that criminalizes migration. Moved by greed, power holders known as Ogres build a border wall on stolen land. Mobilizing their grandmothers' wisdom, the youth win over the opponents' attack dogs and take to the streets to demand justice and social change—"All cages must break!" "Power to the Children!" "Keep our families together!" Through collective action, the empowered youth reunite forcefully separated children with their parents, reverse the power dynamic by caging the Ogres, and advocate for a world that upholds migrant dignity, community, and solidarity. In my view, Rebeldita's call to action for immigrant justice also applies to the need for greater diversity and equitable representation in YA publishing.

Building on previous chapters that examine the migrant journey and undocumented youth experiences in fiction by cultural insiders and outsiders, here I analyze a growing corpus of "own voices" Latinx YA novels that denounce the "border security-industrial complex" (De León). Aligning with the We Need Diverse Books organization's choice to forgo the term "own voices," I discuss the authors' identities as matching those of their protagonists.[1] To trace how the Latinx YA journey has itself come of age by creating

1. See Cristina Rhodes's summary of the term in "Multicultural Children's and Young Adult Literature."

a body of work that uplifts counternarratives amid the structural violence of detention and deportation regimes, I divide my argument in three parts. First, I examine how *Gaby, Lost and Found* (2013) by Angela Cervantes, *Efrén Divided* (2020) by Ernesto Cisneros, and *Indivisible* (2021) and *Brighter than the Sun* (2023) by Daniel Aleman depict youth agency in mixed-status families and give readers and inside view of how they experience one or both parents' deportation. Expanding on this depiction of state inflicted violence, in the second section, I study how the Latinx counternarratives in *The Crossroads* (2018) and *Santiago's Road Home* (2019) by Alexandra Diaz, *We Are Not from Here* (2020) by Jenny Torres Sanchez, *Land of the Cranes* (2020) by Aida Salazar, *Illegal* (2020) by Francisco X. Stork, *Ander & Santi Were Here* (2023) by Jonny Garza Villa, and the historical fantasy romance *The Secret of the Moon Conch* (2023) by award-winning authors David Bowles and Guadalupe García McCall speak out against the traumatizing jailing of youth while shining a light on neoliberalism's politics of disposability. Last, I reflect on how the YA migrant journey has come of age through a study of Latinx YA novels depicting US Central American girls' own coming of agency by exploring their identities and historical memory. Penned by authors of the Guatemalan and Honduran diaspora, *Shine On, Luz Véliz!* (2022) by Rebecca Balcárcel, *Turtles of the Midnight Moon* (2023) by María José Fitzgerald, *The Weight of Everything* (2023) by Marcia Argueta Mickelson, *Mani Semilla Finds Her Quetzal Voice* (2024) by Anna Lapera, and *Libertad* (2024) by Bessie Flores Zaldívar bring much-needed visibility to a growing US Central American population that has long been underrepresented in both YA literature and Latinx studies.

Living between Two Worlds: Cruelty Is the Point!

Tellingly, *Gaby, Lost and Found, Efrén Divided, Indivisible,* and *Brighter than the Sun* depict youth coming into agency by making personal life choices amid structural violence in the form of enforced family separation from loving, undocumented parents. Mexican American author Angela Cervantes begins her middle-grade novel *Gaby, Lost and Found* with eleven-year-old Gaby Ramirez Howard mourning her mother's deportation to Honduras. Legally excluded from the state through her status (Zimmerman et al. 822), Paloma Ramirez, Gaby's mother, was deported three months earlier after ICE conducted a raid in the factory where she worked. As part of a mixed-status family, Gaby lived with her mother after her parents divorced, so she doesn't feel particularly close to her father, but he moves in to take care of her after the deportation.

As a Mexican American YA author amplifying migration from Honduras, a journey rarely depicted in fiction, Cervantes skillfully balances the pain and precariousness Gaby's feels after her mother's deportation with her coming-of-age(ncy) journey to find her voice and explore her cultural identity. Unfortunately, as in novels discussed in chapter 4, some classmates bully Gaby due to her mother's undocumented status. Their mean-spiritedness is indicative of the wider community's anti-immigrant sentiments. As Gaby gains awareness about the difficulties her mother experiences trying to return home, she acquires new respect for her sacrifices and defends her against cruel bigotry: "My mom is risking her life to come home right now. In case you'd like to spread more gossip or make jokes about that" (Cervantes 186). When her mother is finally able to call Gaby, Gaby learns that she works day and night trying to earn enough for the long journey back to Kansas City. The crossing has become significantly more costly and dangerous than when she left fourteen years ago, so she will need to hire an experienced coyote to increase her chances of clandestinely getting across the US border. Gaby learns that "jobs in Honduras don't pay like they do in the States. . . . In the States, her mom made more for a full day of work at the factory than she did during an entire week in Honduras" (122). Here, Cervantes masterfully identifies poverty wages in Central America and family reunification as key root causes for migration. Abrego and Menjívar specify that CAFTA-DR, the Central American free trade agreement with the United States, allows "multinationals, as well as local elite business owners, to profit from (and maintain) the low wages and poor working conditions of Central American workers" (234). To learn about her mother's intended journey, Gaby studies a world map and uses a school computer to trace the route from San Pedro Sula through Guatemala, learning that many migrants risk their lives riding Mexican cargo trains to reach the United States. She is shocked to learn that her mom was only six years older than Gaby's own current age when she left Honduras; Gaby can't imagine "traveling alone across deserts, mountains, and rivers" (Cervantes 59).

Gaby's coming of age(ncy) occurs when she puts her mother's safety above her own personal needs. She shows new maturity when she realizes "she doesn't have to risk her life again because no matter how far away she is, she's in my heart always" (188). When they talk, Gaby expresses a desire to visit her mother in Honduras in the future, which is something she'll be able to do safely with a US passport. Meanwhile, she researches Honduras to learn more about her cultural background, exploring the food, Mayan pyramids in Copán, the beautiful Roatán Island, and the traditions and ancestral homelands of the Afro-Indigenous Garifuna.

When her father finds a better paying job in Dodge City, Gaby exerts agency by choosing to remain in Kansas City to live with her best friend's family. As a middle-grade novel, *Gaby, Lost and Found* is striking for two reasons. First, it is one of three YA novels in this corpus that specifically represents migration from and deportation to Honduras. And second, it rejects a happy ending by capturing how deportation separates Gaby from her undocumented mother and US citizen father.

Similarly, *Efrén Divided* by California school teacher Ernesto Cisneros and *Indivisible* and *Brighter than the Sun* by Daniel Aleman relate the stories of US-born youth from mixed-status homes who must take on increasingly demanding responsibilities when one or both parents are deported to Mexico. After Efrén Nava's mother is detained during an immigration raid and deported to Mexico, this twelve-year-old assumes care of his younger twin siblings, one of whom has functional needs, in Highland, California, while their father works extra hours to earn enough to help her return home. In *Tactics of Hope* (2022), Jesus Montaño and Regan Postma-Montaño underscore that children are often left out of conversations on immigration. Recalling Aurora Levins Morales's admonishment that children "need us to listen deeply and with respect to the ways they experience the world, validate their sense of injustice, and help them understand the systemic nature of unfairness" (quoted in Montaño and Postma-Montaño 127), they comment on an important discussion Efrén has with a classmate about their fears of deportation. Efrén and Jennifer Huerta disclose to each other that their mothers' don't have papers, but Jennifer nevertheless feels empowered to run for class president because her mother has taught her that "we are seeds," from the Mexican saying "Nos quisieron enterrar, no sabían que éramos semillas" (They tried to bury us, but they didn't know we were seeds). I concur with Montaño and Postma-Montaño that the characters' confiding their shared fears about undocumented status and the threat of deportation "leads to the profound realization that the current world can be transformed" and they can create new realities (128).

Like a seed, Efrén exerts agency as he becomes the primary caregiver for his younger siblings while trying to stay on top of his schoolwork. When his mother's money is stolen in Tijuana, he demonstrates agency by offering to deliver funds to her to pay for a coyote so she can return home. His father is reluctant to allow him to cross the border by himself, but only Efrén has official documentation. Thankfully, a taxi driver named Lalo helps him navigate the unfamiliar border city of Tijuana; Lalo himself was deported and separated from his family, including a baby daughter, after twenty-eight years of living in the US. Lalo proves to be an important character, not only because he serves as Efrén's guide but because he gives voice to deportees who are rarely depicted in US literature. Montaño and Postma-Montaño spotlight this significant absence: "Very rarely do we listen to voices that present the perspectives of those who cannot return. . . . A deportation regime would have us believe that those deported should be forgotten, erased from personal as well as collective memory. *Efrén Divided* offers a powerful dissent by foregrounding novel ways that families in deportation regimes are reimagined" (131). In my view, this reimagining is a central feature of Latinx YA novels, given that they emphasize the intentional cruelty of family separation as a deterrent for unauthorized migration and feature agency over victimization. With Lalo's help, Efrén reunites with his mother, delivers the money, and returns safely to his father on the US side of the border. But unfortunately, his mother's fate is similar to that of Jennifer Huerta's mom and Paloma Ramirez in *Gaby, Lost and Found.* She is apprehended at a border checkpoint, taken to a detention center, and deported back to Mexico—a heavy dose of crimmigration realism for a middle-grade novel.

In his author's note, Cisneros states that his students in California often faced this harsh reality, so he wanted to be faithful to their experiences. Efrén, however, exerts agency by running for class president when Jennifer must step down. Although this decision causes conflict between Efrén and his best friend and unleashes xenophobic bullying and vandalism of his campaign signs, he gathers courage from the idea that seeds flourish even in adversity. Echoing Chicanx writer Gloria Anzaldúa, Montaño and Postma-Montaño note Efrén's resiliency, agency, and transformation into a social justice activist: "Instead of powerless victims who need to be protected from challenging matters such as deportability, the novel posits that children, if provided avenues of conocimiento, that is, knowledge and awareness, can find means to empower themselves and those around them" (132).[2] Clearly, Latinx authors and scholars are making important contributions to YA literature by speaking out against cruel detention and deportation regimes based on white supremacist exclusion.

Daniel Aleman's debut YA novel *Indivisible* (2021) takes place in New York City with sixteen-year-old Mateo García as the first-person narrator and protagonist who dreams of attending New York University to become an actor. Mateo is one of the few openly queer protagonists in this corpus of YA Latinx fiction, and it is heartening to see that his Catholic Mexican

2. On a personal note, author Jesus Montaño identifies with Efrén's embodiment of hope for the possibilities of agency in the service of societal transformation: "Not a day goes by that I (Jesus) am not reminded of the ways that living as undocumented as a child has marked my life. What racks my heart these days is not so much my own situation; instead, it is the way that fear, anxiety, and loss have been weaponized and aimed at young Latinx people. When I think of all the children currently living in fear and anxiety over deportability and the children currently being held in ICE detention centers, my heart truly and truthfully breaks" (133–34).

parents are unreservedly supportive of his identity and sexuality. Every night after dinner, Mateo and his mother watch a telenovela featuring a gay character. Seeing himself mirrored in pop culture echoes the importance of having LGBTQ+ protagonists widely available for young readers. Mateo reflects, "seeing someone fall in love with another man on-screen somehow made me feel less alone" (Aleman 25). Curiously, although Mateo is out about his sexuality to his family and close friends, he chooses to keep his parents' undocumented status a secret. When his parents are arrested by ICE at the bodega they've owned for almost ten years, Mateo must cope with this life-shattering change completely on his own. Like Efrén in Cisneros's novel, Mateo experiences a stressful process of adultification (Diaz-Strong et al. 3) as the older child who must care for a traumatized younger sibling. A statement from Sonia Alejandra Rodríguez's and Ingrid Campos's insightful review of *Efrén Divided* rings equally true for *Indivisible*: "While the story focuses on immigration, it is also about finding self-empowerment while living in a system determined to disenfranchise people. . . . It's also evident that ICE is terrorizing communities and ultimately, traumatizing people. And one of the ways this happens is by not allowing parents to parent their children by forcefully removing the parent from the picture because of citizenship status." As Mateo struggles to care for Sophie, his traumatized sibling who is in second grade, we witness their initial shock, confusion, and anxiety over their parents' deportation. They enter a grieving period as Mateo reflects on all the sacrifices his parents made in the more than twenty years they'd lived in the US. When they run out of food at home, he feels overwhelmed: "I'll have to stock the fridge, and do our laundry, and clean the apartment, on top of everything else I already have to do. How am I gonna find the time for all that? How will I manage to pay for food and rent?" (Aleman 70). At first, people in the community drop off food and remind them that they are not alone, but Mateo—indoctrinated in a capitalist neoliberal ideology rooted in individualism—is reluctant to ask for help. He is ashamed to tell his close friends that his parents were taken away in handcuffs like criminals. When he visits his mother in detention in Buffalo, he barely recognizes her. Visiting his father is just as traumatic, given the glass wall that divides them. He is outraged by the injustice: "This is the sort of room where you would visit a murderer or a drug dealer. . . . All he ever did was work hard and look after our family" (168). Even though Mateo testifies at his father's hearing about his role as family provider and upstanding member of the community, the judge orders his deportation, and his mother chooses voluntary departure to accompany him. Mateo and Sophie are US-born children, and their lives are shattered. Mateo finally admits, "I don't have the energy to tell any more lies. I just let the truth leave my mouth without putting up any resistance. . . . I feel empty. No hope, no light, no heartbeat. Nothing" (228). Like the other protagonists discussed here, he comes of age when he gains critical consciousness of the world beyond himself. Once he decides to confide in his friends, he receives support and grows closer to Adam as they begin a loving relationship without secrets or shame. With Adam's support, Mateo tells his father he wants to remain in New York to finish high school and attend college. Despite his fears, Mateo learns that he and his family across the border are seeds in loving soil, capable of transformation: "And no matter how hard they tried to separate us, how much the distance hurt, or how it nearly broke us, we are really, truly indivisible" (386). Latinx authors Cervantes, Cisneros, and Aleman underscore the systemic cruelty of detention and deportation along with the resiliency and agency of young protagonists who suffer family separation yet emerge with a more empowered sense of self.

Like *Indivisible,* Aleman's second cross-border novel, *Brighter than the Sun,* also features family separation, premature adultification, and a budding romance. At age sixteen, Sol, short for María de la Soledad, feels the weight of US citizenship as she crosses the border daily from Tijuana to Chula Vista for high school. As the family mourns their mother's recent death to cancer, Sol becomes the primary caregiver for her younger brother Diego, who is bullied at school. She feels the tension between her right to cross the border for school and work as a US citizen as opposed to her father and brothers. The daily crossing takes a personal toll on Sol, in line with Ray Acheson's characterization of the states using borders to criminalize racialized migrant labor, suppress workers' wages, and intimidate them, thereby preventing them from organizing resistance: "This enables the capitalist class to . . . politically divide them between citizen and migrant. . . . Freedom for some is predicated on the exclusion of others" (Acheson 7). Immersed in this exploitative capitalist system, Sol uses her cross-border agency to become the family's primary breadwinner by getting a part-time job at a department store in San Diego before and after school.

The school's anti-immigrant climate lands Sol's friend Bruno Rodríguez in the hospital for demanding that Jack Akers apologize for telling her to "speak English. This isn't Mexico" (Aleman 109). When Jack beats Bruno, he isn't even suspended, yet Bruno faces expulsion, putting his graduation from an American high school and college opportunities at risk. Jack's family, however, insists on a disciplinary hearing, which Sol views as white privilege since "people like him can have a way of getting under our skin, of making us feel like we never fully belong" (131). Although she is afraid of public speaking,

Sol agrees to speak to the school board about the fight she witnessed. Many students and community members come out to support Bruno, and her words convince the board to allow him to stay in school.

When the daily crossing becomes too burdensome, Sol decides to stay with her best friend Ari and her mother in San Diego. This relocation allows her to pick up early morning and late night shifts, but Sol feels guilty for leaving Diego, especially since the school bullying he experiences distances him from their *machista* father.

As the debts pile up at home and the family permanently closes the restaurant, the pressure on Sol escalates. But in YA romance fashion, Sol feels a spark when she meets her coworker Nick, who empathizes with her as his mother's caregiver. She "feels something exploding—a warm glow that breaks through the hopelessness. . . . All I could possibly care about is the glow of the stars and the feeling of our lips touching" (213, 224). As she becomes more self-aware, she resents pondering whether she should give up her dream of studying engineering to work full time to help the family: "I wish they would remember that I'm not the only one who's responsible for feeding the family, and that I'm not the adult here, but it's probably too late for that" (266). Her expression of frustration over the shouldering of financial responsibilities along with the unfairness of the burden point to systemic socioeconomic inequalities that the border zone magnifies, and the ripple effects they have on family dynamics.

After coming home with bruises on his face, Diego confides that he is teased about his friendship with Andrés; they are called "boyfriends" by their Mexican classmates. Modeling solidarity and a culture of care, Sol wisely counters their machismo and homophobia by advising him to enjoy the friendship and to be there for his friend. Her wise advice is especially necessary during a stressful time of economic disparity, disposability, and family separation.

Jonny Garza Villa's *Ander & Santi Were Here* (2023) takes up the important themes of undocumented status, family separation, and coming into creative agency. Garza Villa's protagonist is eighteen-year-old Ander Justino Martínez, a talented queer muralist who lives with their Mexican parents in the Santos Vista neighborhood of San Antonio, Texas. Ander is an accomplished artist who enjoys working at the family's restaurant, cheekily accepting a fifty-dollar tip from "some Beckys and Karens. The type of white women who think they can empathize with brown people because they read *American Dirt*" (Garza Villa 12), a best seller that prompted calls for Latinx "own voices" representation from the publishing industry. Ander's decision to defer acceptance to the School of the Art Institute in Chicago to remain in San Antonio for a one-year residency program disappoints and angers their parents. Deep down, Ander fears being stereotyped as a young Mexican muralist, so their plan is to devote the year working on local commissions while reflecting on what kind of artist they truly want to be. Ander's fear that "Mexican aesthetic wasn't seen as serious art" is triggered during a meeting with their adviser, who displays "passive racism" (224) by mentioning only Latinx neighborhoods such as Little Village, South Lawndale, and Pilsen as spaces where they will find inspiration. Feeling tokenized, Ander hangs up on the adviser after shouting, "We wouldn't be having this conversation if I was white" (225). Ander's racialized and queer consciousness empower them to speak out against bias as they gain a deeper understanding of citizenship privileges and the creative power of agency when they fall in love.

Sparks fly when Ander trains the new waiter after their parents fire them to ensure that they will focus on their art during the gap year. What Ander doesn't see, given their new crush on Santi, is the way the family maneuvers to shield undocumented workers from anti-immigrant policies of detention and deportation. At the dinner table, Ander's parents and grandmother discuss a recent raid and a neighbor from Honduras who was denied asylum. Feeling infuriated by the injustice, Ander reflects: "This stuff is fucking angering. . . . Actual born-here citizens feel scared about walking around at night not because of gangs or criminals but because they might end up accidentally in a cage when these pinche terrorists want to act first and give us their half-assed apologies later" (15). Ander's understanding of immigration politics deepens when they fall in love with Santi and learn that he is undocumented. Ander uses their agency to protect Santi when ICE agents come into the restaurant while Santi is in the restroom. Ander quickly goes to him so they can exchange T-shirts, and Ander pretends to be a server while Santi sits at a booth as a self-absorbed customer, playing with Ander's iPad. Temporarily trading places compels Ander to grasp the terror of the situation: "I hate seeing how fear sinks immediately into every part of his body. How it's a physical thing that comes out of him like a gust of wind hitting my body" (143). During the incident with ICE, Ander's grandmother advises them on how to be an ally: "Recuerda, we belong here. Show them that you can't be bothered and be a shield. Take up as much space as possible so we can get people out the back" (144). This solidarity draws the young couple closer, as Santi shares more about his frightening experiences of narcoviolence in Mexico, where his father and brother were killed and his mother, sister, and he were almost abducted and were forced to flee in the middle of the night. The anxiety of the moment and physical attraction arouse their desire to have sex when they are home alone. Unlike other authors in this corpus, Garza Villa writes explicitly about sex. On the day before Ander's nineteenth birthday, they note, "There's only us, here together in a moment that is both beautiful and frightening, for however long the world wants to give us. And we're going to make the most of it" (154). Yet when Ander becomes overprotective, Santi exerts agency by pushing back:

> You don't have to protect me. I'm not your responsibility. . . . You get to live with a different set of rules and I know you know that, but, Cielo, that doesn't mean I want you fighting my battles for me. You being in the middle means you're in front of me, and I don't want that. Side by side I can live with. Me in front of you, having a chance to keep you from some of it, that's better. (204, 205)

That Garza Villa points out the different set of rules between them from the perspective of the undocumented character is also unique and much needed in YA fiction. But things quickly escalate when an ICE van follows them to question Santi. Thankfully, family and the community protect them as Ander cries and screams at the thought of losing Santi. Traumatized, they shower together: "And with every touch, I am reminded that we are powerful. That our existence is powerful. And no men or government or racist ideology can ruin this. At least not right now" (149). Feeling closer, Ander asks Santi to go with him to Chicago, but their plans are truncated when Santi's mother disappears in Mexico, so he must return to take care of his younger sister. Fortunately, an uncle in Reynosa agrees to care for her, but Ander is enraged by the obstacles that conspire to draw them apart. Everything changes when Santi steps out to buy a snack at a convenience store and is detained by ICE. Again, family and friends mobilize to help, thinking that he can apply for asylum given his mother's recent disappearance. Ander's younger sister and friend plan a protest at the detention center where he is held, with posters stating "Abolish ICE," "No one is illegal on stolen land," and "Free Santi." Ander delivers a speech underscoring the humanity of those in detention and the power of their collective voices to resist. They protest each afternoon, but when Santi appears in court, the judge issues a deportation order. As an act of resistance against displacement and disposability, Ander uses creative agency to paint a mural of Santi "resting on me, his eyes closed as we hold hands, an arm outstretched, like we're dancing. Like he's finally being allowed to be at peace" (347). The novel concludes with a final act of agency—Ander withdraws from art school and moves to Mexico City to live with Santi and study Mexican muralism. Ander's decision to abandon the US to live with Santi in Mexico underscores the impossibility of living with dignity in a white supremacist anti-immigrant society. Recalling Rebeldita's proclamations in Siu's picture book, Ander and Santi break free of unjust immigration policies to remain together, envisioning a life where they can both move freely with dignity.

Abolish ICE! An Inside View of Dehumanizing Baby Jails and Youth Detention

Land of the Cranes by Aida Salazar, an arts activist who was born in Mexico and grew up in California, is a middle-grade novel written in verse that takes place in East Los Angeles. Roberta Quintero, the bilingual protagonist and nine-year-old fourth grader, is named after her father but affectionately called Betita. Plumita is her father's nickname for her, referring simultaneously to a crane's feather and her creative writing skills.

To instill pride in her rich Indigenous cultural heritage, he tells Betita stories about mythical Aztlán, which translates to "the land of the cranes," referring to a prophecy that one day they will return home. Salazar extends the notion of home by situating the narrative in the Indigenous context of Aztlán before and beyond the creation of colonial geopolitical borders. Montaño and Postma-Montaño relate the mythical land of Aztlán to highlight that Latinx and Chicanx people are not intruders to the US, but rather, "rightful heirs to their homeland": "Betita and her parents belong to these people coming 'home,' not as migrants fleeing . . . but as people seeking to reclaim both the land and the history of their ancestors" (116). Insightfully, they relay that "Betita seizes historical agency to refashion her world, one in which families are separated, to reimagine a better world in which cranes, like the Quintero family, can move freely about their ancestral lands, following the origin story of Aztán" (117). I relate the connections between these Mesoamerican texts—*Land of the Cranes, Journey of the Sparrows, Return to Sender*'s swallows and monarch butterflies, and the phoenix in *The Radius of Us*—to the Maya context pointed by Barillas Chón: migration is survival. Envisioning a land without borders, these works underscore Salazar's standpoint in her note to the reader: "The history of humanity across the globe is one of migration. . . . If we look at migration patterns—not only of people, but of cranes and other species—we will notice what all migrants have in common: They migrate to survive changes to their environment and for their well-being. It is humans who have drawn the lines in the sand, erected walls and borders around their territories, and deemed people 'illegal' when they cross those walls and borders." This statement delegitimizes colonizing borders and white supremacist notions of illegality. Moreover, Salazar not only condemns the Trump administration's "zero tolerance" policy that forcibly separated children from parents as a deliberately cruel deterrence measure, she also connects her personal experience as a woman of color who was born in Mexico and brought to the US as a baby to the power of storytelling: "I wrote *Land of the Cranes* with an understanding of the long and devastating history of raids, separations, deportations, incarcerations, and deaths my community has suffered." As a prize-winning author and Latinx ally well acquainted with a childhood fear of la migra or immigration enforcement, Salazar emphasizes the need for more Central American representation in the publishing industry: "I am hopeful more #ownvoices stories from the Central American perspective will rise to speak to the deep tragedies and sufferings these people have endured. These stories need to be told, especially because these communities—many of which are Indigenous—make up the largest group of migrants coming to the border today." Without a doubt, this call for more Central American and specifically Indigenous voices is needed in academia and the publishing industry.

With the critical awareness and sensitivity of a Latinx YA author, Salazar goes beyond depicting Betita's parents as hardworking immigrants with multiple jobs; she depicts them as affirming her creative agency by proudly displaying her new poems and drawings all over their one-bedroom rental. Betita's worst fear materializes when her father is detained by immigration officials, so her mother explains that in El Norte, there are walls that people like them are not supposed to cross: "We are sin papeles, undocumented, 'without permission'" (Salazar 35). The idea of borders and cages as structural power to restrict mobility is at odds with her self-identification as dignified cranes who are free. Given Betita's anxiety and confusion about her father, her supportive teacher makes her aware of the history of solidarity and sanctuary, explaining that "laws are not always fair. But there are others who might help him. They are fighting for all those who migrate" (39). When they learn where her father is detained, a lawyer explains that he won't be able to return for ten years because he failed to appear in court to have his asylum petition heard. This infraction calls for immediate deportation, even though he never received a notice. An aunt and uncle drive Betita and her mother to the San Diego–Tijuana border so the family can briefly reunite at Friendship Park to see each other across the fence. Regrettably, the uncle misses the exit and the aunt, mother, and Betita are detained by border patrol.

Readers get an inside view of the dehumanizing conditions in an immigration detention facility in the second part of the novel, titled "Mictlan," the Nahuatl word for the underworld in Aztec mythology. It's heartbreaking to view the frightening ordeal through a child's perspective, seeking to make sense of a system purposefully designed to be cruel.[3] She assumes, for example, that the building, which people refer to as *la hielera,* or "the freezer," is made of ICE because of the subzero temperature. After they are processed and placed in chain-link cages, her creative lens views the reusable foil blanket as a silver cape as she tries to hold on to *la dulzura,* the sweetness of life that her father taught her, but she feels it dying in this terrible place where mothers and children with lice are always crying, hungry, and cold from sleeping on the concrete floor.

The novel denounces the terrible conditions, ranging from moldy, half-frozen burritos to a lack of running water that forces detainees to drink from the toilet tank. Abusive guards exert their power by calling them "burros" and "wetbacks" without repercussions. Despite this dehumanizing treatment, the children use their agency in resistance by making armpit fart noises, spreading laughter "like a wildfire of uncontrollable joy from every crane in the cages! Our laughter is an applause the guards can't do anything to stop" (Salazar 154). This daring act of resistance ends when guards bring in a rebellious young woman wearing a T-shirt that says #AbolishICE who is savagely beaten and kicked repeatedly in the stomach.

In "Anáhuac," Nahuatl for "close to water," we meet the assertive newcomer, Marisel Dominguez, who understands the purpose behind the government's dehumanizing tactics. She explains that the frigid temperature, traumatizing family separation, and abusive treatment are all forms of torture designed to make them leave the country: "Pero, what they don't want to admit is that our people have been here since before there were borders. We are indigenous to this land and they, THEY are the illegal immigrants who came to this continent without an invitation and colonized" (Salazar 166). She defies the white supremacist narrative that imposes borders on stolen land. As a Dreamer who had to meet several requirements to obtain DACA, Marisel was targeted for making a speech at an immigration rally about ICE's abuse, so now she faces deportation. Betita is inspired by Marisel's leadership: "I've never met a crane like her before. . . . Sprouting truths, I can feel my wings regrowing in real time" (168). Given the deplorable conditions, they begin a hunger strike and social media campaign with the help of a lawyer and Marisel's girlfriend. Exerting agency and leadership of her own, Betita teaches kids how to create picture poems to express their sadness or trauma from riding La Bestia or crossing a river on a raft during their migration journey. Betitia's agency and their nonviolent direct action strategies for social change are successful: "Our

3. According to Harsha Walia, "a record 69,550 migrant children were incarcerated in the US in 2019, more children separated from their families and detained than in any other country on the planet" (20).

picture poems campaign is starting to go viral! And people are protesting because they saw the pictures and words of our nightmares and it scares them too" (220). Reporters and government officials come to inspect the detention center and transfer some children to temporary family shelters run by charities. Finally, Betita meets her baby sister, born in detention, as they opt for "voluntary departure" to reunite with their father.

The idea of "voluntary departure" takes on liberatory significance in David Bowles's and Guadalupe García McCall's *Secret of the Moon Conch,* along with themes of agency, family separation, detention, and belongingness in this Mesoamerican romance and historical fantasy YA novel. *Secret of the Moon Conch* abolishes borders by alternating the narrative between Sitlali Morales, who flees present-day narcoviolence in Mexico and crosses the Río Grande to find her father in San Antonio in 2019, and Calizto, a Nahuatl speaking warrior who fights the Spanish invasion of Tenochtitlan in 1521. This fusing of the past and present masterfully aligns coloniality and current immigration politics. In *Border and Rule,* Harsha Walia traces the roots of forced migration back four centuries, when "nearly eighty million Europeans became settler-colonists across the Americas and Oceania, while four million indentured laborers from Asia were scattered across the globe and the transatlantic slave trade kidnapped and enslaved fifteen million Africans" (6). Although the dominant US immigration narrative conveniently overlooks historical violences such as colonialism, genocide, slavery, and indentureship, Walia, Bowles, and García McCall expose them as "the *very* conditions of possibility for the West's preciously guarded imperial sovereignty" (Walia 6). Immersed in a layered context of structural violence, Sitlali and Calizto come into agency when they meet and fall in love as seventeen-year-olds who each encounter a moon conch that magically brings them together, defying the five hundred years that separate them.

Secret of the Moon Conch resonates with *Land of the Cranes* in that the characters share a critical Indigenous consciousness that rejects neocolonial and neoliberal borders. Like Betita, Sitlali knows Nahuatl and is aware of Mexican history. Sitlali, whose name means Little Star in Nahuatl, was born and raised in Veracruz, but her mother died seven years ago and her grandmother passed away recently. This painful loss, along with the pressure to marry a local drug lord, compel her to search for her father, who went to the US to find work twelve years ago without fulfilling his promise to send for his wife and daughter. Sitlali plans to cross the border to reach her godmother in Texas. On the migrant journey, she learns that her godmother is part of a network that helps others cross the border. Fortunately, along the way Sitlali encounters kind people who extend solidarity and hospitality. After crossing the river, she joins twelve other undocumented immigrants in the back of a dark, miserably hot trailer, hoping they will make it through the border checkpoints.

Despite their separation across time and space, Sitlali's experiences in the borderlands mirror Calizto's confrontations with the Spanish invaders. As the only survivor in his family after the smallpox plague that the Spanish brought and used to decimate the Indigenous population, he is haunted by the loss of his people. He treasures the conch left to him by his mother, a priestess, and honors his promise to his father to care for Ofirin, an African Yoruba youth who was enslaved by the Spanish and learned their language. Depending on the moon cycle and whether they hold the conch at the same time, Sitlali and Calizto can hear each other's thoughts, communicate mentally, see what the other observes, and even touch. When Sitlali makes it to the border, for example, Calizto sees the river and border wall made of iron slats, which he decries as a monument to isolation that declares, "You're not wanted here" (Bowles and García McCall 131). His interpretation coincides with Walia's contention that the US-Mexico border is a racist tool rooted in imperialist expansion, Indigenous genocide, and anti-Black enslavement, "thus solidifying the white settler power of racial exclusion and migrant expulsion" (21). This is precisely the context in which Sitlali sees Calizto fighting for his life, training unhoused orphan boys to fight the invaders, and leading hundreds of refugees to safety. Despite the surrounding violence, when he sees Sitlali he finds her breathtaking and yearns to touch her, recalling Central American critiques of *mestizaje*: "All that is beautiful about my people, blended with the imperious dazzle of our enemy. A perfect balance. Divine, incomparable" (Bowles and García McCall 103).[4] She exoticizes him as well, feeling strongly attracted to his lean, muscular body, covered only by a loincloth.

By setting the YA novel's plot simultaneously in 1521 and 2019, Bowles and García McCall critique white settler colonization and the neoliberal cycle that exploits and displaces the vulnerable. Sitlali's reunion with her undocumented father is distressing because his American wife Samantha fears Sitlali will put her US-born sons in jeopardy. Samantha claims neighbors will call ICE if they see her at the house, so she separates her again from her father, who meekly complies with her wishes. Samantha tips off ICE to raid the restaurant where Sitlali waits for her father, who doesn't show up. Sitlali is taken to a freezing

4. Shannon Speed observes that *mestizaje* played out differently: "Mexico is notably different from Guatemala, where settler culture lent itself to a more apartheid regime, leading eventually to a genocide in the latter twentieth century. In other countries of Central America, logics and practices of elimination were also at work, both through combinations of the ideology of *mestizaje* combined with overt killings and repression, as in El Salvador in the 1930s, or *mestizaje* and geographic isolation, as Afro-descendant and indigenous groups on the Atlantic Coast were largely shut out of the mestizo state in Honduras, Nicaragua, and Costa Rica" (788).

cold room to be processed, then taken to a detention center. At the same time, Calizto and Ofirin are captured and imprisoned on a Spanish brigantine. When Calizto blows the conch, he feels Sitlali's humiliation and anger. Since she kept a fragment of the conch in her pocket, the sound of the trumpet gives her strength to maintain her dignity in a warehouse full of chain-link cages that resemble kennels. As she and the other women denounce the deplorable conditions, they critique the fact that "these facilities create 'jobs.' These white people are getting rich off our suffering. Every fearful soul shoved in these cages, every wall, every tear, is one more dollar in the bank for the big corporations running this place" (314). Sitlali explains to Calizto, "*No surprise. Cruelty is the point: part of their strategy, not some side effect. . . . Greed. . . . That's what the people controlling the government worship. Riches and power*" (337). He confides that his father once said the same, "*after drinking too much agave wine in the privacy of our home, about Emperor Moteuczoma*" (337). Their critique underscores the timeless, systemic use of cruelty as a tactic by the powerful and a strategy of control that prioritizes profits over human dignity.

When a new detainee manages to smuggle her phone in, Sitlali begs to borrow it. Using her agency, she quickly records a video denouncing the inhumane conditions and shares it on social media, announcing that they are going on a hunger strike and urging people to come out to protest. As in *Land of the Cranes,* the video goes viral and outraged people demand change. When reporters arrive, Sitlali is taken to isolation, where the cruelty escalates. She is strip-searched, and Calizto comforts her as they kiss passionately, but the Spanish soldiers on horseback mirror the police's cruelty in the detention center. As Sitlali and Calizto each press the crane glyph on the magical conch, a portal opens for them so they can finally be together. They vow to care for others in need: "We go back for the rest of them. The ones in cages in the US. The ones hiding in the rubble in Tenochtitlan. . . . We save them all. We bring them home" (390). Defying borders, this YA novel will surely serve as a mirror, window, or sliding glass door for readers of all ages.

We reencounter Jaime Rivera, a Guatemalan Indigenous protagonist in *The Crossroads,* the sequel to *The Only Road,* a Pura Belpré Honor Book discussed in chapter 2. Twelve-year-old Jaime Rivera lives in a trailer on a ranch in southern New Mexico with his older brother Tomás and fifteen-year-old cousin Angela. This narrative begins a week after Guatemalan cousins Jaime and Angela survive the dangerous migrant journey across Mexico and border crossing, after Angela's brother and Jaime's best friend Miguel was killed by gang members. Jaime's first act of agency occurs as he mourns Miguel's killing. When he learns that the Alphas attacked and killed his grandmother, he uses his creative spirit to cope with so much tragic loss, and draws her portrait to honor and remember her.

At school, which resembles a prison with a pointed iron fence, Jaime navigates a scaled-down version of the white supremacist system that forced him to flee home and imposed structural barriers to keep him from reaching the US. Now he must negotiate the language barrier and anti-immigrant sentiment as he learns English. Tomás explains that in the US, children are required by law to go to school, as opposed to Guatemala, where many kids Jaime's age abandon their education to help support their families. Tomás also informs him about current anti-immigrant debates regarding "a massive wall and deportation" (Diaz, *Crossroads* 16). Like other YA authors discussed, Alexandra Diaz illustrates the challenges of adapting to a new school, language, and culture in a country heavily steeped in white supremacy. Fortunately, Jaime's social studies teacher challenges the dominant narrative that the US was built by immigrants. Bearing in mind that Jaime identifies as part Mayan, the exploitative working conditions his teacher describes echo both Guatemala's race-based hierarchy that pays Indigenous peoples the lowest wages and committed genocide when they demanded change, and the exploitative wages paid to immigrants in the US. Jaime learns more about the US immigration system from Don Vicente, an older Mexican from Chihuahua who runs the ranch where Jaime lives. He crossed the border decades ago, before restrictive walls were erected, but with drastic changes in immigration politics including heavy federal investment in border security, militarization, detention, and deportation, Don Vicente's life changes unexpectedly when he is stopped at a pop-up border checkpoint. Although Jaime is not allowed to visit Don Vicente in detention, he identifies with him because of his own illegalized status. His emerging critical consciousness is an effective mirror and window to readers: "Sure, he entered this country without permission, swimming across the Río Bravo that separated Mexico from El Norte. The act might have been illegal, but as a person, he was no different than any other human. How could anyone actually be 'illegal?'" (145). With this awareness, Jaime breaks through the oppressive structural barrier of illiteracy by sending drawings to Don Vicente to communicate that he is valued and remembered. Jaime's drawings are shared with the immigration judge to persuade him that Don Vicente is a highly respected asset to the community.

Jaime uses his art to cope with anti-immigrant sentiment at school. Diego, for example, who claims not to speak Spanish, parrots a white supremacist myth that goes unchallenged by the teacher: "Doesn't matter what you call them. They're all here to take away our jobs" (153). Acting on his internalized racism, Diego steals Jaime's sketchbook, tears the pages in the bathroom then pees on the drawings, and threatens him: "you can't say anything to anyone about it or I'll have you deported" (185). When Diego's father picks him up from the principal's office, it's clear that they speak Spanish at home, implying that he is ashamed to speak Spanish because he associates it with second-class status. When they discuss the difference between an immigrant and a refugee in class, Jaime identifies as a refugee because fleeing Guatemala due to gang violence was the only choice: a choice "between definitely dying and possibly dying" (156).

Centering *We Are Not from Here* in tragic migrant deaths, Jenny Torres Sanchez dedicates her YA novel to seven Indigenous Maya and Salvadoran child migrants who lost their lives in ICE custody and to "all the children whose names we do not know, whose existence and demise have been hidden."[5] Echoing the structural inequalities that triggered the Central American civil wars examined in chapter 1, the deaths of Indigenous Maya children in the borderlands connect neoliberalism to racial, gendered, and ethnic violence compounded by increased border militarization and inhumane conditions in detention centers. In this context, I view Torres Sanchez's naming of the deceased children in her dedication as a condemnation of transnational state necropolitics responsible for their deaths. Likewise, Walia situates the death of Jakelin Amei Rosmery Caal Maquin, a seven-year-old Q'eqchi' Maya girl who died in border patrol custody in 2018, in the larger context of "territories destroyed by the cumulative impacts of Spanish colonial invasion, genocidal massacres during the civil war targeting Q'eqchi' communities, large biofuel and sugar plantations displacing Indigenous livelihoods, and now one of the areas in Guatemala most vulnerable to climate change" (27). As discussed in chapter 2, it is crucial to examine the perilous migrant journey in this critical multilayered context.

Here, I focus on the novel's final section, when Pequeña and Pulga exert agency to ensure their survival. As they face death in the desert, they run away from border patrol agents, but Pulga is caught and taken to an immigration detention center. Pequeña, however, takes back her agency with a gut-wrenching scream, marking her survival by identifying with her given name, Flor. Two women hear her liberating scream and stop their car to help her. Pulga, on the other hand, is near death in a detention center as he freezes in his wet clothes with only a government-issued foil blanket to keep him warm. When he's taken to a large warehouse with metal cages, he is haunted by Chico's voice and wakes up screaming, just as many children cry out for their parents. As noted in the other novels, the conditions in the detention

5. Darlyn Cristabel Cordova-Valle was a 10-year-old Salvadoran girl. From Guatemala and ranging from toddlers to teenagers were Mariee Juarez (19 months), Jakelin Caal Maquin (Q'eqchi' girl, age 7), Felipe Gómez Alonzo (Chuj, age 8), Juan de León Gutiérrez (age 16), Wilmer Josué Ramirez Vásquez (age 2½), Carlos Gregorio Hernández Vásquez (Maya Achi, age 16).

center are purposefully dehumanizing. He observes that the detainees are all wearing filthy clothes and smell of rotten fruit. Recalling Libertad's precarious existence in the Guatemala City garbage dump discussed in chapter 1, this signals that migrant children are also considered disposable. Eventually, a guard takes Pulga to meet his lawyer because Flor called her mother, who reached out to his aunt in the US, and she will serve as his asylum sponsor. As his trauma-healing journey begins, he calls his mother in Guatemala in a state of shock. His aunt holds him as he screams to release the horrors of the journey. Echoing *Rebeldita the Fearless in Ogreland,* the novel ends with his desire that all the detained children collectively scream for liberation.

In the same vein, *Santiago's Road Home* (2020) by Alexandra Diaz tells the story of Santiago García Reyes, a twelve-year-old Mexican boy who is turned away from his aunt and uncle's home in Chihuahua due to their extreme poverty. Rather than return to his abusive grandmother, he bonds with a mother and her five-year-old daughter, Alegría, along the migrant journey. María Dolores Piedra Reyes from Culiacán empathizes with Santiago since she recently left an abusive relationship, so they decide to journey together. During the desert crossing, police and paramedics take María Dolores away in critical condition while Santiago and Alegría hide. He feels guilty for not being able to care for Alegría, but they are separated by gender and not allowed contact in the youth detention center for unaccompanied minors. With "fewer rights than murderers" (Diaz 167), he tries to stay strong but cries in the bathroom, knowing that surveillance is everywhere.

As the other novels attest, the purpose of this cruelty is to deter further migration. Santiago languishes for months in this traumatizing place where guards demean the boys daily, referring to them as "crybabies," "dirtbags," "idiots," or "lazy bums." Santiago is treated with dignity only by a teacher from Honduras who comes to the facility twice a week. Showing agency, Santiago asks the teacher to teach him how to read, and eventually, Santiago introduces tender-age boys to picture books as a respite from the cruelty that surrounds them. Eventually, María Dolores and Alegría come for Santiago after acquiring his birth certificate from Mexico. Since he never received their letters, he feared they had abandoned him. The novel ends happily with Santiago leaving the detention center with his new family.

Diaz's desire to bring about much-needed change by raising awareness resonates with *Illegal* by Francisco X. Stork, the sequel to *Disappeared* (2017), discussed in chapter 3. Sara Zapata, a Mexican journalist who fled Ciudad Juárez with her young brother Emiliano after their home was destroyed, is taken to Fort Stockton Detention Center, run by a private company. She seeks asylum because she was targeted for investigating the disappearance of young girls, including her best friend Linda. Echoing dehumanizing conditions in detention, Sara is constantly harassed by an abusive female guard because powerful people in Mexico responsible for the sexual enslavement of young women want to make sure there is no evidence on Leopoldo Hinojosa's cell phone. As the corrupt head of the Public Security and Crime Prevention Unit of the State Police, Hinojosa is implicated in the kidnapping of young girls in Ciudad Juárez. Emiliano actually has the cell phone and reluctantly joins their father in a suburb of Chicago so that the phone can be used to complete the investigation that was thwarted in Mexico. In fact, Emiliano feels guilty that Sara was attacked in the desert while he was unharmed because of his suspicious business connections. As the narrative fluctuates between Sara's and Emiliano's perspectives, *Disappeared* denounces far-reaching US and Mexican complicity in a transnational human trafficking ring with a high level of government impunity and corrupt business ties. Sara discovers a network of corruption within the detention center, where employees are bribed to go along with wrongdoing. As we saw in *Dream Things True,* under the cover of whiteness and white supremacy, capitalism spurs multiple kinds of illegality, yet undocumented people, who are often made to feel powerless, use their agency for the greater good, as opposed to the privileged, who prey on women as disposable objects for wealthy men's pleasure. Stork's novel is a powerful critique of impunity and neoliberal complicity in gendered violence taking place on both sides of the border.

Although the burgeoning body of literature examined in this chapter depicts painfully realistic topics, we also see young characters respond with empathy and agency during traumatic times of family separation, detention, and deportation. Collectively, these stories by Latinx authors represent global capitalism and white supremacy's structural violence on the one hand and youth agency in the search for safety and liberation in the long history of resistance on the other. Surely there is a long road ahead for writers of color in the white publishing industry, but this growing corpus of Latinx YA novels is a testament to youth as agents of social change. To conclude this chapter, I discuss a growing set of novels that raise the visibility of Central American stories of the diaspora.

"My Story and My History": US Central American Girls Raise Their Quetzal Voices

Past and present come together in an inspiring array of coming-of-age(ncy) novels by authors of the Guatemalan and Honduran diaspora. Strikingly,

Shine On, Luz Véliz! (2022) by Rebecca Balcárcel, *Turtles of the Midnight Moon* (2023) by María José Fitzgerald, *The Weight of Everything* (2023) by Marcia Argueta Mickelson, *Mani Semilla Finds Her Quetzal Voice* (2024) by Anna Lapera, and *Libertad* (2024) by Bessie Flores Zaldívar serve as mirrors and windows for readers exploring their Central American identities and agency. The protagonists introduce readers to Guatemala and Honduras through their varied interests in soccer, robotics, wildlife, photography, poetry, and art, bringing much-needed visibility to a growing diasporic population that is underrepresented in both youth literature and Latinx studies.

Rebecca Balcárcel's *Shine On, Luz Véliz!* is the story of an eleven-year-old sixth grade soccer star in Texas who becomes unable to play after a terrible accident. Lost without sports, Luz Véliz feels distanced from teammates and her Guatemalan father, who coached them. With help from teachers and a neighbor, Luz begins to explore a new facet of her identity through coding and robotics. But life takes another turn when she learns that her father has a thirteen-year-old daughter in Guatemala who he didn't know about from a previous relationship, and she's coming to live with them. Welcoming an older half sister isn't easy, but Solana gives Luz a deeper understanding of her Guatemalan roots. Through Solana's stories and sketches, Luz learns about the beautiful volcanoes surrounding Lake Atitlán, the *barriletes* de Sumpango, which are giant, intricate kites flown on the Day of the Dead, and paintings by Maya Kaqchikel artist Paula Nicho Cúmez from San Juan Comalapa, or Chixot in Kaqchikel. Since Solana shares Luz's interest in coding, she tells her about a Mayan horoscope she made using the Tzolk'in, a sacred 260-day calendar: "You put in your birthday, and it tells you your Nahual—your day sign and animal guide" (149). This uplifting of Indigenous knowledge is unique in Latinx YA because it decenters the Ladino or non-Maya experience. Although Luz and Solana do not identify as Maya, their respect for Indigenous knowledge strengthens their relationship. When Solana disappears after seeing an ICE vehicle in front of the house, Luz understands that she must be afraid of deportation, having heard stories of people rounded up by ICE only to be killed upon arriving in Guatemala. Tragically, Solana's fears are not unfounded since her own mother was killed by gang members in front of her home while Solana was inside. Balcárcel touches on the migration narrative with sensitivity and nuance, drawing readers in not only with sports, technology, and art but by balancing Guatemala's challenging social reality with its natural beauty and its rich Mayan culture. Tellingly, the story is reflective of the author's experience meeting her own Guatemalan half sister as an adult.

Similarly, Fitzgerald's debut novel, *Turtles of the Midnight Moon,* brings two very different twelve-year-old girls together in an eco-mystery that takes place in Honduras.[6] Barana's beach village of Pataya sits on protected land of Indigenous and Afro-descendant Garifuna peoples on the coast of La Mosquitia, where she cares for a six-hundred-pound *baula*, or sea turtle, named Luna. Passionate about sea life, Barana volunteers at the turtle conservation project and attends Escuela Berta Cáceres, named after Honduras's internationally renowned Indigenous land and water defender who was assassinated in her home in 2016 for speaking out against transnational extractive industries. She is surprised by the announcement that her supervisor María and her husband were threatened by armed poachers from the islands, and learns that Luna's eggs were stolen, so she promises to bring the thieves to justice.

Although they start off on the wrong foot, Barana partners with Abby Durón, who accompanies her father on a medical work trip to Pataya, where he was born. Abby is from a small northern New Jersey town and is passionate about photography. Having lost her only friend, who relocated to London, she's found it hard to make new friends given the judgment she experiences at school for not fitting the Latinx stereotype given her fair skin, inherited from her white mother, and her Honduran father's dark hair and eyes. Although she endures teasing from a mean cheerleader, she corrects a boy who misidentifies her, saying, "I thought you were Spanish." She explains that people from Spain are Spanish, and that she speaks Spanish, but she is actually Honduran.

Asserting her identity initiates Abby's coming-of-age(ncy) journey as she explores her self-identity and gains insight into her heritage during the two-week trip to Honduras, where she is astonished by the mangroves, manatees, howler monkeys, and dolphins. As Barana and Abby join forces to protect the turtle eggs, considered valuable delicacies on the black market given the lack of economic opportunities in the area, they disregard the police as useless due to their corruption and lack of concern for the environment. Instead, they launch their own investigation. With Barana and her brother's help, Abby exerts agency by secretly photographing suspects on the beach, leading to the culprits. Additionally, she creates a social media page for the Pataya Sea Turtle Conservation Center, posting pictures to raise awareness about this unique project. In Fitzgerald's acknowledgments, she thanks the environmental conservation warriors "in Honduras and throughout Central America, who, against all odds, fight for our forests, oceans, rivers, and all their magnificent creatures" (308). This recognition is significant because worldwide, Honduras is one of the most dangerous countries for environmental activists. In a subtle manner for a middle-grade novel, Fitzgerald draws much-needed attention

6. Like Fitzgerald's novel, *Hurricane* by Terry Trueman is one of the few YA novels set in Honduras. It tells the story of devastating Hurricane Mitch in 1998, from the perspective of thirteen-year-old survivor José.

to the Honduran Mosquitia's natural resources and Garifuna communities in need of protection given dangerously powerful economic interests, racialized dispossession, and violence against environmental defenders.[7]

In contrast to Balcárcel's and Fitgerald's depoliticized representations, Mickelson's *The Weight of Everything*, Lapera's *Mani Semilla Finds Her Quetzal Voice*, and Bessie Flores Zaldívar's *Libertad* situate their YA narratives within a critical context to raise awareness about human rights in Guatemala and Honduras, drawing attention to a need for justice that dignifies victims in the digital age (Alvarado et al. 133).

Mickelson, who was born in Guatemala and immigrated to the US as an infant, tells the story of a high school junior whose Mexican American mother died in a car accident six months before. In *The Weight of Everything*, protagonist Sarah Mosley withdraws from her fine arts boarding school in Austin to become her younger brother's primary caregiver in San Antonio after their grieving father, a white history professor, has a nervous breakdown and turns to alcohol to numb his pain. Amid the emotional labor and financial stress at home, she runs an Etsy shop drawing portraits from photographs to keep the family afloat. Although she doesn't have the bandwidth to make new friends, she bonds with a classmate, David Garza, who like her brother Steven loves sports and generously includes him in their outings. As she figures out how much she can handle in terms of a relationship, Sarah begins to explore her mother's Guatemalan roots for a school art project, in what Latinx YA scholarship would call a *conocimiento* narrative given that it's ultimately a journey of self-discovery. Taking inspiration from Gloria Anzaldúa's theorization of conocimiento or knowledge as a healing process, Sonia Alejandra Rodríguez positions conocimiento as "an opportunity to recognize the oppressions that direct the characters' existence and provide a means to challenge and transform them" ("Conocimiento Narratives" 10).

She learns that her great-grandfather was born in Guatemala but fled to Mexico City during the civil war. She begins to draw connections between the CIA's role in the 1954 coup that ended a ten-year democratic period, and US political and financial ties to the United Fruit Company and the Dulles brothers. Aided by her mother's notebook and conversations with her father, Sarah gains an understanding of why Mexican muralist Diego Rivera's painting *Gloriosa Victoria* meant so much to her mother, who was a Latin American studies professor and believed art was about having a voice to tell important

7. Loperena writes about the pillage of environmental resources in Indigenous territories in relation to settler colonial logics, "which render indigenous and black peoples as barriers to national progress and necessitates their removal and even elimination in the pursuit of profit and the extraction of wealth for the national elite" (806).

stories. The painting depicts key players in the US-supported coup, namely US President Dwight D. Eisenhower, CIA Director Allen Dulles (who is whispering into the ear of his brother), and US Secretary of State John Foster Dulles (who shakes hands with Castillo Armas, the newly appointed president of Guatemala). Bloody, dismembered children lie at their feet as armed soldiers, banana workers, and protesters look on. As a fan of Frida Kahlo's self-portraits, Sarah discovers that she shared Rivera's indignation over the coup. In fact, shortly before her death, Frida Kahlo participated in an anti-coup protest in Mexico City, showing solidarity despite her illness. Sarah, in turn, displays agency by telling her great-grandfather's story based on the photographs he took as a journalist in Guatemala. Adding her voice in resistance, she signs an online petition that her mother circulated to rename the Dulles International Airport. Since Guatemala isn't covered in the curriculum and they are never taught about US interventions abroad, including support for genocide, Sarah infuses her art project with nonviolent direct action by taking a stand against the school's neutrality policy. At her art show, she speaks out about the United States' historical intervention in Guatemala and invites people to participate in a walkout to sign the petition which obtains even more signatures once it's shared on social media.

Further widening the scope of Guatemalan American representation, Anna Lapera's debut novel *Mani Semilla Finds Her Quetzal Voice* features a twelve-year-old seventh grader named Manuela Semilla, or Mani, who desperately wants to get her period. A self-described myopic *nerda,* she has much in common with Cristina Herrera's concept of *ChicaNerds* (2021) as a reclamation of Brown girl self-love that combines intelligence and sociopolitical consciousness. Mani identifies as a "half Chinese-Filipino-American half Guatemalan" (Lapera 2) who can't speak any ancestral language well. Feeling self-conscious about her limited Spanish, she develops a negative perception of the language due to family members' inappropriate comments about her developing body, but she hesitates to speak up for herself. Although her grandmother is losing her memory, she encourages Mani to find her quetzal voice, like her Tía Beatriz. Unsure of what that means, Mani knows that the quetzal is Guatemala's national bird and that legend says that ever since the Spanish invasion, they stopped singing and will never find their voice until the country is free. But all she knows about her aunt is that she disappeared one day in Guatemala and never made it home. Compellingly, Mani's home life with an overprotective mother and a hostile school environment begin to mirror political events in Guatemala that she learns about through her mother's letters in the attic. When Mani discovers the letters, she pieces together her aunt's and mother's activist past as journalists who denounced disappearances and femicide.

This critical transnational awareness ultimately gives Mani the strength to denounce the violence that takes place at school: "It seems like all this bad stuff people are doing against girls and women is happening all around me. Not just in Guatemala" (Lapera 146).

Sadly, Mani develops a negative association of Guatemala based on her limited understanding of political disappearances and gendered violence, so she resists the idea of traveling to Guatemala for the first time with her mother on her thirteenth birthday. Although she finds it challenging to talk with her mother, the letters and photographs in the attic help her see a side of her mother that she never imagined, a young woman who protested and wrote songs for marches demanding justice and an end to impunity. Slowly, she develops a deeper, more nuanced understanding of Guatemala as "a magical place where people cry and sing all the time. . . . Where nothing made her throat clench or blocked her voice like a muzzle. Where she smiled often and sang loud" (83). The process of developing historical memory by reviewing the materials in the attic not only shapes her self-identity and liberates her voice and agency to speak her truth; it gives Mani an appreciation of resistance movements embracing sorrow and joy.

Interestingly, her mother's insistence on buying Mani oversized clothing is rooted in her fears of gendered violence, problematically blaming the victim instead of systemic forces, which mirrors the school administration's repressive policies. Knowing that clothing is never an invitation to unwanted attention, Mani nevertheless struggles to speak out against gendered violence. She wants to speak up when popular boys harass and bully young women on the school bus, but she keeps quiet. They disparage girls' bodies—belittling flat breasts while snapping bras, groping, and knocking them down, then posting humiliating videos. One day, Corey slaps A'niya's butt so hard that everyone hears it. Mason pulls A'niya's hair while they make gross sounds, even pinching her breast. Mani is in shock, but she knows they have to report the incident as racialized sexual harassment. Instead of holding the boys accountable, the principal blames the unwanted attention on girls' clothing, so they move A'niya's locker to the basement and change her schedule, while the bullies only get a warning. The message here is that A'niya can easily be displaced and invisibilized, so that the status quo remains untouched. Rhodes's assertion holds true: "The external messages proliferated about girls' bodies, such as the idea they should look and act a certain way, disempowers them and arrests the potential of their activism to truly make change" ("Carmelita" 362). Fortunately, Mani and A'niya don't give up on the quest for justice. A'niya, who is Salvadoran, and Genesis, who is Honduran and is inspired by Indigenous human rights and land defender Berta Cáceres, further awaken

Mani's curiosity about Guatemala: "I ache all over for the women I've never met but somehow feel connected to, like there's an invisible hilo holding us all together" (Lapera 175). As she gains cultural insight and self-awareness she states, "My story and my history. I never thought of either of them forming in Guatemala, a place I've never ever been" (210). This reflection indicates her agency to situate herself in the wider collective context of historical memory. Inspired by her aunt's and mother's feminist consciousness and outraged by the impunity she witnesses at school, Mani resolves to use her agency to create change. Bravely, Mani stands up to the administration and inspires fellow classmates to speak out and take action because "our sense of worth and safety are under attack at this school" (192). Her oppressive school environment reveals how the white supremacist system situates and regulates young women of color, ensuring that they don't achieve full agency (Ventura 91).

During a school meeting in which girls are blamed for wearing provocative clothing, Mani announces that she is going to start a database to document sexual harassment in school as part of her Speak Up Project. Although she is suspended for one week, classmates leave notes in her locker describing assaults and humiliating incidents after which the school issued no consequences to the aggressors. During her public presentation, she acknowledges that although the Guatemalan peace process officially ended the long civil war, the violence continued: "Especially the violence against women. Women were disappearing, being killed, and there was no justice anywhere" (Lapera 265). The audience participates in a walkout she organizes with signs saying "Girl power!" and "Una voz y seremos millones!" Although she doesn't accompany her mother to the opening of a new museum of resistance and memory in Guatemala for her birthday, Mani ultimately uses her quetzal voice to self-identify as Guatemalan American: "I realize now that everything I am is because of everything they were. Their story is my story, and for the first time, I feel connected to Guatemala. But also to here. Definitely to here" (270). Additionally, she learns that "being a woman isn't about periods and body size or shape or how anyone sees you. . . . For me, it's about fighting against all the things that keep us down for being women, like the disrespect and violence against women's bodies" (316). Having found her quetzal voice, Mani knows that the majestic birds in the rainforest will one day sing again.

Taking a more political stance than the other novels, *Libertad* by Bessie Flores Zaldívar is a queer coming-of-age(ncy) story framed between the 2009 Honduras coup and the 2017 presidential election during massive student protests resisting right-wing governments. We meet Libertad Morazán, the first-person narrator, her older brother Maynor, and close friends including Cami, who she kisses in a bathroom bar in February 2017.

As a high school student, Libertad, or Libi for short, is unsure about whether she should attend the national university in Tegucigalpa, leave for college in the US, or join a migration caravan to flee queer discrimination. How free is she to choose? She is named Libertad, after all, because she was born on Independence Day. With all the attention focused on election day and protests against President Juan Orlando Hernández's unconstitutional reelection, the novel draws attention to US support for the 2009 coup despite the Hernández administration's connections to drug cartels, which mean that no one expects a fair election. Given oppressive police violence and homophobia, Libi expresses herself anonymously by posting political poems on social media.

Libi explores what independence means when she meets Dani Castillo, a university student whose parents migrated when she was a child but disappeared right before arriving in Juárez, Mexico, on the way to the US border. With news of migrant caravans leaving the country during military rule, curfews, protests, and the anniversary of Berta Cáceres's assassination, Libi considers migrating as her only option. When she learns that her Tía Martha was killed at a protest three days after the coup, she wonders if she was protesting for queer people's rights and lives. To help her gain clarity, Maynor gives her a tour of the university campus, introducing her to an area devoted to honoring historical memory by featuring the names and faces of the disappeared. This space underscores storytelling's role in bearing witness to injustice and countering erasure.

By framing the storyline between the coup and the fraudulent election, *Libertad* goes the furthest in representing migration as an act of youth agency by connecting Central American displacement to US foreign policy. As Honduran scholar Suyapa Portillo Villeda highlights, "Honduras saw no democratization in tandem with neoliberalization of its economy—resulting in a multitiered economic system that exploited the very poor, made the rich richer, eroded labor protections, and fostered growing corruption" (69). In fact, Portillo Villeda underscores that queer migrants are often invisibilized as they escape violence and state neglect while facing exceptionally life-threatening hardships on the migrant journey. Portillo Villeda clarifies that US policy "also thwarted possibilities for nations like Honduras to be sovereign and democratic and to offer democratic processes and policies for LGBTQ individuals and other disenfranchised communities" (70). As the novels in this YA corpus attest, the US has historically utilized immigration policies to dominate its neighbors while racializing anti-immigrant sentiments at home.

Further illustrating the inner workings of power and neoliberal disposability, Flores Zaldívar's note to the reader mentions Juan Orlando Hernández's capture on February 15, 2022, and his conviction on US drug trafficking charges on March 8, 2024. While referencing the election of Honduras's first woman president, Flores Zaldívar points out that "as a queer person, you still can't be openly queer and completely safe in Honduras, not really." As if embodying all the journeys from previous chapters, Flores Zaldívar writes, "But what Libertad, both the character and the novel, has taught me is this: Our queerness allows us to imagine care and justice beyond the ideals of a ruling political party. We are not free until all of us, everywhere, are free." Like the quetzal, we migrate to exist because we cannot survive in captivity. Collectively, the array of protagonists that come of age in these Latinx YA novels enact agency at great risk, having experienced how a neoliberal white supremacist power structure works to diminish or silence their voices. Yet with an embodied awareness of where they come from and the historical resistance of their ancestors, they add their voices as agents of change.

CONCLUSION

A Long Time Coming

From the Coming-of-Age Journey to Latinx YA(gency)

Following the lead of adolescents and young adults who consistently question, learn, and grow, I bring *Coming of Age(ncy) on the Migrant Trail* to a close eagerly anticipating future directions that the representation of adolescent migration journeys may take in Latinx YA literature. Throughout these pages, we have encountered youth experiencing deep despair as they flee the Salvadoran and Guatemalan civil wars and clandestinely crossing borders as they grieve the deaths, disappearances, and forced separation of friends and family due to immigration detention and deportation regimes. As they come of age within a context of structural violence and racialized oppression, the protagonists at once come into their agency with a critical consciousness of anti-immigrant racism and raise their voices in resistance. Like testimonio rooted in agency, these characters embark on a journey of self-discovery where they find their voice by sharing their stories and use it to connect with others in community. As the protagonists grapple with questions of identity and belonging, they experience bullying due to anti-immigrant discrimination and gendered violence in a school setting, challenging them to use their creative agency to denounce white supremacy and bring about awareness, expressing solidarity in resistance. Likewise, their friendships and romantic relationships in these realistic works of fiction reflect society's exclusionary notions of deservingness, where immigrants are viewed as either angels or trespassers. As protagonists of diverse backgrounds who find and use their voices to advocate for themselves and others, their experiences and perspectives serve as mirrors, windows, and doors for readers of all ages, showcasing various ways of exercising agency.

Framing this study at the intersections of youth literature, Latinx studies, and Central American studies, these YA novels show us that the representation of youth migration goes back several decades. Starting in the 1980s, novelists call attention to youth fleeing the Salvadoran conflict as various others recount the long journeys of Indigenous Maya adolescents fleeing Guatemala's genocidal war. Interestingly, among the earliest novelists to set their stories in Central America, only Omar Castañeda was himself Guatemalan. The others are mostly white authors who could travel more safely to the region and had more access to the publishing industry. The 1990s and 2000s saw an increase in books by Latinx and white writers depicting Guatemalan youth fleeing "peacetime" gang violence and clandestinely crossing Mexico to reach the United States. I include works by insider and outsider authors in my study of Latinx YA fiction because until there is greater own voiced representation, more Latinx, Chicanx, and white solidarity is needed to amplify stories that serve as mirrors to readers of the Central American diaspora. Widening the scope of authors who approach the topic with cultural sensitivity and nuance allows a greater range of narratives about Mexican, Guatemalan, Salvadoran and Honduran youth migration experiences and their coming of age in the US.

A handful of authors have written YA novels as windows into Mexico's terrifying drug war, in addition to heartfelt texts about the impact of femicides in the borderlands. Whether the characters practice subtle resistance by playing marbles and cards games, rooting for an underdog wrestler, or writing to raise public consciousness, their stories point to the strategic absence and complicity of the Mexican state with criminal groups. Several also implicate the US as a market for drugs and exporter of weapons. The gut-wrenching scenes shine a critical light on how racial capitalism renders impoverished youth and women disposable in the neoliberal drug war marketplace.

Likewise, the novels give voice to a young population that speaks up and takes action from the shadows and in the streets. Menjívar and Abrego address the challenges undocumented youth face in school as legal violence because of intense stigmatization "that keeps individuals in these situations bound up with structural violence when it blocks their paths to upward mobility and keeps them on the margins of society" (1408). They experience "legally sanctioned social suffering" precisely because "this type of violence is legal, sanctioned, and legitimated through formal structures of power that are publicly accepted and respected" (1408). As the novels illustrate, collective action and creative agency are very much needed for making social change.

The characters who survive the dangerous transnational journey and make it into the US are fearful of the state's detention and deportation regime, yet they look beyond themselves to form friendships and romantic relationships that point to the power of solidarity and community. These affective ties give them strength to tell their stories, which I read as Latinx YA liberatory narratives that underscore the human side of a deeply divisive political issue. Told with compassion and dignity, the YA novels critique poverty, violence, and injustice, inspiring readers of all ages to work for change, acknowledging that they exert agency within structural constraints.

Within the past decade, more Latinx authors including US Central Americans of the diaspora have published YA novels that give visibility to a growing population of Guatemalans and Hondurans who had not previously seen themselves in literature. With nuance and sensitivity, their fiction is a call for greater protection of the environment along with its Afro-Indigenous land defenders and water protectors. These stories matter especially because references to climate change and violence against environmental activists challenging transnational extractive industries are often absent when addressing migration. Opening a space for Central American visibility within Latinx studies invites solidarity with other marginalized voices, and there is a strong need to lift up Indigenous voices often subsumed as "presently absent" (Barillas Chón). As I see it, this literature contributes to decentering *mestizaje* and complicates the overarching representation of the US-Mexico border by featuring protagonists like Ander, who decides to relocate to Mexico with Santi, and girls from the Central American diaspora who travel to the isthmus. These innovative storylines are certainly something to celebrate, knowing that academia and the publishing industry must work harder to diversify the representation of Latinx people to underscore that we are not a monolith. Looking forward, I would welcome more examples of Latinx diversity in order to hear from Indigenous voices speaking back to history and power.

Perhaps it's the willingness of authors and protagonists of color to denounce the deportation regime and imagine a world without borders, that authoritarian politicians and radicalized parents want to ban YA books, further denying marginalized youth access to stories that mirror their experiences. This white supremacist silencing, however, also affects white teens, who will have limited access to window books that invite them to empathize and reflect on notions of white privilege, white saviorism, and effective allyship. Despite the political polarization, I'm hopeful that this younger generation challenges narratives rooted in US imperialism and neoliberal capitalism while calling for racial reckoning, an end to settler colonialism, and divestment as systemic change. Viewed together, this bold body of fiction attests to the power of an antiracist education that cultivates critical awareness in youth along with pride in the teachings and practices of Indigenous cultures, empowering them to voice their opposition to systemic cruelty while building historical memory.

As the last decades have fostered the growth of neoliberal austerity and the militarization of borders have made the crossing increasingly more dangerous and costly, politicians have demonized immigrants rather than addressing root causes. While they invest in more punitive measures such as mass deportation and larger detention centers, fewer resources are devoted to humanitarian aid and asylum shrinks. Latinx YA, however, responds with critical awareness and a culture of care, conscious of a long history of resistance and the power of community.

This YA literature challenges readers to cultivate awareness and add their voices to critique transnational policies that unjustly result in more migration, such as the loss of democratic rights with the growth in authoritarianism in Central America. In El Salvador, for example, the state of exception has incarcerated more than sixty-five thousand citizens in its crackdown on gang members, although many are not affiliated with gangs. Central American governments have curtailed freedom of the press by imprisoning Guatemalan journalists and human rights activists and forcing former judicial officials into exile.

Primarily, my aim in *Coming of Age(ncy) on the Migrant Trail* has been to give more visibility to Latinx YA and its value for students and educators. While (im)migration will surely continue to be a timely issue of concern to members of the general Latin American and Latinx community, the perspective of adolescents can be particularly insightful to teachers, researchers, school administrators, social workers, human rights advocates, and community activists who work and volunteer with child migrants. I hope this book will serve as a valuable resource for undergraduate and graduate students interested in children's and YA literature and Latinx studies. Hopefully, the general professional and activist community will find it to be a useful tool for engaging youth in more complex discussions of human rights, immigrant justice, and solidarity across borders.

Considering the literary value of the these works and their contribution to the classroom and larger social justice field, I appreciate Sanjuana Rodríguez and Sandra Osorio's assertion in their study of banned and challenged Latinx picture books: "As classrooms become increasingly more diverse, educators need to use all the resources and texts available to meet students where they are and provide moments where culturally and linguistically diverse students see themselves represented in the books they read" (21).

Reflecting on the array of stirring, often heartbreaking stories, it's heartening to see that Latinx YA literature's coming of age has been a long time coming. Its strength lies in its power to imagine better futures, precisely in spite of the turbulent times in which they take place.

ACKNOWLEDGMENTS

There are so many people who accompanied me throughout the long research and writing process, and I am eternally grateful. This book is the result of many years of learning from and working with a loving community that knows no borders, so with humility, I would like to express deep gratitude to the activist community in Chicago who welcomed me into their fair trade and immigrant justice organizations. I learned so much at MayaWorks from Kathleen Morkert, Phyllis Nichols, Sarah Cunningham, and Patricia Krause. I'm grateful to Victoria Cervantes for encouraging me to join the Honduras Delegation and the Honduran Solidarity Network. On that trip in 2014, I was privileged to meet Berta Cáceres, and I have continued to learn from Karen Spring in her guest lectures in my classes and the *Honduras Now* podcast. Volunteering with Interfaith Community for Detained Immigrants and the Wellington United Church of Christ community challenged me to listen, ask questions, and take action. Thanks to the shared space and solidarity with migrants and asylum seekers over the years, I began to believe in this project as much more than academic research. Accompanying young migrants in detention in Chicago broke my heart open and taught me to be present, bearing witness to the power of the arts, especially when glitter was involved. It's been an honor to serve with Consuelo Sandoval, Sara Wohlleb, Chris Inserra, Craig Mousin, Brian and Wendy Carson, Gonzalo and Tina Escobar, Joey Sylvester, Tom and Laura Krainz, Christopher Tirres, Maricruz, Jimmy, Cristina, and Lupita.

I deeply appreciate my supportive network of colleagues and longtime friends. Ann Russo, Sandra Benedet, Lourdes Torres, Wendy Baldwin, and Anita Gallers read early drafts, offering feedback and encouragement. Special thanks to my dear friend and writing coach Wendy Baldwin at Linguaverse who wrote weekly with me from Spain. I've benefited so much from her writing retreats and personalized sessions. Anita Gallers has been a supportive listener since graduate school. I appreciate her helpful feedback and cherish our phone dates.

I owe a debt of gratitude to Dr. Rose Spalding at DePaul University for making it possible for me to take a year off from directing the Peace, Justice and Conflict Studies Program, which has been such a welcoming and healing space for me personally and professionally. Learning from and working with such committed colleagues as Ken Butigan, Tomás Ramírez, Jerica Arents, Tara Betts, Micaela Garrido, and Victoria Agunod has truly been a privilege. I'm thankful for PAX students, alumni, and affiliated faculty for making the world a better place.

I feel deep appreciation for the Social Transformation Research Collaborative for supporting my work as an inaugural fellow in 2022–23, and I am grateful to my research assistant Victoria Alejandra Vega Castañeda. I appreciate the support of the College of Liberal Arts and Social Sciences at DePaul University for summer research grants, a paid leave, and a Late Stage Research Grant. I have enjoyed the solidarity of different writing groups at DePaul: first the Faculty Research Collaborative under the direction of Beth Catlett, then the Social Transformation Research Collaborative's writing group led by Julie Moody Freeman and the Writing Center group with Mark Laboe and Erin Herrmann. I appreciate Katie Brown's support at DePaul's Center for Writing-Based Learning for connecting me with Elias Ahumada, who kindly read and commented on an early draft. Many thanks to Elizabeth Coonrod Martínez and Bill Johnson González for their support as directors of the Center for Latino Research and to Carolina Sternberg as chair of the Department of Latin American and Latino Studies. Jennifer Schwartz at the Richardson Library helped me track down sources. I am especially thankful for Ann Russo, Maria Ferrera, and Julie Moody Freeman, my partners in the Healing Justice Initiative and the Difficult Dialogues Collaborative.

I learned so much about solidarity and collaboration from Lydia Saravia and Jhonathan Gómez during our Humanities X Fellowship in 2023–24. I appreciate the support of Lisa Dush, Amanda Lautermilch, Derek Potts, and Angelina Alvarez for the wonderful coteaching experience.

Life in Chicago is joyous thanks to the unwavering solidarity and friendship of Siobhan O'Donoghue, Kristin Tepas, Morgen MacIntosh Hodgetts,

Jacqueline Lazú, Rocío Ferreira, Claudia Fernández, Tim Gaster, Clara Burgo, Amina Chaudhri, Tim Higgins, Valentina Tikoff, Beatrice Figueroa, Shereen Ilahi, and Anmol Satiani.

Finally, I am forever grateful to my family in Los Angeles for their unwavering support. My parents, José Luis and Clara Luz, left Mexico and Guatemala as young adults and inspired me with their stories. Wholehearted thanks to my sister Clara for always offering me a lovely writing space and planning amazing trips for us. Many thanks to my brother José for taking me to the best bars in Los Angeles and Mexico City and for being such a fun travel partner. I'm thankful for my relatives in Guatemala and Mexico for always welcoming me and sharing their stories with me. Special thanks to my cousin Sandra Martínez for our walks and heart-to-heart conversations. Much gratitude to my aunts Herminia Gallegos and Virginia Meek and uncles Miguel and Felix Martínez.

My most heartfelt thanks to my travel companion Angelica Rodríguez. Thank you Nori Sogomonian for our decades-long friendship.

I deeply appreciate the support and guidance I've received from Kristen Elias Rowley and Becca Bostock at The Ohio State University Press. And special thanks to Billie Smith-Haffener and Elizabeth Zaleski.

Portions of chapter 1 previously appeared as "Contemporary Coming of Age(ncy) Narratives of Political Violence and Death in El Salvador and Guatemala: 'So That Future Generations May Be Aware,'" in *Global Perspectives on Death in Children's Literature,* edited by Lesley D. Clement and Leyli Jamali, Routledge 2016, pp. 130–41. Used with permission of Taylor & Francis Group 2016; permission conveyed through Copyright Clearance Center. Portions of chapter 4 previously appeared as "Patriots and Citizens of the Planet: Friendship and Geopolitics in Julia Alvarez's Young Adult Fiction," in *Inhabiting La Patria: Identity, Agency, and Antojo in the Work of Julia Alvarez,* edited by Rebecca L. Harrison and Emily Hipchen, SUNY Press, 2013, pp. 109–30. Used with permission of SUNY Press.

WORKS CITED

Primary Texts

Aleman, Daniel. *Brighter than the Sun.* Little, Brown Books for Young Readers, 2023.

Aleman, Daniel. *Indivisible.* Little, Brown Books for Young Readers, 2021.

Alvarez, Julia. *Return to Sender.* Turtleback, 2009.

Beatty, Patricia. *Lupita Mañana.* HarperCollins, 1981.

Belcárcel, Rebecca. *Shine On, Luz Véliz.* Chronicle Books, 2022.

Bowles, David, and Guadalupe García McCall. *Secret of the Moon Conch.* Bloomsbury YA, 2023.

Brown, Skila. *Caminar.* Candlewick Press, 2014.

Buss, Fran Leeper. *Journey of the Sparrows.* Puffin Books, 1991.

Cameron, Ann. *Colibrí.* Farrar, Straus and Giroux, 2003.

Castañeda, Omar S. *Among the Volcanoes.* Yearling, 1992.

Castañeda, Omar S. *Imagining Isabel.* Dutton, Lodestar, 1994.

Cisneros, Ernesto. *Efrén Divided.* Quill Tree Books, 2020.

De Leon, Jennifer. *Borderless.* Atheneum/Caitlyn Dlouhy Books, 2023.

De Leon, Jennifer. *Don't Ask Me Where I'm From.* Atheneum/Caitlyn Dlouhy Books, 2020.

Diaz, Alexandra. *The Crossroads.* Simon & Schuster/Paula Wiseman Books, 2018.

Diaz, Alexandra. *The Only Road.* Simon & Schuster/Paula Wiseman Books, 2016.

Diaz, Alexandra. *Santiago's Road Home.* Simon & Schuster/Paula Wiseman Books, 2020.

Diederich, Phillippe. *Playing for the Devil's Fire.* Cinco Puntos Press, 2016.

Fitzgerald, María José. *Turtles of the Midnight Moon.* Yearling, 2023.

Fullerton, Alma. *Libertad.* Fitzhenry and Whiteside, 2008.

Garza Villa, Jonny. *Ander & Santi Were Here.* Wednesday Books, 2023.

Hobbs, Will. *Crossing the Wire.* HarperCollins, 2007.

Jaramillo, Ann. *La Línea.* Macmillan, 2008.

Johnston, Tony, and María Elena Fontanot de Rhoads. *Beast Rider: A Boy's Journey Beyond the Border.* Amulet Books, 2019.

Lapera, Anna. *Mani Semilla Finds Her Quetzal Voice.* Levine Querido, 2024.

Marquardt, Marie. *Dream Things True.* St. Martin's Griffin, 2015.

Marquardt, Marie. *The Radius of Us.* St. Martin's Griffin, 2017.

Martinez, Manuel L. *Crossing.* Bilingual Review Press, 1998.

McNeal, Laura. *Dark Water.* Alfred A. Knopf, 2010.

Mickelson, Marcia A. *The Weight of Everything.* Lerner Publishing Group, 2023.

Mickelson, Marcia A. *Where I Belong.* Carolrhoda Lab, 2021.

Mikaelsen, Ben. *Red Midnight.* HarperCollins, 2002.

Mikaelsen, Ben. *Tree Girl.* HarperTeen, 2004.

Narváez Varela, Alessandra. *Thirty Talks Weird Love.* Cinco Puntos Press, 2021.

Pellegrino, Marge. *Journey of Dreams.* Frances Lincoln Children's Books, 2009.

Resau, Laura. *Red Glass.* Delacorte Books for Young Readers, 2007.

Salazar, Aida. *Land of the Cranes.* Scholastic Press, 2020.

Schafer, Steve. *The Border.* Sourcebooks Fire, 2017.

Sedgwick, Marcus. *Saint Death.* Orion Children's Book, 2016.

Stork, Francisco X. *Disappeared.* Arthur A. Levine Books, 2017.

Stork, Francisco X. *Illegal.* Scholastic Press, 2020.

Temple, Frances. *Grab Hands and Run.* HarperCollins, 1995.

Torres Sanchez, Jennifer. *We Are Not from Here.* Philomel Books, 2021.

Zaldívar, Bessie Flores. *Libertad.* Dial Books, 2024.

Zéleny, Sylvia. *The Everything I Have Lost.* Cinco Puntos Press, 2019.

Secondary Sources

Abrego, Leisy J. "Narratives of Migration and Integration of Central American Migrants in the US and Canada." *North and Central American Task Force on Migration,* 2021, pp. 1–12.

Abrego, Leisy J. "On Silences: Salvadoran Refugees Then and Now." *Latino Studies,* vol. 15, 2017, pp. 73–85, https://doi.org/10.1057/s41276-017-0044-4.

Abrego, Leisy J. "Relational Legal Consciousness of US Citizenship: Privileges, Responsibility, Guilt, and Love in Latino Mixed-Status Families." *Law & Society Review,* vol. 53, no. 3, 2019, pp. 641–70, https://doi.org/10.1111/lasr.12414.

Abrego, Leisy J., and Cecilia Menjívar. "Central American Migration to the United States: Historical Roots and Current Conditions." *The Routledge History of Modern Latin American Migration,* edited by Andreas E. Feldmann, Routledge, 2023, pp. 232–45.

Acheson, Ray. *Abolishing State Violence: A World beyond Bombs, Borders, and Cages.* Haymarket, 2022.

Administration for Children and Families. Unaccompanied Children Bureau Fact Sheet. 3 Jan. 2025.

Akom, A. A. "Critical Hip Hop Pedagogy as a Form of Liberatory Praxis." *Equity & Excellence in Education,* vol. 42, no. 1, 2009, pp. 52–66, https://doi.org/10.1080/10665680802612519.

Aldama, Frederick Luis. *Latino/a Children's and Young Adult Writers on the Art of Storytelling.* U of Pittsburgh P, 2018.

Allweiss, Alexandra. "'Too Dangerous to Help': White Supremacy, Coloniality, and Maya Youth." *Comparative Education Review,* vol. 65, no. 2, 2021, pp. 207–26.

Alma, Karina. *Central American Counterpoetics: Diaspora and Rememory.* U of Arizona P, 2024.

Alter, Rebecca. "Why Is Everyone Arguing about the Novel *American Dirt*?" *Vulture,* 7 Feb. 2020, https://www.vulture.com/article/american-dirt-book-controversy-explained.html.

Alvarado, Karina O., et al. *U.S. Central Americans: Reconstructing Memories, Struggles, and Communities of Resistance.* U of Arizona P, 2017.

Amaya, Hector. *Trafficking: Narcoculture in Mexico and the United States.* Duke UP, 2020.

Aquilina, Tyler, and Jessica Wang. "Oprah Defends Keeping *American Dirt* in Book Club after Controversy: 'I Really Loved the Book.'" *Entertainment Weekly,* 2 May 2022, https://ew.com/books/oprah-defends-american-dirt-in-book-club-after-controversy/.

Arias, Arturo, and Claudia Milian. "US Central Americans: Representations, Agency, and Communities." *Latino Studies,* vol. 11, 2013, pp. 131–49.

Avilés, William. "Trump and U.S. Drug Policy in the Americas: No End in Sight of War and Repression." *The Future of the U.S. Empire in the Americas,* edited by Timothy M. Gill, Routledge, 2020, pp. 286–306.

Barba, Lloyd D., and Tatyana Castillo-Ramos. "Latinx Leadership and Legacies in the U.S. Sanctuary Movement, 1980–2020." *American Religion,* vol. 3, no. 1, 2021, pp. 1–24.

Barillas Chón, David W. "K'iche', Mam, and Nahua Migrant Youth Navigating Colonial Codes of Power." *Urban Education,* vol. 59, no. 4, 2024, pp. 1224–51.

Barillas Chón, David W. "When Children of Tecum and the Quetzal Travel North: Cultivating Spaces for their Survival." *Educational Studies,* vol. 57, no. 3, 2021, pp. 287–98.

Barnet, Elizabeth. *Reunion: Finding the Disappeared Children of El Salvador.* U of California P, 2023.

Barry, Arlene L. "Hispanic Representation in Literature for Children and Young Adults." *Journal of Adolescent and Adult Literacy,* vol. 41, no. 8, 1998, pp. 630–37.

Batz, Giovanni. "Maya Cultural Resistance in Los Angeles: The Recovery of Identity and Culture among Maya Youth." *Latin American Perspectives,* vol. 41, no. 3, 2014, pp. 194–207.

Bauder, Harald. "Why We Should Use the Term 'Illegalized' Refugee or Immigrant: A Commentary." *International Journal of Refugee Law,* vol. 25, no. 3, 2014, pp. 327–32.

Bickford, Donna M. "Using Testimonial Novels to Think about Social Justice." *Education, Citizenship and Social Justice,* vol. 3, no. 2, 2008, pp. 131–46, https://doi.org/10.1177/1746197908090007.

Bishop, Rudine Sims. "Mirrors, Windows, and Sliding Glass Doors," *Perspectives: Choosing and Using Books for the Classroom,* vol. 6, no. 3, 1990, pp. 9–11.

Bishop, Rudine Sims. "What Has Happened to the 'All-White' World of Children's Books?" *Phi Delta Kappan,* vol. 64, no. 9, 1983, pp. 650–53.

Boffone, Trevor, and Cristina Herrera. *Nerds, Goths, Geeks, and Freaks: Outsiders in Chicanx and Latinx Young Adult Literature.* U of Mississippi P, 2020.

Bolt, Julie. "Toward an Active Utopia: Truth-Making in Menchú, Stoll, and the Classroom." *Review of Education/Pedagogy/Cultural Studies,* vol. 21, no. 3, 1999, pp. 265–79.

Bonilla-Silva, Eduardo. "Toward a New Political Praxis for Trumpamerica: New Directions in Critical Race Theory." *American Behavioral Scientist,* vol. 63, no. 13, 2019, pp. 1776–88.

Botelho, M. J. "Reframing Mirrors, Windows, and Doors: A Critical Analysis of the Metaphors for Multicultural Children's Literature." *Journal of Children's Literature,* vol. 47, no. 1, 2021, pp. 119–26.

Bowles, David. "American Dirt Is Proof the Publishing Industry Is Broken." *New York Times,* 27 Jan. 2020, https://www.nytimes.com/2020/01/27/opinion/american-dirt-book.html.

Bravo, Vanessa, and María De Moya. "Contesting the 'Bad Hombres' Narrative: U.S. and Mexican Media Diplomacy and Presidential Strategic Narratives about Immigrants." *Diplomatica: A Journal of Diplomacy and Society,* vol. 3, no. 1, 2021, pp. 47–73, https://doi.org/10.1163/25891774-03010003.

Brennan, Desine, and Citlalli Alvarez Almendariz. "Life without Papers as a State of Emergency in the Trump Era." *LASA Forum,* vol. 48, no. 3, 2017, pp. 24–29.

Brett, Roddy. "In the Aftermath of Genocide: Guatemala's Failed Reconciliation." *Peacebuilding,* vol. 10, 2022, pp. 1–21.

Brigden, Noelle K. "A Visible Geography of Invisible Journeys: Central American Migration and the Politics of Survival." *International Journal of Migration and Border Studies,* vol. 4, 2018.

Brigden, Noelle K., and Wendy Vogt. "Homeland Heroes: Migrants and Soldiers in the Neoliberal Era." *Antipode,* vol. 47, no. 2, 2014, pp. 303–22.

Brock, Rose. *Young Adult Literature in Action: A Librarian's Guide.* 3rd ed., Libraries Unlimited, 2019.

Bruce, Heather E. "Subversive Acts of Revision: Writing and Justice." *English Journal,* vol. 102, no. 6, 2013, pp. 31–39.

Buehler, Jennifer. "The Critical Work of YA Literature." *National Council of Teachers of English,* vol. 27, no. 4, 2020, pp. 19–23.

Burt, Jo-Marie. "Historic Verdict in Guatemala's Genocide Case Overturned by Forces of Impunity." *NACLA Report on the Americas,* vol. 46, no. 2, 2013, pp. 1–3.

Burt, Jo-Marie, and Paulo Estrada. "Trial for 'Death Squad Dossier' Ties Guatemalan Wartime Atrocities to Current Criminal Networks." Washington Office on Latin America, 29 Apr. 2022, https://www.wola.org/analysis/trial-death-squad-dossier-guatemala-wartime-atrocities-criminal-networks.

Bushmen, John H., and Shelley McNerny. "Moral Choices: Building a Bridge between YA Literature and Life." *ALAN,* vol. 32, no. 1, 2004, https://doi.org/10.21061/alan.v32i1.a.6.

Butcher, Kasey. "Constructing Girlhood, Narrating Violence: *Desert Blood, If I Die in Juárez,* and 'Women of Juárez.'" *Latino Studies,* vol. 13, no. 3, 2015, pp. 402–20, https://doi.org/10.1057/lst.2015.33.

Butler, Judith. *Precarious Life: The Powers of Mourning and Violence.* Verso, 2004.

Cáceres, Berta. Goldman Environmental Prize Acceptance Speech. *YouTube,* 22 Apr. 2024, https://youtu.be/AR1kwx8boms?si=JC7ELCzXjw9h-sG5.

Cardona, Julián, and Alice Leora Briggs. *Abecedario de Juárez: An Illustrated Lexicon,* translated and illustrated by Alice L. Driver. U of Texas P, 2022.

Caruth, Cathy. *Trauma: Explorations in Memory.* Johns Hopkins UP, 1995.

Caruth, Cathy. *Unclaimed Experience: Trauma, Narrative, and History.* Johns Hopkins UP, 1996.

Cervantes, Alejandro. "Testimonios." *Liberation Psychology: Theory, Method, Practice, and Social Justice,* edited by Lilian Comas-Díaz and Edil Torres Rivera, American Psychological Association, 2020, pp. 133–47.

Chacón, Gloria E. "Indian Trouble." *Cultural Dynamics,* vol. 31, no. 1–2, 2019, pp. 50–61.

Chacón, Gloria E. "Metamestizaje and the Narration of Political Movements from the South." *Latino Studies,* vol. 15, no. 2, 2017, pp. 182–200.

Chacón, Gloria Elizabeth, and Mónica Albizúrez Gil. *Teaching Central American Literature in a Global Context.* Modern Language Association of America, 2022.

Chaudhri, Amina. "#OwnVoices for Young Readers." *Book Links,* 2019, pp. 35.

Chávez, Karma R., and Hana Masri. "The Rhetoric of Family in the U.S. Immigration Movement: A Queer Migration Analysis of the 2014 Central American Child Migrant 'Crisis.'" *Queer and Trans Migrations: Dynamics of Illegalization, Detention, and Deportation,* edited by Karma R. Chavez and Eithne Luibheid, U of Illinois P, 2020, pp. 209–25. *JSTOR,* https://doi.org/10.5406/j.ctv18oh78v.21.

Chomsky, Aviva. Foreword. *Teachers as Allies: Transformative Practices for Teaching Dreamers & Undocumented Students,* edited by Shelley Wong, Elaisa Sánchez Gosnell, Anne Marie Foerster Luu, and Lori Dodson. Teachers College P, 2018.

Coats, Karen. "Teaching the Conflicts: Diverse Responses to Diverse Children's Books." *The Edinburgh Companion to Children's Literature,* edited by Clémentine Beauvais and Maria Nikolajeva, Edinburgh UP, vol. 1, 2017, pp. 13–28.

Cole, Pam B. *Young Adult Literature in the 21st Century.* McGraw-Hill Higher Education, 2009.

Cornejo, Kency. *Visual Disobedience: Art and Decoloniality in Central America.* Duke UP, 2024.

Coutin, Susan. "Borders and Crossings: Lessons of the 1980s Central American Solidarity Movement for 2010s Sanctuary Practices." *Critical Dialogues in Latinx Studies: A Reader,* edited by Ana Y. Ramos-Zayas and Mérida M. Rúa. New York UP, 2021.

Cruz-Malavé, Arnaldo. "Testimonio." *Keywords for Latina/o Studies,* edited by Deborah R. Vargas, Lawrence La Fountain-Stokes, and Nancy Raquel Mirabal, New York UP, 2017, pp. 228–31.

Cummins, Amy. "Border Crossings: Undocumented Migration between Mexico and the United States in Contemporary Young Adult Literature." *Children's Literature in Education,* vol. 44, 2013, pp. 57–73.

Cummins, Jeanine. *American Dirt.* Flatiron Books, 2019.

Curcic, Dimitrije. "Young Adult Book Sales Statistics." *Wordsrated,* 30 Jan. 2023, https://wordsrated.com/young-adult-book-sales/.

De León, Jason. *The Land of Open Graves: Living and Dying on the Migrant Trail.* With photographs by Michael Wells, 1st ed., U of California P, 2015.

De Nadie. Directed by Tin Dirdamal. Producciones Tranvia, 2005.

Deahl, Rachel. "Publishing's *American Dirt* Problem." *Publishers Weekly,* 3 Feb. 2020, https://www.publishersweekly.com/pw/by-topic/industry-news/publisher-news/article/82312-publishing-s-american-dirt-problem.html.

Dezenski, Lauren. "Sessions: Many Unaccompanied Minors Are 'Wolves in Sheep's Clothing.'" *Politico,* 25 Sept. 20, https://www.politico.com/story/2017/09/21/jeff-sessions-border-unaccompanied-minors-wolves-242991.

DiAngelo, Robin. *White Fragility: Why Is it So Hard for White People to Talk about Racism?* Beacon Press, 2018.

Diaz-Strong, Daysi Ximena, Ivón Padilla-Rodríguez, Stephanie Torres. "Beyond Infantilization and Adultification: The Binary Representations of Child Migrants in the United States and How They Harm Young Migrants." *Children & Society,* 2024, pp. 1–17.

"#DignidadLiteraria and PRESENTE Respond to 30-Day Follow-Up Meeting with Macmillan USA." *Latino Rebels,* 12 Mar. 2020, https://www.latinorebels.com/2020/03/12/dignidadliterariamacmillan/.

Donovan, Marie Ann. "Mirrors, Windows, and Springboards: Choosing and Using Quality Literature with the Young Children We Know." *Contemporary Challenges in Teaching Young Children: Meeting the Needs of All Students,* edited by Gayle Mindes, Routledge, 2020, pp. 170–83.

Drabinski, Emily. "The Fight Against Book Bans Is Mobilizing a New Generation of Student Activists." *Truthout,* 25 May 2023, https://truthout.org/articles/the-fight-against-book-bans-is-mobilizing-a-new-generation-of-student-activists/.

Durant, E. Sybil, and Marilisa Jiménez García, "Unsettling Representations of Identities: A Critical Review of Diverse Youth Literature." *Research on Diversity in Youth Literature,* vol. 1, no. 1, 2018, pp. 1–24.

Edison, Jaden, and Patrick Svitek. "At Least 50 Migrants Found Dead in Abandoned 18-Wheeler in San Antonio." *Texas Tribune,* 27 June 2022, https://www.texastribune.org/2022/06/27/bodies-18-wheeler-san-antonio-lackland/.

Ellstrand, Nathan. "Politicized Refuge: Chicago and the Transformation of the Sanctuary Movement." *Middle West Review,* vol. 9, no. 1, 2022, pp. 25–48.

Enriquez, Grace. "Foggy Mirrors, Tiny Windows, and Heavy Doors: Beyond Diverse Books toward Meaningful Literacy Instruction." *Reading Teacher,* vol. 75, no. 1, 2021, pp. 103–6.

Enriquez, Laura E. *Of Love and Papers: How Immigration Policy Affects Romance and Family.* 1st ed., U of California P, 2020.

Fife, John. "From The Sanctuary Movement to No More Deaths." *Religious and Ethical Perspectives on Global Migration,* edited by Elizabeth W. Collier and Charles R. Strain. Lexington Books, 2014.

Figueroa, Ariana Mangual. "¡Hay que hablar! Testimonio in the Everyday Lives of Migrant Mothers." *Language & Communication,* vol. 33, no. 4, 2013, pp. 559–72.

Finnegan, Amy C. "Growing Up White Saviors." *Journal of Applied Social Science,* vol. 16, no. 3, 2022, pp. 617–36.

Flores, Edwin. "A Quarter of All Children in the U.S. Are Latino, U.S. Census Study Finds." *NBC News,* 2 June 2023, https://www.nbcnews.com/news/latino/quarter-children-us-are-latino-us-census-study-finds-rcna87253.

Fregoso, Rosa Linda. "The Complexities of 'Feminicide' on the Border." *Color of Violence: The INCITE! Anthology,* edited by INCITE! Women of Color Against Violence, Duke UP, 2016, pp. 130–34.

Fregoso, Rosa L., and Cynthia Bejarano. *Terrorizing Women: Feminicide in the Americas.* Duke UP, 2010.

"Full text: Obama's Statement Following Trump's Ending of DACA." *Politico,* 5 Sept. 2017, https://www.politico.com/story/2017/09/05/obamas-statement-following-trumps-ending-of-daca-transcript-242339.

García, Marilisa Jiménez. "The Lens of Latinx Literature." *Children's Literature,* vol. 47, 2019, pp. 1–8.

Gibbons, Elizabeth. "Wings of the Phoenix: The Legacy of Violence for Adolescents in Post-Conflict Reconstruction." *Human Rights and Adolescence,* edited by Jacqueline Bhabha, U of Pennsylvania P, 2014, pp. 149–69.

Gibler, John. *To Die in Mexico: Dispatches from Inside the Drug War.* Lights Bookstore, 2011.

Giroux, Henry A. "Beyond the Biopolitics of Disposability: Rethinking Neoliberalism in the New Gilded Age." *Social Identities,* vol. 14, no. 5, 2008, pp. 587–620.

Giroux, Henry A. "US Fascism Is Spreading under the Guise of Patriotic Education." *Truthout,* 10 Apr. 2023, https://truthout.org/articles/us-fascism-is-spreading-under-the-guise-of-patriotic-education/.

Giroux, Henry A. *Youth in a Suspect Society: Democracy or Disposability?* Palgrave Macmillan, 2009.

Golash-Boza, Tanya M. *Deported: Immigrant Policing, Disposable Labor, and Global Capitalism.* New York UP, 2015.

Golash-Boza, Tanya M. *Forced Out and Fenced In: Immigration Tales from the Field.* Oxford UP, 2017.

Golash-Boza, Tanya M. "National Insecurities: The Apprehension of Criminal and Fugitive Aliens." *The Immigrant Other: Lived Experiences in a Transnational World,* edited by Rich Furman, Greg Lamphear, and Douglas Epps, Columbia UP, 2016, pp. 19–33.

Golash-Boza, Tanya M. "Punishment beyond the Deportee: The Collateral Consequence of Deportation." *American Behavioral Scientist,* vol. 63, no. 9, 2019, pp. 1331–49, https://doi.org/10.1177/0002764219835259.

Golden, Renny. "Sanctuary and Women." *Journal of Feminist Studies in Religion,* vol. 2, no. 1, 1986, pp. 131–49.

Gonzales, Roberto G. *Lives in Limbo: Undocumented and Coming of Age in America.* U of California P, 2016.

Gonzales, Roberto G., et al. "Unauthorized Status and Youth Development in the United States: Consensus Statement of the Society for Research on Adolescence." *Journal of Research on Adolescence,* vol. 27, no. 1, 2016, pp. 4–19, https://doi.org/10.1111/jora.12272.

Gonzalez-Barrera, Ana, et al. "Path to Legal Status for the Unauthorized Is Top Immigration Policy Goal for Hispanics in U.S." *Pew Research Center,* 11 Feb. 2020, https://www.pewresearch.org/short-reads/2020/02/11/path-to-legal-status-for-the-unauthorized-is-top-immigration-policy-goal-for-hispanics-in-u-s/.

González Izás, Matilde. "Arbitrary Power and Sexual Violence." *The Guatemala Reader: History, Culture, Politics,* edited by Greg Grandin, Deborah T. Levenson, and Elizabeth Oglesby, Duke UP, 2011, pp. 405–10.

Graizbord, Diana. "U.S.-Mexico Relations in the Trump Era and Beyond: Racial Capitalist Rearticulated." *The Future of U.S. Empire in the Americas,* edited by Timothy M. Gill, Routledge, 2020, pp. 286–306.

Grande, Reyna. "*American Dirt* Isn't the Problem: The Publishing Industry's Views of Immigrant Narratives Is Slow to Change." *New York Times,* 2 Feb. 2020.

Grandin, Greg, Deborah T. Levenson, and Elizabeth Oglesby, eds. *The Guatemala Reader: History, Culture, Politics.* Duke UP, 2011.

Green, Linda. *Fear as a Way of Life: Mayan Widows in Rural Guatemala.* Columbia UP, 1999.

Green, Linda. "The Nobodies: Neoliberalism, Violence, and Migration." *Medical Anthropology,* vol. 30, no. 4, 2011, pp. 366–85.

Green, Linda. "A Wink and a Nod: Notes from the Arizona Borderlands." *Dialectical Anthropology,* vol. 32, 2008, pp. 161–67.

Gurba, Myriam. "Pendeja, You Ain't Steinbeck: My Bronca with Fake-Ass Social Justice Literature." *Tropics of Meta,* 12 Dec. 2019, https://tropicsofmeta.com/2019/12/12/pendeja-you-aint-steinbeck-my-bronca-with-fake-ass-social-justice-literature/.

Heidbrink, Lauren. *Migranthood: Youth in a New Era of Deportation.* Stanford UP, 2020.

Herrera, Cristina. *ChicaNerds in Chicana Young Adult Literature: Brown and Nerdy.* Routledge, 2021.

Hinton, Mary, and Maria Nikolajeva. *Contemporary Adolescent Literature and Culture: The Emergent Adult.* 1st ed., Routledge, 2012.

Irizarry, Ylse. "The Ethics of Writing the Caribbean: Latina Narrative as Testimonio." *Literature Interpretation Theory,* vol. 16, no. 3, 2005, pp. 263–84.

Jars-Thomas, Susie. "Beyond Tamales, Tacos, and Our Southern Neighbors: Exploring Latino Culture in Child and Young Adult Literature." *Making Connections,* vol. 11, no. 1, 2009, pp. 33–39.

Jonas, Susanne. "Reflections on the Great Immigration Battle of 2006 and the Future of the Americas." *Social Justice,* vol. 33, no. 1, 2006, pp. 6–20.

Kornfield, John, and Laurie Prothero. "Envisioning Possibility: Schooling and Student Agency in Children and Young Adult Literature." *Children's Literature in Education,* vol. 36, no. 3, 2005, pp. 217–39, https://doi.org/10.1007/s10583-005-5971-2.

Landt, Susan M. "Multicultural Literature and Young Adolescents: A Kaleidoscope of Opportunity." *Journal of Adolescent & Adult Literacy,* vol. 49, no. 8, 2006, pp. 690–97.

Laub, Dori, and Shoshana Feldman. *Testimony: Crisis of Witnessing in Literature, Psychoanalysis, and History.* Routledge, 1992.

Lauria-Santiago, Aldo A. "The Culture and Politics of State Terror and Repression in El Salvador." *When States Kill: Latin America, the U.S., and Technologies of Terror,* edited by Cecilia Menjívar and Néstor Rodríguez, U of Texas P, 2005, pp. 85–114.

Levenson, Deborah T. *Adiós Niño: The Gangs of Guatemala City and the Politics of Death.* Duke UP, 2013.

Lewis, Cynthia, et al. *Reframing Sociocultural Research on Literacy: Identity, Agency, and Power.* 1st ed., Routledge, 2007.

Lim, Clarissa-Jan. "There's a Lot of Controversy Around the New Novel 'American Dirt.' Here's Everything You Need to Know About It." *BuzzFeed News,* 22 Jan. 2020, https://www.buzzfeednews.com/article/clarissajanlim/american-dirt-jeanine-cummins-controversy-explained.

Loperena, Christopher A. "Settler Violence? Racial and Emergent Frontiers of Progress in Honduras." *American Studies Association,* 2017, pp. 801–7.

Lopez, Mark H., et al. "Who Is Hispanic?" *Pew Research Center,* 15 Sept. 2022, https://www.pewresearch.org/short-reads/2022/09/15/who-is-hispanic/.

Lopez, William D. *Separated: Family and Community in the Aftermath of an Immigration Raid.* Johns Hopkins UP, 2019.

MacGregor, Amanda. "The Transformative Power of Books, a Guest Post by Daniel Aleman." *School Library Journal,* 24 Mar. 2023, https://teenlibrariantoolbox.com/2023/03/24/a-guest-post-by-daniel-aleman/.

Macías-Rojas, Patricia. *From Deportation to Prison: The Politics of Immigration Enforcement in Post-Civil Rights America.* New York UP, 2016.

Manz, Beatriz. "Reflections on Remembrance: Voices from an Ixcán Village." *What Justice? Whose Justice? Fighting for Fairness in Latin America,* edited by Susan Eva Eckstein and Timothy P. Wickham-Crowley, U of California P, 2003, pp. 313–36.

Manz, Beatriz. "Terror, Grief, and Recovery: Genocidal Trauma in a Mayan Village in Guatemala." *Annihilating Difference: The Anthropology of Genocide,* edited by A. L. Hinton, U of California P, 2002, pp. 292–309.

Márquez, John D. "Latinos as the 'Living Dead': Raciality, Expendability, and Border Militarization." *Latino Studies,* vol. 10, no. 4, 2012, pp. 473–98.

Martin, Michelle H. "Of Publications, Pickaninnies, and Literary Soup Lines: Reflections on Diversity in Children's Literature." *Children's Literature,* vol. 50, 2022, pp. 32–48.

McClennen, Sophia A. "Young People Are No Longer at Risk: They Are the Risk." *Symploke,* vol. 17, 2010, pp. 317–22.

McGuire, Randall H., and Ruth M. Van Dyke. "Crossing la Línea: Bodily Encounters with the U.S.-México Border in Ambos Nogales. *The Border and Its Bodies: The Embodiment of Risk along the U.S.-México Line,* edited by Thomas E. Sheridan and Randall H. McGuire, U of Arizona P, 2019, pp. 41–70.

McNair, Jonda C., and Edwards, Patricia A. "The Lasting Legacy of Rudine Sims Bishop: Mirrors, Windows, Sliding Glass Doors and More." *Literacy Research,* vol. 70, no. 1, 2021, pp. 202–12, https://doi.org/10.1177/23813377211028256.

Meehan, Kasey, and Jonathan Friedman. "Update on Book Bans in the 2022–2023 School Year Shows Expanded Censorship on Themes Centered on Race, History, Sexual Orientation and Gender." *PEN America,* https://pen.org/report/banned-in-the-usa-state-laws-supercharge-book-suppression-in-schools/.

Mendoza, Marcos. "The Tyranny of Narco-Power: Political Rule and Austere Domination in Michoacán, Mexico." *Journal of Latin American and Caribbean Anthropology,* vol. 26, no. 3–4, 2021, pp. 408–26.

Menjívar, Cecilia. *Enduring Violence: Ladina Women's Lives in Guatemala.* U of California P, 2011.

Menjívar, Cecilia. "Guatemalan-Origin Children's Transnational Ties." *Critical Dialogues in Latinx Studies: A Reader,* edited by Ana Y. Ramos-Zayas, and Mérida M. Rúa. New York UP, 2021, pp. 121–33.

Menjívar, Cecilia, and Leisy Abrego. "Legal Violence: Immigration Law and the Lives of Central American Immigrants." *American Journal of Sociology,* vol. 117, no. 5, 2012, pp. 1380–421.

Menjívar, Cecilia, and Krista M. Perreira. "Undocumented and Unaccompanied: Children of Migration in the European Union and the United States." *Journal of Ethnic and Migration Studies,* vol. 45, no. 2, 2019, pp. 197–217.

Michelson, Anna. "The Politics of Happily-Ever-After: Romance Genre Fiction as Aesthetic Public Sphere." *American Journal of Cultural Sociology,* vol. 9, no. 2, 2021, pp. 177–210.

Misra, Tanvi. "No Children Here." *The Baffler,* no. 71, Nov. 2023, https://thebaffler.com/salvos/no-children-here-misra.

Mobius, Janina. "Wrestling for Their Lives." *Lucha libre relatos sin límite de tiempo,* edited by Margarita de Orellana, Richard Moszka, Alberto Ruy, Artes de México, 2015, pp. 65–80.

Montaño, Jesus, and Regan Postma-Montaño. *Tactics of Hope in Latinx Children's and Young Adult Literature.* New Mexico UP, 2022.

Montes, Verónica, and Maria Dolores Paris Pombo. "Ethics of Care, Emotional Work, and Collective Action of Solidarity: The Patronas in Mexico." *Gender, Place, and Culture: A Journal of Feminist Geography,* vol. 26, no. 4, 2019, pp. 559–80.

Montgomery, David, et al. "Journey Fatal for 9 Migrants Found in a San Antonio Parking Lot." *New York Times,* 23 July 2017, https://www.nytimes.com/2017/07/23/us/san-antonio-truck-walmart-trafficking.html.

Murphy, Kaitlin M. "Against Precarious Abstraction Bearing Witness to Migration through Moysés Zúñiga Santiago's La Bestia Photographs." *Latin American and Latinx Visual Culture,* vol. 1, no. 1, 2019, pp. 7–22.

Naidoo, Jaime C. "Opening Doors: Visual and Textual Analyses of Diverse Latino Subcultures in Américas Picture Books." *Children and Libraries,* vol. 6, no. 2, 2008, pp. 27–35.

Nelson, Diana M. "Reckoning the After/math of War in Guatemala." *Anthropological Theory,* vol. 10, no. 1–2, 2010, pp. 87–95.

Nevins, Joseph. "Migration as Reparations." *NACLA*, 24 May 2016.

Osuna, Steven. "Manifest Destiny: Mexico's War on Drugs, Crisis of Legitimacy, and Global Capitalism." *Journal of World-Systems Research*, vol. 27, no. 1, 2021, pp. 12–34, https://doi.org/10.5195/JWSR.2021.1023.

Osuna, Steven. "Transnational Moral Panic: Neoliberalism and the Spectre of MS-13." *Race & Class*, vol. 61, no. 4, 2020, pp. 1–26.

Padilla, Yajaira M. "The Central American Transnational Imaginary: Defining the Transnational and Gendered Contours of Central American Immigrant Experience." *Latino Studies*, vol. 11, no. 2, 2013, pp. 150–66.

Padilla, Yajaira M. *From Threatening Guerrillas to Forever Illegals: US Central Americans and the Cultural Politics of Non-Belonging*. U of Texas P, 2022.

Paik, A. Naomi. *Bans, Wall, Raids, Sanctuary: Understanding U.S. Immigration for the Twenty-First Century*. U of California P, 2020.

Paley, Dawn M. "Cold War, Neoliberal War, and Disappearance: Observations from Mexico." *Latin American Perspectives*, 48, no. 1, 2021, pp. 145–62.

Paley, Dawn M. *Drug War Capitalism*. AK Press, 2014.

Paley, Dawn M. "Mexican Disappearance, U.S. Incarceration." *Commune*, 2020, https://communemag.com/mexican-disappearance-u-s-incarceration/.

Paley, Dawn M. "Response: Fear and Terror as Tools of Capitalism." *NACLA Report on the Americas*, vol. 48, no. 2, 2016, pp. 140–43.

Park, Jungwon. "Bare Life in Contemporary Mexico: Everyday Violence and Folk Saints." *A Post-Neoliberal Era in Latin America?*, edited by Daniel Nehring and Magdalena López, Policy Press, 2019.

Passel, Jeffrey S., et al. "U.S. Hispanic Population Continued Its Geographic Spread in the 2010s." *Pew Research Center*, 3 Feb. 2022.

Peterson, Anna, and Kay A. Read. "Victims, Heroes, Enemies: Children in Central American Wars." *Minor Omissions: Children in Latin American History and Society*, edited by Tobias Hecht, U of Wisconsin P, 2002, pp. 215–30.

Pierce, Ramona. "Fighting Book Bans in Kentucky Schools—and Beyond." *The Nation*, 18 Feb. 2023.

Pineda, Dorany. "Publisher Commits to Making Changes; After *American Dirt* Outcry, Macmillan Vows to Work on Latinx Representation." *Los Angeles Times*, 5 Feb. 2020, https://www.latimes.com/entertainment-arts/books/story/2020-02-04/american-dirt-publishers-dignidadliteraria-meet.

Polit-Dueñas, Gabriela. "The Place of the Journalist in Contemporary Mexico: A Case in Juárez." *Revista de Estudios Hispánicos*, vol. 53, no. 1, 2019, pp. 77–97.

Portes, Alejandro. "Migration in the Contemporary History of Latin America: An Overview of Recent Trends." *LASAForum*, vol. 58, no. 2, 2017, pp. 12–14.

Portillo Villeda, Suyapa G. "Central American Migrants: LGBTI Asylum Cases Seeking Justice and Making History." *Queer and Trans Migrations: Dynamics of Illegalization, Detention, and Deportation*, edited by Eithne Luibhéid and Karma R. Chavez, 2020, pp. 67–73.

Preston, Julia. "U.S. Continues to Deport Central American Migrants." *New York Times*, 9 Mar. 2016, https://www.nytimes.com/2016/03/10/us/us-continues-to-deport-central-american-migrants.html.

Reagan, Maggie. "Let's Talk about Love." *The Booklist*, vol. 118, no. 2, 15 Sept. 2021, pp. 62–63.

Rhodes, Cristina. "Book Review: *The Only Road* by Alexandra Diaz." *Latinxs in Kid Lit*, 16 Mar. 2017.

Rhodes, Cristina. "Carmelita Tropicana and Bodies of Resistance: Reclaiming Young Latinas' Bodies within Hegemonic Discourse." *Latino Studies,* vol. 19, no. 3, 2021, 358–73.

Rhodes, Cristina. "Corporeal, Phenomenological, and Activist Transformations in Pam Muñoz Ryan's *Esperanza Rising.*" *Children's Literature Association Quarterly,* 2021, pp. 41–56.

Rhodes, Cristina. "Multicultural Children's and Young Adult Literature of the United States: From Painful Histories to Action and Progress." *A Companion to Multiethnic Literature of the United States,* edited by Gary Totten, Wiley-Blackwell, 2023, pp. 269–80.

Rhodes, Cristina. "Processes of Transformation: Theorizing Activism and Change through Gloria Anzaldúa's Picture Books." *Children's Literature in Education,* vol. 52, 2021, pp. 464–77.

Rivera Garza, Cristina. "On Our Toes: Women against the Femicide Machine in Mexico." *WLT,* vol. 94, no. 1, 2020, pp. 50–54.

Rocco, Raymond. "Disposable Subjects: The Racial Normativity of Neoliberalism and Latino Immigrants." *Latino Studies,* vol. 14, no. 1, 2016, pp. 99–117.

Rodríguez, Ana Patricia. "The Fictions of Solidarity: *Transfronterista* Feminisms and Anti Imperialist Struggles in Central American Transnational Narratives." *Feminist Studies,* vol. 34, 2008, pp. 199–226.

Rodríguez, Ana Patricia. "Wasted Opportunities: Conflictive Peacetime Narratives of Central America." *Globalization of U.S.-Latin American Relations: Democracy, Intervention, and Human Rights,* edited by Virginia M. Bouvier, Greenwood/Praeger, 2002, pp. 227–47.

Rodríguez, Néstor, et al. "Unaccompanied Minors from the Northern Central American Countries in the Migrant Stream: Social Differentials and Institutional Contexts." *Journal of Ethnic and Migration Studies,* vol. 45, no. 3, 2019, pp. 218–34.

Rodriguez, Sabrina. "Harris' Blunt Message in Guatemala: 'Do Not Come' to U.S." *Politico,* 20 June 2021, https://www.politico.com/news/2021/06/07/harris-message-in-guatemala-do-not-come-492047.

Rodriguez, Sanjuana C., and Eliza Gabrielle Braden. "Representation of Latinx Immigrants and Immigration in Children's Literature: A Critical Content Analysis." *Journal of Children's Literature,* vol. 44, no. 2, 2018, pp. 46–61.

Rodriguez, Sanjuana, and Sandra Osorio. "Censorship in Early Childhood: A Critical Content Analysis of Banned and Challenged Latine Picture Books." *Research on Diversity in Youth Literature,* vol. 6, no. 1, 2024, pp. 1–26.

Rodríguez, Sonia Alejandra, and Ingrid Campos. "Book Review: *Efrén Divided* by Ernesto Cisneros." *Latinxs in Kid Lit,* 17 Sept. 2020, https://latinosinkidlit.com/2020/09/17/book-review-efren-divided-by-ernesto-cisneros/.

Rodríguez, Sonia Alejandra, and Ingrid Campos. "Book Review: *We Are Not from Here.*" *Latinxs in Kid Lit,* 24 Aug. 2020.

Rodríguez, Sonia Alejandra. "Conocimiento Narratives: Creative Acts and Healing in Latinx Children's and Young Adult Literature." *Children's Literature,* vol. 47, no. 1, 2019, pp. 9–29.

Rojas Wiesner, Martha L., and Ailsa Winton. "Precarious Mobility in Central American and Southern Mexico: Crises and the Struggle to Survive." *The Oxford Handbook of Migration Crises,* edited by Cecilia Menjívar, Marie Ruiz, and Immanuel Ness, Oxford UP, 2018, pp. 245–60.

Rosen, Jill. "U.S. Textbooks Miss Opportunities to Teach Latino History." *Johns Hopkins U,* 16 May 2023, https://hub.jhu.edu/2023/05/16/latino-history-textbooks-report/.

Rothenberg, David. *Memory of Silence: The Guatemalan Truth Commission Report.* Palgrave Macmillan, 2012.

Roush, Laura. "Santa Muerte, Protection and Desamparo: A View from a Mexico City Altar." *Latin American Research Review,* vol. 49, 2014, pp. 129–48.

Roy, Nilanjana. "*American Dirt* and the Risks of Writing Other People's Stories." *Financial Times*, 20 Feb. 2020, https://www.ft.com/content/77241e5c-5242-11ea-a1ef-da1721a0541e.

Russo, Ann. "Resisting the 'Savior' Complex." *Feminist Accountability: Disrupting Violence and Transforming Power*, New York UP, 2018, pp. 214–42, https://doi.org/10.18574/nyu/9780814777169.003.0010.

Salama, Viviana. "Trump to Mexico, 'Take Care of Bad Hombres' or US Might." *AP News*, 1 Feb. 2017, https://apnews.com/united-states-government-0b3f5db59b2e4aa78cdbbf008f27fb49.

Sánchez, Rosaura. "The Toxic Tonic: Narratives of Xenophobia." *Latino Studies*, vol. 9, 2011, pp. 126–44.

Sánchez Prado, Ignacio M. "*American Dirt* Gets Mexico Very Wrong. It's the Latest in a Long Trend." *Washington Post*, 23 Jan. 2020, https://www.washingtonpost.com/opinions/2020/01/23/american-dirt-gets-mexico-very-wrong-its-latest-long-trend/.

Sánchez Prado, Ignacio M. "Commodifying Mexico: On *American Dirt* and the Cultural Politics of a Manufactured Bestseller." *American Literary History*, vol. 33, no. 2, 2021, pp. 371–93.

Sánchez Prado, Ignacio M. "Mexico: The Essential Neighbor." *Public Books*, 8 Apr. 2020, https://www.publicbooks.org/mexico-the-essential-neighbor/.

Sanford, Victoria. *Buried Secrets: Truth and Human Rights in Guatemala*. Palgrave Macmillan, 2003.

Sanford, Victoria. "Command Responsibility and the Guatemalan Genocide: Genocide as a Military Plan of the Guatemalan Army under the Dictatorships of Generals Lucan Garcia, Rios Montt, and Mejia Victores." *Genocide Studies International*, vol. 8, no. 1, 2014, pp. 86–101.

Sanford, Victoria. *Textures of Terror: The Murder of Claudina Isabel Velásquez and Her Father's Quest for Justice*. U of California P, 2023.

Sciurba, Katie, et al. "Humanizing the Journey across the Mexico-U.S. Border: Multimodal Analysis of Children's Picture Books and the Restorying of Latinx (Im)migration." *Children's Literature in Education*, vol. 52, no. 3, 2021, 411–29.

Seif, H. "'Coming Out of the Shadows' and 'Undocuqueer': Undocumented Immigrants Transforming Sexuality Discourse and Activism." *Journal of Language and Sexuality: Queering Borders: Language, Sexuality and Migration*, vol. 3, no. 1, 10 Mar. 2014.

Sheridan, Thomas E., and Randall H. McGuire. *The Border and Its Bodies: The Embodiment of Risk along the U.S.-México Line*. Arizona UP, 2019.

Siu, Oriel María. *Rebeldita the Fearless in Ogreland*. Rebeldita the Fearless, 2021.

Smyth, Frank. "The Untouchable Narco-State." *The Guatemalan Reader: History, Culture, Politics*, edited by Greg Grandin, Deborah T. Levenson, and Elizabeth Oglesby, Duke UP, 2021, pp. 480–86.

Socolovsky, Maya. *Troubling Nationhood in U.S. Latina Literature: Explorations of Place and Belonging*. Rutgers UP, 2013.

Sorensen, Ninna N. "Wars and Migration Crises in Central America: On Missing Persons during Armed Conflict and International Migration." *The Oxford Handbook of Migration Crises*, edited by Cecilia Menjívar, Marie Ruiz, and Immanuel Ness, Oxford UP, 2018, pp. 389–406.

Speed, Shannon. "Structures of Settler Capitalism in Abya Yala." *American Studies Association*, 2017, pp. 783–90.

Spring, Karen. "Government Reforms Face Corporate Backlash in Honduras." *NACLA Report on the Americas*, vol. 55, no. 4, 2023, pp. 350–54.

Stewart, Mary A. "Giving Voice to Valeria's Story: Support, Value, and Agency for Immigrant Adolescents." *Journal of Adolescent & Adult Literacy*, vol. 57, no. 1, 2013, pp. 42–50, https://doi.org/10.1002/jaal.217.

Swanson, Kate, and Rebecca Maria Torres. "Child Migration and Transnationalized Violence in Central and North America." *Journal of Latin American Geography*, vol. 15, no. 3, 2016, pp. 23–48.

Thomas, Ebony Elizabeth and Marquise Jamond Griffin. "Children's Literature and the Future: Fifty Years and Beyond." *Children's Literature*, vol. 50, 2022, pp. 85–97.

Thompson, Amy, et al. "Re-Conceptualizing Agency in Migrant Children from Central America and Mexico." *Journal of Ethnic and Migration Studies*, vol. 45, no. 2, 2019, pp. 235–52, https://doi.org/10.1080/1369183X.2017.1404258.

Torres, Lourdes. "Centering Subjugated Knowledges." *Latino Studies*, vol. 15, 2017, pp. 1–3.

Truax, Eileen. *Dreamers: An Immigrant Generation's Fight for Their American Dream*. Beacon Press, 2015.

Tzul, Gladys T. "The Continuation of Exploitation in Central America." *NACLA Report of the Americas*, vol. 48, no. 2, 2016, pp. 138–40.

United Nations Department of Public Information. *El Salvador Agreements: The Path to Peace*, United Nations, 1992.

Varga-Dobai, Kinga. "Gender Issues in Multicultural Children's Literature—Black and Third World Feminist Critiques of Appropriation, Essentialism, and US/Other Binary Oppositions." *Multicultural Perspectives*, vol. 15, no. 3, 2013, pp. 141–47.

Vaughn, Margaret. "Making Sense of Student Agency and Why Is It Needed Now More Than Ever. Student Agency: Theoretical Implications for Practice." *Theory into Practice*, vol. 59, no. 2, 2020, pp. 62–66.

Vaughn, Margaret, et al. "Examining Agency in Children's Nonfiction Picture Books." *Children's Literature in Education*, vol. 55, 2022, pp. 33–51.

Velásquez Estrada, Elizabeth R. "Intersectional Justice Denied: Racist Warring Masculinity, Negative Peace, and Violence in Post-Peace Accords El Salvador." *American Anthropologist*, vol. 124, 2022, pp. 39–52.

Velásquez Nimatuj, Irma A. "Transnationalism and Maya Dress." *The Guatemala Reader: History, Culture, Politics*, edited by Greg Grandin, Deborah T. Levenson, and Elizabeth Oglesby, Duke UP, 2011, pp. 523–31.

Ventura, Abbie E. "An Intersectional Coming-of-Age: On Body Positivity, Agency, and Self-Expression in *Fat Chance, Charlie Vega*." *Children's Literature*, vol. 52, 2024, pp. 85–103.

Vogt, Wendy A. "Crossing Mexico: Structural Violence and the Commodification of Undocumented Central American Migrants." *American Ethnologist*, vol. 40, no. 4, 2013, pp. 764–80, https://doi.org/10.1111/amet.12053.

Vogt, Wendy A. "Dirty Work, Dangerous Others: The Politics of Outsourced Immigration Enforcement in Mexico." *Migration and Society: Advances in Research*, vol. 3, no. 1, 2020, pp. 50–63.

Vogt, Wendy A. *Lives in Transit: Violence and Intimacy on the Migrant Journey*. California UP, 2018.

Walia, Harsha. *Border and Rule: Global Migration, Capitalism, and the Rise of Racist Nationalism*. Haymarket, 2021.

White, Jackie K. "Latino/a Young Adult and Children's Literature." *Latino/a Literature in the Classroom: 21st Century Approaches to Teaching*, edited by Frederick Luis Aldama, Routledge, 2015, pp. 192–201.

Wolf, Sonja. "Distorting the MS-13 Threat." *NACLA Report on the Americas*, vol. 49, no. 3, 2017, pp. 290–97.

Wolk, Steven. "Reading for a Better World: Teaching for Social Responsibility with Young Adult Literature." *Journal of Adolescent & Adult Literacy,* vol. 52, no. 8, 2009, pp. 664–73.

Yúdice, George. "Testimonio and Postmodernism." *The Real Thing: The Testimonial Debate in Latin America,* edited by George Gugelberger. Duke UP, 1996, pp. 49–64.

Zakaria, Rafia. "*American Dirt* Has an American Problem." *CNN,* 23 Jan. 2020, https://www.cnn.com/2020/01/23/opinions/american-dirt-oprah-book-controversy-zakaria/index.html.

Zavala, Oswaldo. *Drug Cartels Do Not Exist: Narcotrafficking in the U.S. and Mexican Culture.* Translated by William Savinar, Vanderbilt UP, 2020.

Zimmerman, Arely, Joanna Perez, and Leisy J. Abrego. "Complexities of Belonging: Compounded Foreignness and Racial Cover among Undocumented Central American Youth." *Ethnicities,* vol. 23, no. 6, 2023, pp. 822–42.

INDEX

GLOBAL LATIN/O AMERICAS

FREDERICK LUIS ALDAMA AND LOURDES TORRES, SERIES EDITORS

This series focuses on the Latino experience in its totality as set within a global dimension. The series showcases the variety and vitality of the presence and significant influence of Latinos in the shaping of the culture, history, politics and policies, and language of the Americas—and beyond. It welcomes scholarship regarding the arts, literature, philosophy, popular culture, history, politics, law, history, and language studies, among others.

Coming of Age(ncy) on the Migrant Trail: Adolescent Journeys in Contemporary Latinx Young Adult Literature
SUSANA S. MARTÍNEZ

Replaying Marc Anthony: Sonic, Political, and Cultural Resonances
FRANCES R. APARICIO

Zones of Encuentro: Language and Identities in Northern New Mexico
LILLIAN GORMAN

Sanctuary: Exclusion, Violence, and Indigenous Migrants in the East Bay
CRUZ MEDINA

Everyday Dirty Work: Invisibility, Communication, and Immigrant Labor
WILFREDO ALVAREZ

Building Confianza: Empowering Latinos/as Through Transcultural Health Care Communication
DALIA MAGAÑA

Fictions of Migration: Narratives of Displacement in Peru and Bolivia
LORENA CUYA GAVILANO

Baseball as Mediated Latinidad: Race, Masculinity, Nationalism, and Performances of Identity
JENNIFER DOMINO RUDOLPH

False Documents: Inter-American Cultural History, Literature, and the Lost Decade (1975–1992)
FRANS WEISER

Public Negotiations: Gender and Journalism in Contemporary US Latina/o Literature
ARIANA E. VIGIL

Democracy on the Wall: Street Art of the Post-Dictatorship Era in Chile
GUISELA LATORRE

Gothic Geoculture: Nineteenth-Century Representations of Cuba in the Transamerican Imaginary
IVONNE M. GARCÍA

Affective Intellectuals and the Space of Catastrophe in the Americas
JUDITH SIERRA-RIVERA

Spanish Perspectives on Chicano Literature: Literary and Cultural Essays
EDITED BY JESÚS ROSALES AND VANESSA FONSECA

Sponsored Migration: The State and Puerto Rican Postwar Migration to the United States
EDGARDO MELÉNDEZ

La Verdad: An International Dialogue on Hip Hop Latinidades
EDITED BY MELISSA CASTILLO-GARSOW AND JASON NICHOLS